Addenda to the
Popular Dive Guide Series

The first volume of my Popular Dive Guide Series was published in 1988 (*Shipwrecks of New Jersey*). Sixteen additional volumes followed over the next thirty years. Since that first slender volume was published, dedicated wreck-divers have discovered and identified shipwrecks all along the eastern seaboard. They have watched shipwrecks collapse in extreme slow motion. They have found lost relics which materially added to the rich history of maritime events.

As I have written elsewhere, shipwrecks are not static resources as archaeologists would like the uninformed public to believe. They cannot be preserved in a saltwater environment. The best that wreck-divers can do is to remember and record the way they used to look at a single moment in time. For in the next moment they will have changed for the worse.

Shipwreck Potpourri covers some of the changes, discoveries, and identifications that have occurred since the volumes in my Popular Dive Guide Series were originally published. This book also adds shipwreck histories that did not fit into those books due to space constraints, or because other shipwrecks merited coverage than those that were omitted did not.

In other words, *Shipwreck Potpourri* is an addendum to the Popular Dive Guide Series. It covers shipwrecks from Maine to South Carolina, presenting new or supplementary information about many East Coast shipwrecks.

Just because I wrote a book about shipwrecks off a certain State does not mean that I quit researching shipwrecks off that State, including shipwrecks that I covered in previous books. Often I have found facts and photos that I did not possess at the time of publication. Some of these facts and photos are included in this volume.

I have written three other books that touched upon shipwrecks in the same or similar veins: *Shipwreck Sagas* (2008), *Shipwreck Heresies* (2009), and *Underwater Reflections* (2011). These books covered major facts, trivia, and minutiae about local shipwrecks in addition to well-known and little-known wrecks around the world. The current volume covers only wrecks that lie on or off East Coast States. In that sense, it starts where the other books ended.

Plus, in relation to the artwork that graces the front cover, I have included a chapter about the origin and history of mermaids. This chapter also explains the background of the Sirens that illustrated the front cover of *Underwater Reflections*.

The pursuit of shipwreck knowledge is a never-ending quest. So sit back, relax, and peruse the new material that awaits you in the following fact-filled pages.

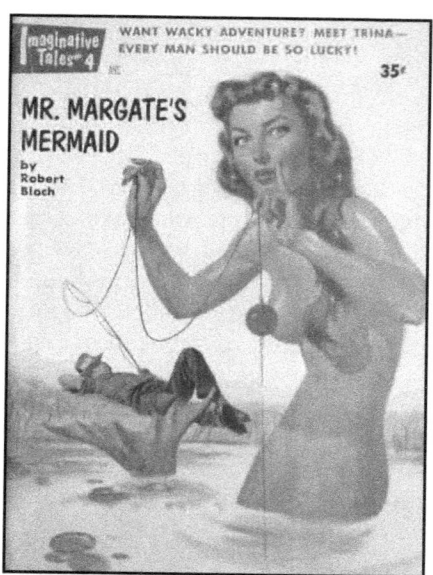

This assortment of mermaid images comes from many times and walks of life. Upper left shows a postcard picture from circa 1900, when female chubbiness was considered the height of pulchritude. Upper right shows the cover of a science fiction digest from 1955. Lower left shows a cartoon panel from an unidentified magazine circa 1940. Lower right shows a German postcard picture from 1918; note that these mermaids possess separated buttocks and midriff lateral fins. The opposite page features a photograph of a scrimshaw jewelry box that was made in India (date unknown).

SHIPWRECK POTPOURRI

by Gary Gentile

Gary Gentile Productions

Copyright 2018 by Gary Gentile

All rights reserved. Except for the use of brief quotations embodied in critical articles and reviews, this book may not be reproduced in part or in whole, in any manner (including mechanical, electronic, photographic, and photocopy means), transmitted in any form, or recorded by any data storage and/or retrieval device, without express written permission from the author. Address all queries to:

Gary Gentile Productions
500 Lehigh Gorge Drive
Jim Thorpe, PA 18229

Additional copies of this book may be purchased from the same address by sending a check or money order in the amount of $20 U.S. for each copy (plus $4 postage per order, not per book, in the U.S. Inquire for shipping cost to foreign countries). Alternatively, copies may be ordered from the author's website and paid by credit card:

http://www.ggentile.com/index.html

Picture Credits

The front cover art was painted by Albert Guillaume (1873-1942), circa 1910. The back cover images are from old product brochures or picture postcards. The image below is taken from an undated picture postcard. All uncredited photographs were taken by the author.

International Standard Book Numbers (ISBN)
1-883056-54-3
978-1-883056-54-4

First Edition

Printed in U.S.A.

Contents

Introduction to Mermaids		7
New Hampshire	William H. Machen	21
Massachusetts	Andrea Doria	22
	Nezinscot	28
	U-550	33
	White Squall	35
New York	Herbert Parker	39
	San Diego	41
New Jersey	Lucy Evelyn	52
	Montgomery (alias Max's Wreck?)	63
	Robert J. Walker (alias $25 Wreck)	65
Pennsylvania ?	United States (and others)	67
Delaware	Amazing Grace and Pilgrim's Progress	73
	Northern Pacific	87
Virginia	Cuyahoga	88
	Despatch	90
	Francis E. Powell	100
	Gere	102
	Hermod	104
	Juno (plus Galga)	107
	Menominee	116
	Olinda	118
	S. G. Wilder (plus Brunswick and Whitehaven)	120
	Saginaw	122
	Unidentified Wrecks	126

North Carolina	Agnes E. Fry (plus *Virginius*)	138
	Alligator Creek Barges	154
	Curlew	158
	Estelle Randall	163
	Home	170
	Pulaski	171
	Queen Anne's Revenge	172
	Mixed-up Merchant Vessels	174
South Carolina	H. C. Brooks	176
	Leif Eriksson	178
	Ozama	182
	Philadelphia	187
	Ringborg (and *Runa*)	191
	Sailing Yacht	197
	Valour	204

The United States of NOAA — 212

Books by the Author — 235
Author's Bio — 238

This drawing from an old-time book is supposed to be a likeness of the first mermaid, Atargatis. She differs somewhat from modern and more appealing representations.

Mermaids

Mermaids have a long and fabulous history. They have been part of human mythology ever since mankind took to the sea.

Simply stated, a mermaid is pictured as a female marine mammal (or person) that (or who) is human in form from the waist up yet aquatic in form from the waist down. That is, she has the head, tresses, face, arms, hands, torso, and breasts of a woman, but the lower abdomen and tail of a porpoise. She is often described as fishlike because the lower part of her body has an integument of scales (although the upper part of her body has an epidermis of skin). "Fishlike" is a misnomer because the tail of a fish is aligned vertically and moves from side to side, whereas the tail of a mermaid is aligned horizontally, as in the porpoise, and moves up and down.

It is the mermaid's foible that an artist invariably drew her tail on the horizontal plain even when the writer describes the tail as fishlike: a case in which the artist is smarter than the writer.

Legend has it that the mermaid lives under water, yet she is never depicted with gills. We must stretch our imagination of this anatomical anomaly by presuming that she breathes through her mouth the way landside mammals do, but has internal gills in place of lungs in order to accomplish the transfer of oxygen. Either that, or she can hold her breath for an uncommonly long time in the manner of deep-diving whales.

Folklore seldom bothers to explain such peculiarities. What you see (or fancy) is what you get. One inherent feature of myths is that they don't have to explain anything and are never bound by logic. A myth is accepted on faith, and reason or logic be damned.

I have always wondered how mermaids could function without the anatomical orifices that women have between their legs for, er . . . well, I don't need to go there. You know what I mean.

Entomologists should note that the derivation of the word "mermaid" likely originated from a combination of the French word "mer," (meaning "sea," as in the phrase "mal de mer," translated literally as "bad of the sea," and meaning "seasickness") and the English word "maid" (an unwed female; and judging by the artful portrayals, a comely one at that).

Mermaids are generally perceived to be good-natured feminine creatures who betoken kindness, love, and compassion. They were probably conjured into existence by imaginative sailors who had been too long at sea without the fair sex – or any sex, for that matter. They were so hard up after weeks and months afloat that they suffered from the same delusion that they suffered in onshore pubs after having their minds numbed by too much alcohol. After a few drinks too many, anyone wearing a skirt began to look appealing, even bag ladies and Scotsmen.

Historians generally agree that the Occidental mermaid myth originated from sightings of one of several marine mammals whose appearance resembles the human form if not the human face. These marine mammals are seals or sea lions, and dugongs or manatees (both known as sea cows).

I doubt that manatees were responsible for creating the mermaid myth. Mermaids have been part of European legend since at least Assyrian times: 1,000 BCE (before current era). In those days, the land around the Mediterranean Sea was thought to com-

Florida manatee.

Below: This nineteenth-century postcard picture of a dugong dressed in feminine finery is a failed attempt to beautify an ugly marine mammal in order to sell it a mermaid.

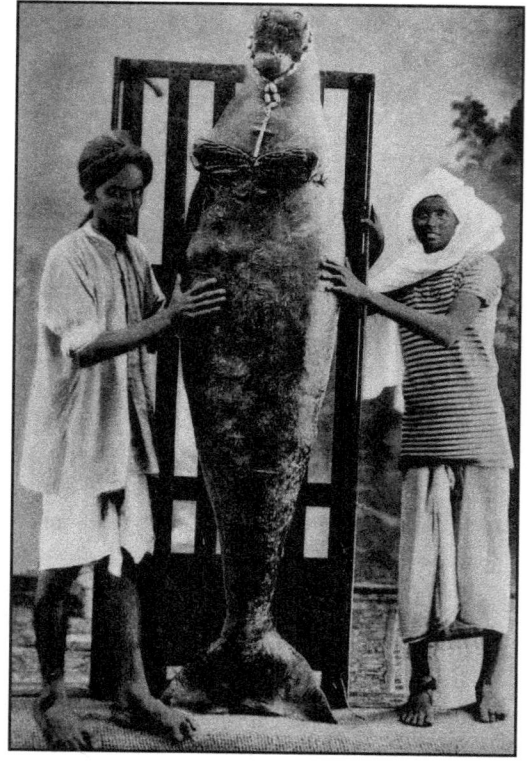

prise the entire world. Adventurers plied the Mediterranean Sea as well as those that surrounded it: the Black Sea, the Aegean Sea, the Adriatic Sea, and the Tyrrhenian Sea; plus the Red Sea that separates Africa from Asia, and which leads to the Indian Ocean. It was commonly accepted that nothing existed beyond these waterways, and that to explore beyond them led to sailing over the edge of the world.

Manatees live only in the New World (the Americas): continents that were then not known by Europeans to exist. In any case, I've seen wild manatees face to face – or what serves as a face on the manatee – and I cannot imagine kissing that ugly puss under any circumstances short of impending death. On second thought, I'll take death. But then, I'm not a hard-up sailor who's been at sea for forever and a day.

Dugongs live along the shores of the Indian Ocean, both in south Asia and east Africa. It is very possible that stories from Indian Ocean travelers reached the ears of European inhabitants via caravans that transported goods and cultural ideas across the vast land connection from Asia to Europe. According to most authorities, there's a better than even chance that these unsightly creatures were responsible for the myth of the mermaid, despite the fact that they are as homely as their western hemisphere brethren (or sistern, but definitely not cistern).

Seals and sea lions are known throughout most of the world. Unlike land mammals, these pinnipeds (as they are known to science) have flippers instead of hands and feet. The muzzle looks more like that of a dog than that of a human female: an extended snout that might have been compressed when seen through the eyes of a grog-filled sailor.

It is my personal opinion that seals or sea lions were responsible for the creation of the mermaid myth. My reasoning is that they commonly surface and submerge as they swim in the sea so that their heads and snouts alternately appear and disappear in the water. This means of propulsion is similar to cavorting: an attribute that is often ascribed to mermaids. Whereas manatees and dugongs take deep breaths and hold it as they swim beneath the surface for long distances. I have swum with manatees and observed them from river banks, so I know whereof I speak. I've also seen seals and sea lions playing and gamboling in the ocean.

Furthermore, even though the faces of seals and sea lions are doglike, they are less homely than dugongs and manatees (which look very much alike, and whose faces are porcine or piglike), because the skin or integument of the latter pair of creatures is not smooth (as in the former pair), but distinctly rough and parchmentlike and usually coated with algae.

No matter. This could all be pure speculation, especially as the Ancients were known to create whole pantheons of gods and goddesses, one for every occasion. Historians should not hold credence with such olden societies. Perhaps they inserted mermaids into the overcrowded ménage of warring and interrelated deities, and believed in mermaids the same as they believed in hundreds of other creatures such as satyrs and unicorns and dragons and cockatrices and cyclops and centaurs and a host of a multitude of different mythological creatures of which fossil remains have never been found by paleontologists.

I never held much faith in a civilization whose people who could look up at the

This cavorting sea lion posed its head and flippers as if were impersonating a mermaid.

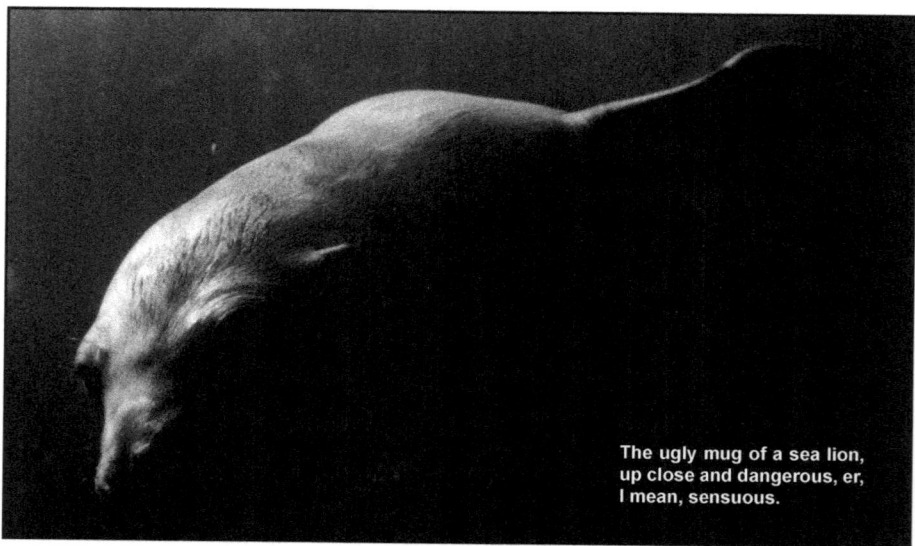

The ugly mug of a sea lion, up close and dangerous, er, I mean, sensuous.

nighttime stars and see a constellation that looks exactly like a Big Dipper, yet connect the stellar dots to perceive a Big Bear (Ursa Major). A water ladle and a furry ursine mammal look nothing alike.

And so, mermaids existed in opium-filled minds and vivid imaginations if not in earthbound reality. (The war on drugs is thousands of years old, perhaps even preceding the holy wars in the Middle East. Maybe not.) In his 37-volume *Historiae Naturalis*, Pliny the Elder claimed that mermaids were "no fabulous tale."

The earliest mention of a humanoid that could possibly be ascribed to mermaid folklore appeared in a fable or fairy tale (take your pick. with or without a moral) that was told in Assyria a thousand years or so before the time of Christ. The tale – and the tail – differs as it does in all myths and legends. Basically, a goddess named Atargatis fell in love with a shepherd. Either she killed him accidentally, or she got pregnant after their miscegenetic union, and committed suicide by leaping into a lake. Due to her profound beauty, the water changed her form into a quasi-fish that could live comfortably in the liquid environment: part human and part fish, although which part was which is open to interpretation.

The same tale – with different tails – was passed down through generations to resurface (no pun intended) in subsequent languages such as Babylonian, Phoenician, Greek, Roman, and Indian. In the latter language, the compilation of *The Arabian Night's Entertainment* (alias *A Thousand and One Nights*) – noted for the origination of Aladdin's lamp, Ali Baba and the Forty Thieves, the voyages of Sinbad, and other well-known classic narratives – relates "The Adven-

Hieronymus Bosch (c.1450-1516) painted a mermaid in the center panel of the triptych known as *The Garden of Earthly Delights*.

tures of Bulukiya," in which the eponymous protagonist explored the ocean in a search for immortality and stumbles upon a civilization of mermaids. The first English edition of this book dates from 1706, but the actual text is hundreds of years older.

And so it went, with mermaid myths embellishing from one human era to another.

William Shakespeare wrote about mermaidlike creatures in *A Midsummer Night's Dream* (1595). In Act 2, Scene 1, the fairy king Oberon says:

> My gentle Puck, come hither. Thou rememb'rest
> Since once I sat upon a promontory
> And heard a mermaid, on a dolphin's back,
> Uttering such dulcet and harmonious breath
> That the rude sea grew civil at her song
> And certain stars shot madly from their spheres
> To hear the sea-maid's music?

J. M. Barrie wrote about mermaids in *Peter Pan* (1904). Act III is entitled "The Mermaid's Lagoon," where it is stated: "There are many mermaids here, going plop-plop, and one might attempt to count the tails did they not flash and disappear so quickly. At times a lovely girl leaps in the air seeking to get rid of her excess of scales, which fall in a silver shower as she shakes them off. From the coral grottoes beneath the lagoon, where are the mermaids' bed-chambers, comes fitful music." Mermaids are mentioned elsewhere in the play.

Several explorers claim to have actually sighted mermaids: Christopher Columbus, John Smith (of Pocahontas fame), and Henry Hudson, to name a few. Hudson went so far as to describe the mermaid in de*tail*:

> This morning one of our companie looking over boord saw a Mermaid . . . from Navill upward, her back and breasts were like a woman's (as they say that saw her) her body as big as one of us; her skin very white; and long haire hanging down behind, of color blacke; in her going downe they saw her tayle, which was like the tayle of a porposse and speckled like a Macrell.

And the list of such sightings continues, well into the twentieth century.

Warsaw, Poland, has honored the mermaid since the 1300's as the protector of the city. She is pictured on the city's coat of arms, mermaid statues are sequestered throughout the city, and she adorns many of the country's coins and stamps. Always she is shown wielding a sword and shield.

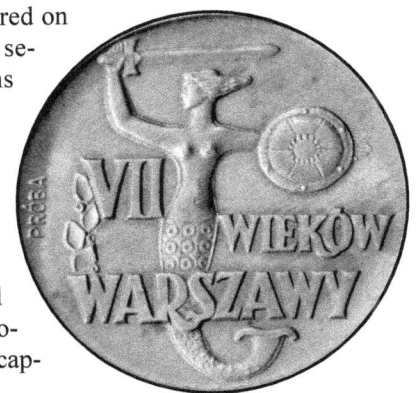

P. T. Barnum took advantage of the popularity of mermaids by displaying a putative mummified one in his circus. Like most of Barnum's exhibits, this one was a hoax: a combination of the head and trunk of a monkey, and the lower body of a fish. According to the promotional literature, the living mermaid had been captured off the Fiji Islands. Therefore, he called it the FeJee Mermaid, or the Feejee Mermaid.

The mummified mermaid scam has been repeated many times in subsequent sideshow carnivals.

Mermaids are pervasive in numerous western cultures. When I typed "mermaid" in the search box on eBay, I got more than 100,000 hits. "Mermaid" on Google got more than three *million* hits.

FEJEE MERMAID, which was exhibited in most of the principal cities of America, in the years 1840, '41, and '42, to the wonder and astonishment of thousands of naturalists and other scientific persons, whose previous doubts of the existence of such an astonishing creation were entirely removed;

Today, mermaids represent a cottage industry, helping to sell thousands of different products from buttons to lunch boxes and everything in between. Mermaid jewelry is a mainstay in women's fashions.

Perhaps the most popular mermaid in the world today is the Little Mermaid. This mermaid was born in 1836, in Denmark, in a fairy tale (or fairy tail) that was written by the most beloved and prolific author of fairy tales in the world: Hans Christian Andersen. He immortalized the mermaid myth in a short story named, appropriately, "The Little Mermaid."

In this tale, the Little Mermaid was the youngest and smallest of six sisters. Together with their king and queen parents – yes, there are mermen too, although they are not anywhere near as popular – they lived under water in a submerged palace that was surrounded by a glorious city. The mother of the females – also a mermaid – told her daughters that they were not allowed to rise to the surface of the sea until they were fifteen years old. One by one, as they reached the prescribed age, they ascended to the interface, saw the sun and the stars and the moon and the activities of humankind, then returned to the seabed and related to their sisters everything that they had observed.

The Little Mermaid could not wait for her turn, but wait she must, while being enthralled by everything that her older sisters told her about the airy world above. Finally, her fifteenth birthday arrived. She scooted to the surface and absorbed the atmospheric wonders. She swam close to shore where she saw a young prince, and immediately fell in love with him.

Every day she returned to the home of the prince in order to watch him. One day the prince and his entourage embarked on a long sea voyage. A great storm arose. The ship was dashed to pieces and everyone onboard drowned. The prince was the last survivor, but was losing his strength to stay afloat. Just as he lost consciousness and slipped beneath the waves, the Little Mermaid – whose name was never given – held onto him, lifted him above the water, and towed him to shore. She placed him on land where a number of girls were gathered. One of the girls spotted the prince, and stood over him as he recovered from his ordeal. The prince then made his way back to his own kingdom.

Hungering for the love of the prince, the Little Mermaid shared her feelings with her mother, and asked if there was any way that she could become human. Her mother told the Little Mermaid that it was impossible for her to do so because humans had im-

Mermaids

The original depiction of the Little Mermaid. In those days, children were not prevented from seeing bare breasts. They grew up normal anyway.

mortal souls and mermaids did not.

Undiscouraged, the Little Mermaid asked a witch if she could have her tail transformed to legs and feet, so that she could meet the prince in person and walk with him, and gain an immortal soul. The witch told the Little Mermaid that she could perform such a transformation, but there was a price attached to it: the Little Mermaid's voice and tongue. The Little Mermaid loved to sing. Of all the mermaids in the world, her voice was the most acclaimed. Nonetheless, she was willing to give up her voice if it would lead to her meeting the prince.

There were other downsides to the operation. Every step the Little Mermaid would take would feel "like a sharp sword going through you." Her feet would bleed. She would never again be able to cavort with her parents and sisters. The transformation was permanent: she could never become a mermaid again. And if the prince married someone other than the Little Mermaid, her heart would break and she would become "foam on the water."

Still the Little Mermaid agreed to the transformation. The witch cut out her tongue and took her voice. From now on she would be mute. And every step indeed felt like swords going through her delicate feet.

The Little Mermaid met the prince and, although she could not speak, they became best friends. They went everywhere together. The Little Mermaid did everything she could to make the prince fall in love with her. One day, the prince confided in her that the girl he wanted to marry was the one who had rescued him from the sea – not the one who towed him to shore, for he knew nothing about that, but the one who found him on the beach and took care of him afterword until he recovered from his experience.

Then the prince met this girl, and married her. The little princess was distraught. Just as she was to be turned into foam and dispersed in the sea, "hundreds of lovely creatures" hovered above her. They were not angels; they were female spirits without wings but who were so light that they could float in the air. They were the "daughters of the air." They did not possess an everlasting soul, but by doing good deeds for three hundred years they could "shape one for themselves."

And so the Little Mermaid became a daughter of the air, till at last she would "come into the heavenly kingdom."

Copenhagen, Denmark – Andersen's birthplace – adopted the Little Mermaid in his honor by placing a bronze statue of her in the city's harbor.

In 1956, Classics Illustrated Junior issued a comic book adaptation of "The Little Mermaid." In this modern children's version, many of the horrific and downbeat elements of Andersen's short story were deleted or changed so that today's sensitive children would not be traumatized.

For example, when the Little Mermaid came of age, her grandmother decorated her tail with seven oyster shells. When she rescued the prince, she left one of the shells in his hand. Although she would feel "great pain" as she walked, the witch did not take her tongue or voice, but warned her that if she spoke, her legs would turn back to a tail. Also, if she could not make the prince marry her within three months, her legs would revert to a tail.

So as not to offend little children (or their parents), the Little Mermaid was shown with green scales that reached above her breasts; her scales magically turned into a dress at the time of the transformation; thus her breasts and nipples were never exposed to pampered eyes. The prince did not marry another, but was in love with the Little

Mermaid; yet he felt that he owed allegiance to the maiden who had saved his life. He came upon the Little Mermaid near the end of three months, when she returned to the spot where she had left the other six shells at the time when her scales had turned into a dress. The prince came upon her, recognized that the shells were the same as his, realized that she was the maiden savior, and asked her to marry him.

The Little Mermaid regained her voice after marriage. She and the prince went to the shore so they could visit with her subaquatic family and friends. And, in modern fairy-tale fashion, they lived happily ever after.

Thus the comic book adaptation affected current feel-good tradition by converting a complex and innovative plot to a simplistic, inoffensive, insipid, and vaporous story that was suitable for modern naive minds.

In Walt Disney's 1989 animated movie, *The Little Mermaid* was given a name: Ariel. (Despite allegations to the contrary, her surname was not Antenna.) Very little of Andersen's original story remained, and justifiably so. Disney's sanitized version utilized the broad basics of Andersen's plotline, but gave the story a twist that converted it from a downer to a "feel good" movie, complete with a happy ending for the hero and heroine (not the recreational drug), and just desserts to the heavy, in this case a female octopus with designs of her own.

Ariel was the youngest of seven sisters. Her father was Triton, who in the Greek pantheon was the messenger of the sea. Ariel's mother was never mentioned. Ariel was always getting into mischief because she rose to the surface to bask in the sun, because she collected human artifacts from sunken ships, and because she wanted to have legs

Mermaids

so she could dance with humans. She wanted to be part of the world of humanity.

One day she watched as a ship got caught in a fierce hurricane. The ship sank. The crew abandoned ship safely in a lifeboat – all but the skipper, who was a prince in a foreign land, and who was looking the world over for a young woman to marry. Ariel saved the prince's life by towing him to a deserted beach. There she sang to him. He awakened and caught a glimpse of her face before she bounded into the sea.

Ariel visited Ursula, the Sea Witch, and pled with her to change her tail to legs and feet. Ursula agreed, but the cost was twofold: she wanted Ariel's voice, and if Ariel did not get the prince to kiss her romantically in three days' time, she would lose her human form, would forfeit her freedom, and would become Ursula's slave. Ariel reluctantly agreed to the witch's conditions.

Ariel found the prince and obtained an audience with him. He recognized her face, but could hear her sing because now she was mute. They went places together, exploring the kingdom. The prince almost kissed her several times, but always something intervened. Seeing how close the pair were to kissing, Ursula changed herself to a beautiful maiden who could sing with Ariel's voice. The prince and Ursula agreed to marry.

On their wedding day, Ariel's friends managed to disrupt the ceremony and punch the voice out of the Sea Witch. The disembodied voice magically entered Ariel's human form. She sang for the prince. The prince was smitten when he recognized her sweet voice. Ursula lost her human form, and reverted to an octopus. But darkness fell before the prince and Ariel could kiss.

Ursula won, and imprisoned Ariel. Triton arrived to fight the ugly Sea Witch. Ursula gained Triton's trident, which gave her power over the sea. But the prince rammed her with his ship. Triton bested Ursula in another duel, and she became a prisoner at the bottom of the sea, while all her erstwhile prisoners were released from bondage. Triton made up with Ariel because he realized that a mermaid must follow her heart wherever it took her. All but Ursula live happily ever after.

If this sounds like typical Disney fare, that is because it is. After all, cartoons are for children, and so are ogres and happy endings. The new tradition for such fare is strictly formulaic. In order for the film to obtain a G rating (for General Audiences: nothing that would offend parents for viewing by children), Ariel wore a brassiere whose cups were small and consisted of a pair of seashells. (I am told by women that hard shells would be *most* uncomfortable.)

It is interesting to note that Ariel was a wreck-diver. She was shown penetrating shipwrecks and recovering relics that she found of interest, but of whose function she was clueless. She had a secret hideaway that was filled with various artifacts.

Ariel was so popular that her likeness was used to adorn a United States postage stamp that was issued in 2005.

Above: A movie poster followed by the novelization under a slightly different title; a digest joke magazine.

Below: A drinking mug; a temporary tattoo (notice reverse printing); ship's figurehead mounted in a museum.

Bottom: Postage stamps from the Congo (note that the mermaid and the whipper in the upper left corner are likenesses of Bettie Page, a famous model from the 1950's); a coin from Palau; a medallion.

Mermaids

Disney published an abbreviated novelization of the movie. It was written by Jan Carr. The film and book spawned a huge franchise in Little Mermaid merchandise that was sold nationwide: the inevitable T-shirt, plus nightgowns, lamp shades, dolls, cake toppers, lapel pins, lunch boxes, purses, collector plates, pajamas, and so on ad infinitum ad nauseam: virtually anything that would appeal to children and would stimulate them or their parents to purchase the items. The Ariel stamp was a merchandising coup that undoubtedly helped Disney's sale of DVD's and associated products.

Mermaids have starred in other movies as well. One of the earliest was *Mr. Peabody and the Mermaid* (1948). Perhaps the most popular was *Splash* (1984). Mermaids have made a splash in hundreds of additional movies that are too numerous to mention. Mermaids have also appeared in books. And in advertisements. And in just about every other form that you can imagine.

Top left: Weeki Wachee was a Florida tourist stop where a school of women conducted underwater ballet's while dressed as mermaids.

Left: Nuclear sub commissioning.

Bottom left: Artist Raphael (1483-1520) painted this mermaid with split legs and fins for feet.

Above: Science Fiction digest cover.

Below: Mermaids are known to be attracted to jewelry, so the fishing line is baited with a pearl necklace.

SIRENS

Whereas mermaids are generally perceived as good or benign, sirens are commonly known as evil. A siren is equivalent to a wicked water witch.

Sirens are usually depicted as adult females in human form, with legs and feet instead of a mammalian tail. Sometimes they are shown with wings. Sirens were anything but angelic. Invariably they went unadorned, or nearly so.

Sirens first appeared in Greek mythology, where they were blamed for the drowning of mariners after they were lured onto rocky shores by the siren's sweet songs and instrumental music, typically played on a lyre. The most famous instance of this kind of catastrophe was described by Homer in *The Odyssey*.

During his return home from the Trojan War – a voyage that lasted more than two decades – Odysseus passed the island of the sirens. He was well aware of their deadly musical talents, but being inquisitive, he wanted to hear them sing. He had his crew lash him to the mast of his ship. He ordered them to stuff their ears with beeswax so that they could not hear their alluring voices that would force the men to wreck the ship. He also ordered them not to release him no matter how much he begged to be untied, until the ship had sailed safely out of range of their singing. Their voices were so hypnotic that Odysseus cried and screamed and struggled to be released, but his crew paid him no heed. Thus the ship was saved from running aground and being dashed to pieces on the rocks.

Jason and his Argonauts clashed with sirens during their infamous quest to steal the golden fleece from the kingdom of Colchis. When the sirens started to sing, he ordered crewmember Orpheus, who was also a musician, to play his music so loud that it drowned out that of the sirens. All were saved from their lethal devices.

Less well known is the story of Leander. He was helmsman on a Greek ship. A siren fell in love with his handsome face and muscular body. She wanted him so badly that she evoked a storm which caused the ship to founder. Leander drowned, so the siren coveted his body in her lap.

The justly earned reputation of the sirens has been maintained for thousands of years. As a result, a siren is defined today as "a beautiful, seductive woman; temptress." The kind of woman who brings men to ruin.

Ironically, a sirenian is "any herbivorous aquatic mammal of the order Sirenia, which includes the manatee and the dugong." These are the very mammals that most scholars claim to be the origin of the mermaid.

This chapter is dedicated to mermaids not only because they adorn the cover, but because my previous book about miscellaneous shipwrecks posed sirens on the cover: *Underwater Reflections*. The sirens on that cover are luring mariners to shore in hopes that their ship will crash so the sirens can recover their treasure and add it to the wealth that they have already accumulated and hidden in their cave.

The present cover shows mermaids who are gamboling innocently on the ocean floor: examining a treasure chest, gazing into a mirror, or swimming through seaweed.

All these images have been handed down through tradition. The creatures they portray are part of mankind's ancient mythology, kept very much alive in vivid paintings, prose, and verse. I wanted to help keep these images alive by passing them along to my readers, and by explaining their multifaceted origin – in order to preserve them for future generations.

Mermaids

Left: This painting of Ulysses and the Sirens was painted by Herbert Draper in 1910. Ulysses was the Roman version of Greek Odysseus, and was written by Vergel instead of by Homer. Note that one of the Sirens is depicted with a tail.

Below left: A Siren playing a lyre was painted by Josef Suess (1867-1937).

Below right: This detailed sculpture of The Siren and the drowned Leander was done by Joseph Durham in 1871.

People no longer believe in mermaids and sirens, but it's fun to dream about mythological creatures even if they never existed.

Santa Claus, on the other hand . . .

NAIADS AND WATER NYMPHS

The names of these two types of female creatures are interchangeable. They are portrayed as nude or partially nude human-looking women who live on, in, or around bodies of freshwater such as streams, swamps, fountains, and wells. Once again we have the Greeks to thank for their creation.

Although they were sometimes responsible for tragedies, they were never evil. For example, consider this passage about Jason's quest to steal the golden fleece, which was recounted in *Bulfinch's Mythology*:

"Hercules left the expedition at Mysia, for Hylas, a youth beloved by him, having gone for water, was laid hold of and kept by the nymphs of the spring, who were fascinated by his beauty." Hylas was a crewmember of the *Argo*.

Thus naiads were known to possess emotional failings such as desire, jealousy, and revenge. These passionate turmoils placed them closer to humanity than to devils.

After their Greek invention, naiads were generally featured as beautiful, wistful, fun-loving beings in female form. They did not go out of their way to be bad. When they acted in immoral ways, it was only because they could not control their emotions: much like people throughout the ages.

Just last week, as we were trekking through the woods, my dog and I drank from a spring that was gushing clear cold water. We were not taunted by any water nymphs. A month ago I paddled down a whitewater river. Of naiads there were none. I suspect that naiads and water nymphs no longer interact with modern sophisticated people.

Continuing the theme, perhaps I will illustrate the front cover of my next shipwreck book with an image of a water nymph. Or better yet, perhaps I will meet and photograph one on a future hike or canoeing venture.

Sigh . . .

This naiad or water nymph who is supported by lily pads in a forest pond is entertaining two young women who appear to be dressed for a Sunday outing to catch fish with a net. (Painted by Hans Zatzka, 1859-1945 or 1949).

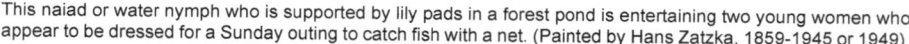

William H. Machen

I have always thought of the *William H. Machen* as the phantom wreck of New Hampshire. The official description of its loss occupied less than a dozen words. Two locations were given at spots that lay 25 miles apart, and the nautical chart had a wreck symbol in yet another location that lay close to shore.

In *Shipwrecks of Maine and New Hampshire*, I speculated about the probable location of this missing collier, which was believed to lie in shallow water near an outlying island: "My best guess is that the wreck lies in deep water."

I am pleased to announce that my speculation has been borne out by a group of intrepid divers who located the wreck at a depth of nearly 300 feet.

Jeff Goodreau sent me an email with a link to a page that provided information about the discovery of the wreck. The search group consisted divers Danny Allan, Jeff Goodreau, and Ryan King, with Scott Morency at the helm. They spent a number of days in 2015 in dragging a magnetometer – a highly sophisticated metal detector – back and forth within a grid in which they thought the wreck might lie. After many days of monotonous searching, they determined precisely where the *William H. Machen* was not.

In 2016 the group worked on other projects. In 2017, they resumed their search for the phantom wreck. Although they located a suitably-sized target, chances were that it was nothing more than a geological formation such as a large rock outcrop. As my dive buddy Ken Clayton used to say, "This is where the neoprene meets the water." In Goudreau's words, they decided to "have a look."

The first dive team consisted of Danny Allan, Bob Foster, and Jeff Goodreau, while Ryan King manned (or personneled, to be politically correct) the helm.

It wasn't until they passed 260 feet in depth that they saw the definite outline of a shipwreck. Although the wreck was not positively identified on that dive, the odds were good that they had found the final resting place of the *William H. Machen*.

Over the succeeding months, the dive team grew in size as others descended to the bottom in order to examine the wreck and look for identifying characteristics. Additional divers included Mike Barnett, Mark Bowers, Josh Cummings, Nate Garrett, Ryan King, and Scott Morency. Foster and King conducted video and still photography.

The wreck was similar to if not the perfect picture of the *William H. Machen* with regard to dimensions. Then, as Goodreau noted, "But it wasn't until a dish bearing the Pocahontas Steamship Company logo that the team felt certain that this was actually the *Machen*."

Hoods off for a job well done.

The *William H. Machen* was a freighter that was sunk after a collision with the *Maid of Stirling*, on July 7, 1942.

Location withheld by Jeff Goodreau.

Andrea Doria

Much has happened with regard to the Grand Dame of the Sea since I published *Deep, Dark, and Dangerous* in 2005. The hull has continued to collapse, more divers have died on the wreck, new discoveries have been made, and a commercial outfit started an abortive effort to take non-diving tourists to the wreck in a five-seat submarine. This may sound like a lot of territory to cover in a chapter, but some of the events are short and to the point.

OceanGate

OceanGate is the name of an outfit that took tourists to see the wreck in 2016. One of the company's promotional gambits was to take advantage of the 60th anniversary of the sinking in its advertisements. Another was to announce its intention to conduct a side-scan sonar survey of the site. A third was to make the claim that it was going to establish a baseline that would enable the company to monitor the rate of collapse from year to year, as it intended to return to the wreck on an annual basis.

I called these lofty goals "gambits" not because they lacked true scientific devotion, but because they were grossly exaggerated. The company issued ingenuous statements for correspondents and newscasters who were hungry for bold-faced headlines and graphic teasers and promises. I don't mean to sound as if I am pooh-poohing its efforts. I accept that a company start-up requires much more than capital. Recognition is essential in any large-scale commercial endeavor. To avoid draining its finances with expensive commercials, reaching the public requires a big presence in the media, even if that presence is manufactured from whole cloth.

But I take exception to some of the company's preambulary statements. For what it's worth, recognizing the 60th anniversary of the sinking of the *Doria* was somewhat irrelevant, as the Italian ocean liner sank on July 26, while the OceanGate tour took place during the second week in June.

In *DDD*, I noted that the optimum weather window for diving on the wreck was from the last week in June through the first week in August. I did not mean to imply that good weather was absent the rest of the year. I meant that diveable weather was less likely and less reliable at other times.

An OceanGate representative called me on the phone as a courtesy, in order to make me aware of upcoming events. He told me that he had read both of my *Doria* books. Had he paid attention to my weather warning, the tour might have met with greater success. In the event, foul weather prevented the surface support vessel and the submersible in tow from staying more than three days. And subsequent trips, with different complements of tourists, were scrapped at the dock. In any case, no tourists had signed up for those following trips.

Only two tourists were willing to spend $10,000 to ride alongside the wreck in the *Cyclops I*. Nonetheless, I cannot remark that they did not get their money's worth. They made only two dives of the planned eight dives, each of three hours' duration. That must have been an awesome experience for both of them, plus the pilot of the submarine. Viewed as a purely economic investment, they may have gotten more for their money than an avid wreck-diver.

The *Ile de France* (right) assisting the *Andrea Doria*. (From the author's collection.)

On average, a wreck-diver makes three twenty-five minutes dives per trip: sometimes more, but often less. Thus he spends around $1,500 for an hour and a quarter of bottom time per trip, and must suffer three cumulative hours of decompression. To get six hours of bottom time, a wreck-diver must therefore go on five four-day trips, at a total cost of $7,500. While it seems as if a wreck-diver spends less than the OceanGate tourists spent, he also must sacrifice twenty days of work, not counting preparation time and all the preliminary dives that are necessary in order to have the experience that is required to make deep dives on the wreck.

A tourist needs no preparation or expertise. He simply walks onboard and enjoys the ride.

In addition to proving the viability of operating a tourist submarine on the *Doria*, OceanGate's support vessel made seventeen side-scan sonar passes, creating images of the wreck in all its collapsing glory. Yet again I must take exception, this time in what the OceanGate rep said to me on the phone. He claimed that they were making a *baseline* of the *Doria's* ongoing state of collapse.

I did not bother to inform him – or remind him, if he had truly read my books – that I had already started the baseline: one that was founded on my personal observations throughout nearly forty years of annual dives on and inside the wreck.

Take this headline as an example of OceanGate's hypocrisy: "New Footage Shows Rapid Breakdown of Shipwreck 'Andrea Doria'." This is unadulterated hogwash. I described the wreck's initial breakdown progress in *Andrea Doria: Dive to an* Era (1989). Then, *DDD* included a comprehensive Collapse Chronology with detailed descriptions of precisely how and when the wreck was collapsing on a year-by-year basis. For OceanGate to claim that this had just been discovered was the height (or depth) of egotistical folly.

Or take this headline: "*Andrea Doria* Shipwreck More Badly Deteriorated Than Expected." This was followed by OceanGate's so-called discovery "of the bow and the catastrophic break when the bow separated from the hull." I made this discovery in

2004. Others – including OceanGate – could have read about it in 2005, when I published DDD. Because an OceanGate rep told me that he had read my books, it seems that he excerpted this fact from my Collapse Chronology, and took credit for my discovery.

OceanGate's promise to return in 2017 was never realized, so the big splash that it made the previous year was it's only splash, and there was no follow-up to its so-called baseline.

STOCKHOLM BELL

In the spring of 2014, the bell from the *Stockholm* was posted for sale on eBay. The seller's eBay name was tomhugre. The buy-it-now price started at $100,000. According to the description, the bell "was recovered from the Andrea Doria sunken Ship wreckage a Short time later by a Private diver," whose name was not provided. In response to a question that was posed by an interested party, the seller revealed that the owner's name was Duffy. Whether this was a given name or a surname was not disclosed.

According to the ungrammatical explanation, "It is easy to see on the right side of the Bell the dent and a crease that was caused by the collision of the 2 ships, resulting in the bell being yanked off its perch and onto the deck of the Doria. The wreckage of the Andrea Doria is one of the most popular and well-known shipwreck sites in the world. The M/S Stockholm Bell was traded by the original diver for needed boat parts to the present owner's Father now willing Sell this Original Real Famous Nautical Treasure."

I had little reason to doubt the authenticity of the bell, but I knew for sure and for certain that it was not recovered from the *Andrea Doria*. Photographs of the crushed bow of the *Stockholm* in dry-dock after the collision clearly show the bell among the wreckage on the forecastle. Thus the history and provenance of the bell were faked.

One Thomas A. Hug posted some video footage of the bell on YouTube: https://www.youtube.com/watch?v=TtTUeM0tJWc. The camera circled the bell in order to show it from all sides. In the narration he stated specifically that the bell had been recovered from the *Doria* wreckage by a diver in approximately 1959.

The asking price quickly dropped to $50,000. By 2015, it had dropped to $29,000. The price dropped again to $25,400. Somewhere along the way, the sentence about the bell being recovered by a private diver was deleted from the description. After a year on the market with no takers, the bell was withdrawn from eBay.

I contacted the seller through eBay, and asked, "Whatever happened to the *Stockholm's* bell?"

Tom Hug replied within minutes. "Stockholm Bell was sold to a person that was actually on the ship when I was selling the bell on EBay. If you Google Stockholm bell on YouTube you'll see they had a ceremony saying they recover the bell back to the ship they had a regular ceremony dedicating the bell back to the ship, thanks Tom."

Visit https://www.youtube.com/watch?v=AhE7m_Udtog for the unveiling ceremony. Tom told me that the bell was purchased for $20,000 by the company that then owned and operated the *Stockholm* under the name *Azores*. The ex-*Stockholm* is still in commission and running Caribbean cruises out of London, which was where Tom had to ship the bell.

In this view of the *Stockholm* in dry-dock, the bell is clearly recognizable in the middle of the forecastle wreckage, in the center of the picture. (From the collection of John Moyer.)

I wrote, "I found it. Many thanks for the prompt reply. Are you permitted to reveal the selling price? Also, did you know that there are pictures of the *Stockholm's* forecastle in dry-dock after the collision in which the bell is clearly shown? Therefore, the bell could not have been recovered by a diver on the *Doria*."

Shortly thereafter, Tom called me on the phone. He was completely ingenuous about the bell's history, and willingly told me all that he knew about it. The owner of the bell that was posted on eBay was Duffy Sullivan. Duffy's father (now deceased) obtained the bell from the diver who claimed to have recovered it from the *Doria*. The diver gave it to Duffy's father in trade for boat parts that included a transmission. Tom did not know the name of the diver, and apparently neither did Duffy.

Even more stunning news was what Tom told me next. Although the outside of the bell had been cleaned and polished to a high brilliance that resembled gold, the inside was covered with barnacles. The clapper also had barnacles on it. This implied that the bell had to have resided in seawater long enough for barnacles to attach themselves and grow. Now I was no longer for sure and for certain about the provenance of the bell.

One on hand the bell was shown in the wreckage of the *Stockholm's* forecastle. On the other hand the bell possessed barnacles. Tom suggested that the bell in the photograph of the *Stockholm's* forecastle must be a different bell from the one that he sold. I admit to being totally confused. I firmly believe that Tom told me the truth about the bell's history; he knows only what Duffy told him. Duffy must have known only what his father told him. In other words, the bell's history was secondhand knowledge; or, as they say in court, the testimony's information was hearsay, and therefore inadmissible.

And there the matter rests.

I also learned from Tom that he had received requests from museums that wanted him to donate the bell and pay the expense of shipping. (On eBay he offered free shipping to anywhere in the world). This constituted a win-lose situation: a win for the museum, a loss for Tom. He diplomatically declined.

Tom also received a request from the television show that went like this: "Hello, Whitney Parshall here. I am the casting producer for History Channel's 'Pawn Stars.' We are on the hunt for some exciting items for sale and took interest in your ship bell. A bit about our program. Pawn Stars is an actual live-sale show. It films transactions at a pawn shop in Las Vegas. You would be filmed interacting with the shop owner, negotiating the sale of your item and discussing the exciting history of the piece. This would be one day for about 3-4 hours."

Lest this sound like a deal made in heaven, "Pawn Stars" wanted Tom to pay all the expenses for shipping the bell to Las Vegas and for his own flight and lodging, with no guarantee that the bell would sell at Tom's opening price. The only expense that the show would incur was the shooting time, with no way to lose on the proposition because the show got an episode out of the deal whether the bell sold or not. No wonder this kind of cable show is proliferating: it makes money no matter what happens, on practically no investment. Again, Tom politely declined.

By the way, the *Stockholm* went through a number of name changes during her long and eventful career: *Volkerfreundschaft, Volker, Fridtjof Nansen, Italia I, Italia Prima, Valtur Prima, Caribe, Athena, Azores, Astoria*. The last name change occurred in March of 2016. During the *Stockholm's* long career, she also underwent numerous refits and modernizations.

Ironically, despite being called the "ship of death" in Italy, for ten years the *Stockholm* was owned and operated by an Italian company: Nina Cia. di Navigazione.

This year (2018) she will be seventy years old. She is still going strong.

The Death Bell Still Tolls

In *Deep, Dark, and Dangerous: Adventures and Reflections on the Andrea Doria* (2005), I appended a statistical sidebar that enumerated the diver fatalities that occurred on or were attributed to the Grand Dame of the Sea. I did this in order to quell the gross exaggeration that byline hungry reporters were wont to make in order to substantiate headlines that made the wreck appear more dangerous than it is. They claimed that more divers had died while diving on the wreck than had been killed in the collision and the tragic aftermath: specifically, more than fifty persons.

At the time of publication, the number of diver fatalities had reached thirteen. Sadly, five more divers have met their demise on or over the *Doria* during the intervening years. I don't wish to dwell on unfortunate death, but I do want to keep the record straight. Thus the following statistics:

14) 2006 July 9   < *Serena* >   Dave Bright (DB=none)
     reached surface alive after uncontrolled ascent with rebreather, lost consciousness on surface, died on boat.

15) 2008 July 30   < *John Jack* >   Terry DeWolf (DB=none)
     rebreather, plummeted to bottom due to loss of buoyancy, landed on seabed off wreck; recovered by Danny Moens and Danny Huyge (both Belgian)

16) 2011 July 24   *< John Jack >*   Michael LaPrade (DB=none)
   rebreather diluent tank empty; recovered by Richie Kohler

17) 2015 July 21   *< John Jack >*   Thomas Pritchard (DB=solo but at the same time as Terry Martzall and Shawn Sweeney).
   Pritchard was using a rebreather
   Cause unknown (possibly dropped off anchor line while decompressing, but his marker strobe was found still attached to the bottom of the anchor line)
   Body not recovered

18) 2017 July 27   *< Old Salty II >*   Steve Slater (DB=not known by me)
   Unknown (possibly rebreather, drysuit, or other equipment failure)
   Reached surface unconscious, retrieved by Robert Thomas

Collapse Chronology Continuation

Not much of the hull has collapsed since my last dive on the *Andrea Doria*, in 2011. The bow has continued to roll over and separate from the main hull. The stern has separated more and is also rolling away, although more slowly and not as much as the bow due to the rounded bottom hull instead of the narrow and pointed hull of the bow; plus the fact that the starboard propeller and rudder are resting on the sand.

Eventually, the wreck will separate into three distinct components: bow, midriff, and stern. The port hull will continue to compress downward as internal supports buckle. None of this comes as any surprise except to landlubbers who are looking to make a splash in the printed and audiovisual media.

Shipwrecks collapse. That's what they do. This is no more of a discovery than the acceptance that old age leads to death.

Future generations of divers should know that the ongoing collapse of the *Doria* does not mean the end of exploration. Although every part of the *Doria* that I visited for 37 years no longer exists, new areas have been will inevitably continue to become exposed. Decks and compartments that I could not reach are now becoming attainable.

Collapse of a shipwreck – any shipwreck – is not equivalent to death. It is instead reincarnation into a new and different form.

Although archaeologists believe, and would like others to believe, that wrecks are preserved into perpetuity, the *Andrea Doria* doesn't look like this any more. (From the author's collection.)

Nezinscot

Space constraints prevented me from including the wreck of this steel-hulled tug in *Shipwrecks of Massachusetts: North*. Here and now I can make up for the deficit.

The tug in question was expressly built for the Moran Towing Company in 1897. She was named *De Witt C. Ivins*, and was immediately put to work as a coastwise tug that operated out of her home port in New York City.

On December 12, 1897, the tug was towing a pair of barges when she ran low on coal off Chatham Light, Massachusetts. She anchored her barges, then departed for Provincetown where she could obtain enough coal to complete her passage.

After a while, the two barges – *Barge No. 48* and *Barge No. 75* – commenced to drag their anchors and proceeded to head offshore. The barges were held together by a towing hawser, but soon the hawser parted and the barges drifted apart. The barge crews lost sight of each other after the fall of darkness. By that time the barges were located some thirty miles from shore.

At noon the following day, "the schooner *Gertrude* sighted *Barge No. 48* and took off the crew [of three men, plus Captain Charles Olsen]. The whereabouts of *Barge 75* is not known but a tug will be sent out to find her. Capt. Charles Peterson is in command, and she carries a crew of four men."

The fishing schooner *Gertrude* transported the barge's captain and crew to Boston, Massachusetts. As no casualty report was issued, it must be presumed that the other barge was located and placed under tow. Neither barge was in danger at any time.

With the onset of the Spanish-American War, the U.S. Navy found itself short of vessels that were needed to prosecute hostilities. The Navy purchased vessels of all kinds from the merchant fleet. The *De Witt C. Ivins* was bought from the Moran Towing Company for $30,000, and renamed *Nezinscot*, after a river in western Maine.

According to the Navy's brief history of the *Nezinscot*: "Serving with the North Atlantic Fleet during the Spanish-American War, operating out of Key West, *Nezinscot* remained in that port following the end of hostilities until the middle of 1900 when she sailed first to Norfolk and then early in 1901 to the Navy Yard, Portsmouth, N.H. [New Hampshire]. For the next eight and one half years, the tug operated out of Portsmouth, towing numerous ships, from the battleship *Missouri* (BB-11) to the smallest auxiliary barge, and making brief voyages to New York Navy Yard, ports in Maine, and most frequently to Boston."

The Navy had fitted the *Nezinscot* with a 16-pounder Colt rifle.

After the war, the Moran Towing Company commissioned the construction of another tug which was named *De Witt C. Ivins*. She was a nearly identical sister to the original *De Witt C. Ivins*. Yet another tug named *De Witt C. Ivins* was constructed for Moran by the same yard in 1920.

According to Ivins' obituary, "Mr. Ivins was at one time connected" with the Moran Towing Company. By "connected" I presume that Ivins was an investor in the company. Nearly every other Moran tug, then and today, bore names of a Moran family member.

The ultimate demise of the *Nezinscot* occurred on August 11, 1909. She departed from Portsmouth at three o'clock in the morning, bound for Boston at ten knots with a heavy cargo of anchor chain, two anchors, and searchlights for delivery to the battleship *Missouri*: altogether some twenty tons of cargo. In command was Captain Thomas Edward Evans. In addition to the crew, also on board were the skipper's wife, their son, and Dr. Charles Trotter.

According to Chief Boatswain's Mate Frank Bitter, "The weather was clear when we left Portsmouth at 3 a m, but there was a strong breeze from the north-northwest. The run was without incident until we reached Halibut point, when a sea boarded the tug, rolling her over on her side.

"Instead of righting, the tug curbed down, probably through some shifting of her deck load. The tug remained in that position for about two minutes, and then sank. In that brief period, while she was above water, Capt Evans had ordered all hands on deck and the crew came tumbling up, but two of them, cook White and a seaman named Taylor, did not appear, and I think they went down with the ship.

"When the tug sank we were all thrown into the water. The captain shouted: 'Save my wife and boy.' I managed to find the woman struggling in the water, but had some difficulty in getting a life belt around her. Then we managed to get hold of a plank, to which we found the boy clinging.

"In the meantime, Capt Evans, Dr. Trotter and the chief engineer had got hold of an oak grating, while four of the crew had found the tug's boat floating and righted her. Mrs Evans, the boy and myself were clinging to the plank and I was supporting Mrs. Evans when one of the negro deck hands came drifting by on a piece of wreckage, but instead of holding on he grasped my leg and I felt myself being pulled down.

"I could only shake my leg feebly and it took all my strength to keep the woman up, but the boy, who was about 14 years old, seeing that the negro was likely to drown all of us by his struggles, reached over and pushed him off, telling him to go back to his own plank. The negro disappeared and we did not see him again.

"After we had been floundering about in the water for about an hour, and Mrs Evans was almost unconscious from exhaustion, the sailors came up with the boat, which they had righted, and hauled all three of us onboard. We could see nothing of the three men on the grating, so we reluctantly pulled ashore in order to obtain medical aid for Mrs Evans. The boy seemed to have withstood the long struggle without difficulty." After reaching shore, "Mrs Evans was taken to the home of a local physician, where at noon it was stated that she was in fair condition, although much prostrated."

Rescue operations were initiated as soon as news of the catastrophe was received

USS *Nezinscot*. (Courtesy of Dave Clancy.)

by those on shore. "Word was at once telegraphed to Admiral Swift at Boston." Swift immediately orchestrated search and rescue operations to search the area for those who might be adrift at sea. He dispatched the torpedo boat *Davis*, the naval tugs *Sioux*, *Iwana*, and *Potomac*, the revenue cutter *Androscoggin*, and the customhouse tug *Winnisimmet*.

In addition, boats were deployed from the life-saving stations at both Old House Cove and Rockport.

Captain Evans, Machinist's Mate Second Class A. Belfric, and Dr. Trotter caught a grating that floated up from the wreck. They clung to this for several hours as it drifted away from the wreck site. Dr. Trotter eventually lost his grip, was swept away, and drowned. Evans and Belfric spotted the tug's pilot house, which had also floated up from the wreck, swam to it, and crawled onto the barely exposed roof. Evans lost consciousness, but Belfric held onto him as he clung to the roof of the pilot house.

At 9:30 in the morning, Captain Nelson King and the crew from the Old House Cove Life-Saving Station rescued Evans and Belfric from their precarious perch.

Captain Evans was still unconscious, and could not be revived until after he was landed and taken to the house of Dr. Rowley. "It was several hours before he was fully conscious, and at the reunion between the captain and his wife the rescue was regarded as a miracle. Each had believed the other lost."

Four men lost their lives in the catastrophe: Leroy Edwards (ordinary seaman), C. L. Taylor (ordinary seaman), Dr. Charles Trotter (acting assistant naval surgeon), and C. F. White (ship's cook).

Those who survived were: A. Belfric (machinist's mate, second class), Frank Bitter (chief boatswain's mate), Captain T. E. Evans, Mrs. Evans, son of Captain and Mrs. Evans, W. H. Fitzgerald (ordinary seaman), C. H. Pratt (chief machinist's mate), V. F. Tillotson (fireman first class), and C. F. Underdown (fireman second class).

"The tug *M. Mitchell Davis*, with wrecking gear and a diver, arrived at the scene of the *Nezinscot's* capsize at 10:30, to see if she can be raised." The depth was given as 205 feet, "seven miles north by east of Lanesville." The location was also given as "seven miles north by east of Halibut Point.

Local river men attributed the foundering of the *Nezinscot* to overloading, "as gross carelessness on the part of someone at the navy yard in sending a tug so heavily freighted to sea."

According to one account, "The *Nezinscot* has met with various mishaps and on the trial trip of the USS *Denver* was sent to sea as one of the stake boats, fouling with one of the other vessels of the fleet and narrowly escaping being sunk.

"About three years ago a fire pump, which weighed two and one-half tons, was placed aboard the tug. After the pump was tested it was found that the boat was practically useless as a fireboat, but the pump was allowed to remain onboard.

"The tug when loaded for a trip with 40 tons of coal in her bunkers and her water tanks had a carrying capacity of 11,000 gallons. Capt C. O. Olsen, who was master of tugs before the appointment of Capt Evans, once refused to put to sea in the craft, telling the executive officer of the yard he would not take the responsibility for the safety of his crew.

"The shipment of cables, anchors, and stores on the deck of the tug, weighing 30 or more tons, on a craft designed for towing purposes and not as a freighter is criticized by river men."

The Navy was also critical of the loss of the *Nezinscot*. A court of inquiry was immediately organized in order to determine the reason for the loss of the tug, or to assign blame to an individual so as not to reflect on the Navy. The board of inquiry chose to take the latter course by designating a scapegoat.

"The Navy department will try to hold Naval Constructor J. G. Tawresey responsible for the disaster to the tug *Nezinscot*, which foundered between Portsmouth and Boston on Aug. 11, when Acting Assistant Surgeon D. E. Trotter, attached to the Portsmouth Naval Hospital, and three other men lost their lives. The tug capsized because she was overloaded. Constructor Tawresey's alleged responsibility lies in the fact that he happened to see her before she left the Portsmouth yard and suggested to her Captain that she was too heavily loaded. Now the department seeks to hold that, having such a suspicion, the full performance of duty on the part of Constructor Tawresey required that he should insist upon a listing test before permitting the tug to sail, and that when he did not insist he became responsible for the subsequent disaster."

Shifting the blame by sacrificing Tawresey took the Navy off the hook. But that was not all.

"Five enlisted men are to be tried at the same time on charges of neglect of duty in connection with the loss of life. *But so far no court has been appointed to try anybody for overloading the vessel* [my italics]. The enlisted men to be tried are Frank H. Bitter, chief boatswain's mate, who was second in command on the tug and had charge of the boat after the *Nezinscot* capsized [sic], the master having been lost [sic]; George H. Pratt, chief machinist's mate; William Fitzgerald, seaman, and V. F. Tillotson and C. F. Underwood, firemen. The charge against these men is one of the most unusual in the naval service, that of deserting comrades in danger of their lives and of failing to attempt a rescue."

According to the Navy whitewash, "When the department heard about Tawresey's connection with the matter he was asked about it, and at once replied, confirming the report of his suggestion." Tawresey's honesty gave the Navy a way out of the situation without seeking to ascertain who authorized the overloading of the tug.

As for the enlisted men, "The charges against the enlisted men are based upon the statements of one of the survivors of the *Nezinscot*, who accuses them of what amounts to cowardice. His charge has special reference to the loss of Surgeon Trotter. It is charged that Dr. Trotter left his place on a life raft which he had procured and went to the assistance of one of the accused men, who was struggling in the sea. He got a sailor to the raft and the man took the place Dr. Trotter had relinquished. But when Dr. Trotter sought to get on the raft again he found he made one too many and the raft would not sustain them all. The result was that before he could get any other means of support he became exhausted and sank. During this struggle it is charged the other four enlisted men made stronger efforts to save themselves than they did to help any of the officers who were in danger.

"Altogether this will be one of the most remarkable navy courts-martial ever held."

At the trial, "Chief boatswain's mate Frank R. Bitter testified in his court martial at Portsmouth navy yard yesterday in connection with the loss of the tug *Nezinscot*. His story of saving Mrs Evans and the loss of the four men differed materially from that told by Capt Evans. He was corroborated by seaman Fitzgerald."

Ultimately, Tawresey was acquitted, perhaps because the Navy was unable to stick him with a responsibility that was not his to possess. Still, the Navy made no attempt to learn who was responsible for overloading the tug.

Lacking any follow-up news items, it seems likely that the four enlisted men were also acquitted. Thus ended the Navy's investigation into the circumstances surrounding the loss of the *Nezinscot*: not with a bang but a whimper.

But that was not the end of the matter. On October 7, it was reported: "Capt Thomas E. Evans, master of tugs at the Portsmouth navy yard, was arrested here [Portsmouth] tonight upon a charge of capias issued by Col John H. Bartlett, J. B. Mitchell and E. L. Guptill, attorneys for Ellen S. Edwards, administratrix of the estate of Leroy M. Edwards. The writ claims damages in the sum of $5000, charging that Capt Evans, as master of the tug *Nezinscot*, so negligently loaded and managed the tug on Aug 11 last that it foundered at Halibut point, and that because of the negligence of Capt Evans, Edwards, who was a member of the crew of the tug, was lost." ("Capias" is a legal term that means "a writ authorizing an officer to arrest the person specified therein.")

Again, as there was no follow-up, we may presume that the case – if there ever was one – was quietly quashed.

On the other hand, there was a great hue and cry some six months later when another Navy tug was lost, this time with all hands, totaling thirty-two men: the captain and crew of the *Nina*, and sailors who were using the tug for transport to Boston, where they were to be assigned to various Navy vessels. For details of the "lost and found" of the *Nina*, see *Shipwrecks of Delaware and Maryland*.

According to one editorial: "What makes it harder to bear for those related to the victims of this sea tragedy is the thought that it might have been averted. A wireless outfit on the *Nina* would have made her predicament known and with so many vessels plying along the coast the chances of rescue would have been greatly increased. The government is rich enough to equip every coastwise vessel with wireless. It is to be hoped that the two lessons that stand out prominently as a result of these disasters – that no small vessel should be allowed to proceed until some commissioned officer has personally assumed the responsibility, and that wireless be installed quickly on all vessels – should be put in effect before a third disaster arouses the country to action."

The Navy officially abandoned the *Nezinscot* on August 28, 1909. According to a memo from the Navy's Scientific and Computing Branch of the Bureau of Construction and Repair, bearing that date, "The *Nezinscot* has been stricken from the Navy List."

Statistics

Built: 1897
Previous names: *De Witt C. Ivins*
Gross tonnage: 117
Type of vessel: Propeller driven tugboat
Builder: Neafie & Levy, Philadelphia, Pennsylvania
Owner: U.S. Navy
Cause of loss: Foundered
Location: 42-47-30 N / 70-32-W

Sunk: August 11, 1909
Depth: 250 feet
Dimensions: 88' x 19' x 10'
Power: Coal-fired steam
Armament: One 16-pounder Colt rifle

8 miles, 17 degrees true from Straitsmouth Island Light

U-550

Originally I intended to write a nitty-gritty, in-depth chapter about the discovery of this long-lost U-boat from World War Two: a vessel whose history I covered in three previous volumes: *Track of the Gray Wolf* (1989), *Shipwrecks of Massachusetts: South* (2006), and *The Fuhrer's U-boats in American Waters* (2006). But I postponed completion of *Shipwreck Potpourri* for so long, while working on other projects, that I have since been superseded by an entire book about the subject: *Where Divers Dare: the Hunt for the Last U-boat*, by Randall Peffer.

Nonetheless, I still wish to cover the topic briefly in order to provide a short summary of the discovery, to add some peripheral details, and to promote the book for those who are interested in shipwreck discoveries in general and lost U-boats in particular.

First, I must say that the phrase "the last U-boat" is a gross misnomer to which I take particular exception. There are literally *hundreds* of sunken U-boats from two world wars that have yet to be discovered. The *U-550* was not even the last lost U-boat off the American eastern seaboard.

Yet unfound from World War Two are *U-215*, *U-234*, *U-521*, *U-548*, *U-805*, *U-857*, *U-858*, *U-873*, *U-889*, and *U-1228*. Still missing from World War One is *U-111*.

What makes this issue worse is that Mazraani found the *U-550* on July 23, 2012. *Where Divers Dare* was published on April 5, 2016. Then NOAA discovered the *U-576* off the North Carolina coast on August 24, 2016. This subsequent "last" U-boat was found four years after the discovery of the *U-550*, and a bare four and a half months after the book proclaimed that the *U-550* was the "last" U-boat that existed to be found.

Be that as it may, although the title is a misleading exaggeration, at least the entire book is not an exaggeration, as was the book about the discovery of the *U-869*: *Shadow Divers*, by Robert Kurson. The latter book did contain a kernel of truth, but it was a very small kernel, and even then it was mostly corn.

Cap's off to Peffer for a job well done! He stuck rigidly to facts that were provided by participants who themselves stuck rigidly to facts. The result is a factual account of the search for and discovery of the most elusive U-boat off the New Jersey-New York bight.

I wrote "elusive" because over the years, a number of divers have searched for the *U-550* – including this author. One of the search trips on which I participated helped to pave the way for the discovery of the *U-550*. That is because

The *Pan-Pennsylvania* is burning in the background while the U-boat that torpedoed her is sinking in the foreground. (Courtesy of the National Archives.)

we discovered the tanker that the *U-550* torpedoed: an action which led to the U-boat's ultimate demise.

The location of the *Pan-Pennsylvania* was crucial to locating the final resting place of the *U-550* because after a dramatic running gun battle, the U-boat sank within sight of the *Pan-Pennsylvania*. Even though the tanker did not sink immediately, she did not drift far before she slowly, almost languorously, capsized and settled with her stern on the muddy bottom and her bow protruding above the surface of the sea, still afire. Even then, it took two days of burning, gunning, depth-charging, and aerial bombardment to clear the ocean of a hazard to navigation. For the full story and gruesome details, read the three books that are mentioned above.

The person who was almost solely responsible for finally discovering the U-boat was Joe Mazraani. When he set his course on the *U-550*, he bought a boat, switched from open-circuit scuba to rebreather, organized search trips, obtained side-scan sonar operator Garry Kozak, and plowed the area in the vicinity of the tanker until the wreck was located. That is what I call extreme dedication. Mazraani's boat was appropriately named *Tenacious*.

What I compressed into a paragraph took several years of hard work and effort, to say nothing of the costly monetary investment.

Other divers on the discovery trip were Steve Gatto, Tom Packer, Brad Sheard, Eric Takakjian, and Anthony Tedeshi. The date was July 23, 2012. The depth was 330 feet.

After reading *Where Divers Dare*, I contacted Steve Gatto and told him how much I enjoyed the book. He blasted back, "How could you have read the book already? It won't be published for another two months." Or words to that effect.

I let him stew for a while, then told him that I had bought an uncorrected proof from a seller on eBay. Clearly printed on the top of the front cover were the words, "Limited Distribution – NOT FOR SALE." I suppose that the putative reviewer sought to make some extra money after receiving a free copy from the publisher. Can't trust reviewers. They're worse than critics. . . . wrote a person who has reviewed books himself. I cherished the books that I received for review, gave an honest review, and kept the book for reference. I guess you can't trust *some* reviewers. And no critics.

My advice is: read the book.

Location withheld by Joe Mazraani.

Below: The *U-550* settling by the stern. Note the empty depth-charge rack on the fantail of the destroyer. (Courtesy of the National Archives.)

WHITE SQUALL

The *White Squall* had a short but intense career. She was built in England in 1864 as one of the first iron-hulled barks to slide down the ways. Wood was slowly yielding to iron as a result of lessons that were learned during the American Civil War, when the strength of iron over wood was clearly demonstrated as the Confederate ironclad warship *Virginia* utterly destroyed two Union wooden-hulled warships of vastly greater fire power, and egressed from the conflict practically unscathed. The message was clear: iron was stronger than wood.

The *White Squall* was built for the Oriental trade. In those days, six months or more were required to sail from England to ports in Asia no matter which way she went: around the Cape of Good Hope (Africa) or around Cape Horn (South America). (Construction of the Suez Canal was not completed until 1869.) She was under the command of Captain Thomas Thirkell, who had been a sailing master for more than two decades.

Asia was an emerging market for local ores, fibers, and, of course, tea. In Malaysia and Singapore, the *White Squall* took on a valuable cargo of tin, rattan, and coffee. Her destination was Boston, Massachusetts. Near the end of a long voyage, she rounded Cape Cod when disaster struck. A fire broke out and quickly consumed the vessel. The bark came to rest when her hull touched bottom, stranding her off Cahoon's Hollow, near Wellfleet.

At first it was hoped that the hull could be refloated. Salvors were endeavoring to pump the water out of her bilge when, according to a contemporary article dated February 22, 1867, "The bark *White Squall*, from Singapore for Boston, previously reported ashore on Cape Cod, went entirely to pieces last night, strewing the beach with fragments of the vessel and its East India cargo. The underwriters' steam-pump was also lost."

Local rumor has it that the wreck was partially salvaged shortly after her loss, with particular emphasis placed upon recovering that portion of the cargo that was not ruined by exposure to seawater, as the coffee and rattan were undoubtedly cold-brewed and waterlogged. The freight that was not adversely affected by saltwater submergence was tin.

Local rumor also has it that the government recovered more of the semi-precious metal during World War Two, when that element was so much in demand due to wartime needs, and therefore a valuable commodity, especially as it could be recovered in the pure state in bulk instead of having to be smelted and extracted from ore.

According to the *International Handbook of Underwater Archaeology* (2002), "Like many agencies of her sister states, MBUAR [Massachusetts Board of Underwater Archaeological Resources] was subject to a number of legal challenges during the 1980s and was a codefendant, with two permittees, in the case of Barry Clifford et al. v. Board of Underwater Archaeological Resources. The case dealt with the MBUAR's regulatory authority over shipwreck remains of the vessel *White Squall*. Preliminary research strongly suggested the *White Squall* had significant archaeological and historical importance and integrity. The suit was originally brought in 1983 and was decided in MBUAR's favor in February 1991, and the plaintiff withdrew his appeal, an outcome that demonstrated the fairness and appropriateness of MBUAR's administrative actions and resource management scheme."

As additional information, which was not mentioned in the above paragraph or elsewhere in the book, Clifford challenged the State's amount of taxation that it levied on recovered treasure – 25% – which he considered to be exorbitant, especially as the State did not share any of the financial risk in the salvage operation. In other words, the State profited without making an investment.

Not only that, but such a tax code violated the Congressional mandate of "no taxation without representation." In this respect, it is important to remember that the American Revolution was fomented precisely because England overtaxed American citizens who had no representation in the British government. This issue is just as noteworthy today as it was more than two centuries ago, when American citizens rebelled and went to war against unjust overlords.

Be that as it may, the MBUAR later issued a salvage permit to an outfit known as the Ocean Marine Diving Company. This led to an unfortunate chain of events in which their reconnaissance permit was suspended in 1998. In 2005, their permit was revoked because the Massachusetts Environmental Police "determined that three members of OMDC, Matthew Costa, James Costa, and Parker Barnes had violated the terms of the permit issued to OMDC by selling the tin cargo recovered from the iron bark *White Squall*.... There were deliberate attempts to cover up this sale and to confuse and otherwise deceive the Board. Further, OMDC has been involuntarily dissolved as a corporation by the Secretary of State. There was no evidence to show that Mr. Barnes had prior knowledge of the violation or received any proceeds as a result of these violations. ... Mr. Barnes is now deceased. ... There was no evidence of any involvement in these violations by the other members of OMDC."

It was estimated that OMDC recovered some one hundred ingots of tin that were worth $100,000. This represented a loss – at the 25% taxation rate – of $25,000 to the Commonwealth of Massachusetts.

Attending the September 1, 2005 public meeting of the MBUAR was Oscar Snow, once a member of the OMCD and now the president of Underwater Discoveries Unlimited, which "had submitted a reconnaissance permit application" for the *White Squall*. Snow "left the organization because he did not approve of the manner in which the company was conducting the operation." Now "he feels that he has an obligation to complete the project in a proper manner, which would include a thorough documentation of the site."

According to the regulations, "The Board issues permits to persons who have located a shipwreck or other resource for purposes of investigation, exploration, recovery, reporting and/or conservation of underwater archaeological resources if the Board deems that such operations are in the public interest."

One question to be considered was: what constitutes public interest? One answer was: money for the Commonwealth by way of taxation.

At the very outset of the meeting, it was established that Snow's permit application "does meet the requirements of the Board as stated in the regulations and therefore should be accepted."

However, certain board members whined repeatedly that they wanted more in the application than was required by the regulations: an absurdist concept that tainted this particular permitting process with personal grudges or grievances that were arbitrary and capricious: the very things that regulations seek to condemn.

Those disapproving board members constantly reiterated their dissatisfaction. They either did not understand or failed to accept that the permit application that Snow submitted was for reconnaissance, not for excavation. They wanted a permit application that included a research design, methodology, historical documentation, potential educational opportunities, archaeological significance of the wreck, "means of disseminating the results of its [UDU's] research and sharing the findings of the project. Additionally, the project archaeologist should provide research questions and a methodology that would enable the project to proceed in this manner."

Approving board members reminded the dissenters that, although UDU had secured the services of an archaeologist, an archaeologist was not required by the regulations at this stage of the project: that is, reconnaissance and not excavation. Furthermore, none of the other hoops that the dissenters wanted to put UDU through were applicable at this stage of the project. Putting the cart before the horse, to coin a cliché, was the standard bureaucratic maneuver that was purposely intended to frustrate the success of the project.

Some members wanted the application to contain more information. But no one – not even dissenters – could articulate what that information should be. One consenter noted that it made no sense to deny the application "based on the absence of information that is not technically required.

This ridiculous situation inflamed one member to declare, "If we can't tell him what we are looking for, then we are just throwing up dust in the air and causing a whole big commotion and smokescreen."

Again, this was SOP for bureaucratic dalliers whose goal was to prevent projects from achieving success – or from ever having the opportunity to commence. Those kind of people enjoyed making people fail: a psychological aberration of people who wield authority.

Ah, committees. Can't live without them; can't kill them.

After much, much, much discussion and some vehement argument among board members, it was ultimately determined that because the permit application met the minimum standards and guidelines that the MBUAR required, the permit should be granted. And it was.

Six months later, Snow attended an MBUAR meeting to which he brought "a considerable about [sic] of information that was required by the Board as conditions to the current reconnaissance permit."

Snow made some observations about the condition of the wreck: "The vessel is in three pieces and the site is a mess. . . . most of the non tin artifacts associated with the vessel were either recovered by OMDC or were washed away by currents and storm activity. . . . the vessel's deck, fittings, gear, etc. are gone and . . . the tin is essentially all that remains due to its weight and the fact that it is interlocked."

Most of the artifacts were recovered from the stern quarter. "The rest of the vessel was nothing but open framing."

One member commented, "OMDC did recover some thirty artifacts which are now in the Board's possession."

Snow reminded the board that the tin was not always exposed. Shifting currents sometimes covered the tin with sand. But UDU had the capability to remove the sand.

With respect to the *White Squall*, the meeting went smoothly and without any vituperation or the argumentative spirit that dominated the previous one. Snow's permit was quickly modified from reconnaissance to excavation.

The *White Squall* project appears to have languished over the following decade. According to the MBUAR, "Except for relocating key sections of the hull remains, UDU had not undertaken any excavation or recovery from the site." No reason was given for holding salvage operations in abeyance over such a long timeframe.

Finally, at the MBUAR meeting of January 28, 2016, the course of the sunken sailing vessel took a different tack. UDU informed the board that it would not be renewing the permit. This may have been due in part to the death of Oscar Snow.

On the heels of that announcement, one board member suggested that the board "consider nominating the site of the *White Squall* as the Board's first underwater archaeological preserve."

A board description of the site ran thus: "From previous investigation [from commercial investigators, not from board members] the bow area, stern area with rudder post, and keel with frames. There was also the windlass and some of the cargo. That area has significant sand accretion. There is potential integrity." Elsewhere it noted, also from commercial investigators, "Site survey has indicated the presence of the iron bow and stern (with rudder post), the iron keel (or keelson) and frames, ship's windlass, and cargo."

With regard to imposed restrictions should the nomination be accepted: "You could not collect artifacts from the site, but it would not restrict recreational diving."

The nomination form belies the imposed restrictions in a roundabout way. The form for the Nomination For Underwater Archaeological Preserve requires the nominator to "Indicate the exact location on attached NOAA nautical chart or USGS topographic map, specify technique used to fix position, and note other identifying features which define location of the site."

Yet, on the line for longitude and latitude, instead of providing coordinates, the word **REDACTED** is typed in capital and boldfaced letters. This leaves one to wonder how recreational divers are supposed to dive on a site whose location is withheld.

Statistics

Built: 1864
Previous names: None
Gross tonnage: 537
Type of vessel: Iron-hulled bark
Builder: Patterson & Son, Bristol, England
Owner: Garn'ck & Cassidy & Company, Liverpool, England
Port of Registry: Liverpool, England
Cause of loss: Burned
Location: Off Cahoon's Hollow, near Wellfleet

Sunk: February 1867
Depth: 10 to 30 feet
Dimensions: 164' x 27' x 17'
Power: Sail

GPS: Withheld by the MBUAR

Herbert Parker

Loran: 26621.3 / 43184.6   Maximum depth: 180 feet.

The name is fictitious. This is the wreck of an old steamship that appears to have been constructed prior to World War Two, and possibly as early as World War One. It is likely a freighter. It lies some 60 miles east of Barnegat Inlet.

The wreck is more than 300 feet in length – how much more is indeterminable because there is no recognizable stem. About 100 feet forward of the remains of the midship structure, the hull is so broken down that it dips into the white sandy bottom without exhibiting any recognizable features, such as a forecastle or stem. The original hull could have been as long as 400 feet. The beam is approximately 45 feet.

The highest relief occurs at the remains of the midship structure: about 25 feet. This structure is squared off with definite boundaries fore and aft and to either side. The structure is skeletal so that one can drop down into the lower decks from above; one can also exit through the starboard side, where the hull plates have sloughed off and only the beams (both horizontal and vertical) remain.

A debris field exists on the starboard side of the midship structure, and extends both fore and aft. Very little debris extends from the port side. From these facts, and from the angle of the rudderpost, it appears that the ship listed to some extent onto its starboard side when it sank; then, as the hull deteriorated and collapsed, the midship structure regained some of its horizontal aspect.

Immediately abaft the midship structure lies a centerline boiler. Six to 8 feet abaft this boiler lies a pair of boilers side by side, separated from each other by 2 to 3 feet, and each separated from the adjacent hull by 3 to 5 feet. Each of these three Scotch boilers measures approximately 20 feet in diameter. The forward boiler appears to have the same dimensions as the after pair of boilers; thus it does not seem to be a typical donkey boiler, but might be one that provided additional steam for the propulsion machinery.

Abaft the pair of boilers, and offset to port, lies a condenser. The upper exposed side of this condenser has been stripped or rusted away, revealing the interior tube assembly. The condenser is angled with respect to the fore and aft orientation of the hull – perhaps 30° or more.

A space of 8 to 10 feet separates the after end of the pair of boilers and what appears to be the engine mass. The engine mass appears to be covered with deck plates which themselves are thickly encrusted. Thus the engine itself is largely indistinguishable. Due to the low profile of the engine mass, it is possible that the engine is a steam turbine instead of a triple expansion reciprocating steam engine.

The curvature of the fantail is recognizable. It lies about fifty feet abaft the aft end of the engine mass. The area between the engine mass and the fantail is piled high with large-size debris that is unrecognizable. It could be machinery or cargo. Several portholes were noted in this area, leading to the speculation that the ship possessed a large aft structure such as a poop deck.

Traces of the rudder post are exposed beneath the fantail. The post is angled to starboard about 20°.

Shipwrecked – or Near Wrack and Ruin

One of my dives on this fascinating wreck nearly resulted in disaster. After I reached the seabed I headed straight for the stern, puttering through high wreckage along the way. When I reached the area of the fantail, I held up my gauge panel in order to check my time . . . only to discover that neither of my two dive computers had switched on automatically when I hit the water. Both screens were blank.

Naturally, I panicked. But after a moment's thought I settled down and reasoned out my predicament. I knew the depth from previous dives. Based on the distance I had traveled, I estimated that I had been on the bottom for approximately ten minutes. If I returned right away, it should take me another ten minutes to reach the anchor line. So I moseyed back on a parallel course in visibility that measured 40 feet.

I ascended slowly to a depth that looked like 50 to 40 feet. I was not certain of the depth because that information should have been displayed on my computer screens. For the same reason, neither was I able to watch the time. But I had done enough dives to equivalent depths that I knew by heart how long the decompression penalty should be. I erred on the side of caution by overestimating the depth and over-counting times, and by staying deeper and hanging longer at every stop.

I surfaced without showing systems of decompression injury. This just goes to prove that the best backup is the human brain, and a comprehensive knowledge of decompression penalties for every depth and bottom time.

Below left: The long tubular item appears to be the crankshaft of an engine that has toppled onto its side.
Below right: The midship structure is partially intact. This ladder connects one interior deck with another.

San Diego
Watch and Locket

The Watch Below

With the passage of time, Nature has treated the *San Diego* unmercifully. Since I wrote the book on the warship – *U.S.S. San Diego: the Last Armored Cruiser* (1989) – the wreck has collapsed so much that were I to dive on the shredded remains today, I would not even recognize the hull in which I made more than 150 penetrations. Such is the way of all shipwrecks. We can but mourn the inevitable passing the way we grieve over the death of a loved one.

And I loved the *San Diego*. She sank on July 19, 1918, after striking a mine that was laid by the German U-boat *U-156*. I suppose that was when this story began: when more than a thousand sailors abandoned the capsizing warship and left behind their worldly possessions.

With regard to diving on the *San Diego*, the good old days were indeed the good old days. Seeing the wreck today is like visiting the grave of a friend or family member. Such is life . . . and death.

But some parts of the *San Diego* are very much alive: they are the parts that were rescued by wreck-divers before the armored hull collapsed and either crushed or buried the living relics that produce fond celebration of the *San Diego's* illustrious history.

This chapter is about the travels and ultimate destination of two of those personal and precious relics.

The modern story began on May 2, 1981, when a small group of dedicated wreck-divers squeezed onto the dive boat *Ark* in anticipation of diving on and inside the wreck of the *San Diego*. Owner and skipper Danny Bressette so named the boat because of the wreck-diving "animals" he expected to transport to shipwrecks near the *Ark's* home base of Freeport, on Long Island, New York. These so-called animals were known in the diving community as "gorilla divers," because they dived deeper, stayed down longer, and decompressed more than those who were known colloquially as "tourist divers" (with evident disdain). Danny's expectations were quickly achieved.

All of us eagerly splashed into the cold spring water to be greeted by fantastic visibility: from 50 to 75 feet. We each explored different decks and sections of the wreck. I returned to the boat with two keepsakes: a brass cigarette holder and a leather slipper. Others found different items. But the top artifact of the day belonged to Mike Boring. Out of the mud, muck, and silt of an interior compartment in the aft officers' quarters, he pulled a gold watch.

A person who was unfamiliar with the background of diving might be inclined to claim that Mike was lucky that day. But luck had nothing to do with making his find. He lived in the Washington, DC area. After work on Friday, he packed his gear and drove for five hours reach the dive boat in Freeport. Near midnight, he loaded his gear in the dark. He slept in a dank bunk or on the hard deck until very early in the morning. After the boat left the dock, for two hours he endured the loud noise and vibration that were generated by the diesel engine. Then he donned thousands of dollars' worth of scuba gear, rolled over the gunwale, descended the anchor line, and conducted his reconnaissance and deep penetration . . .

. . . and he did that week after week, month after month, for year after year, for a full decade: gaining confidence with his equipment, honing his skills, keeping a sharp eye open for hazards, and learning the layout of the wreck. By the time he found the watch, he had spent thousands of dollars in gasoline and charter fees. He learned where to look for artifacts, and how to recognize them when they were buried. When he finally spotted the watch, the only part of it that was exposed above the silt, was the pea-sized bail for the chain that would have secured to watch to a button hole as the watch rested in its fob.

No part of sighting that tiny gold hoop had anything to do with luck. It had to do with a huge investment in time and money. It had to do with skill and experience. It was no accident that Mike found himself at the right time at the right place under the right conditions to spot a speck of gold amid a swirl of muck and mud. It was purpose and conscious decision that drove Mike to *go* to the right place.

It was not chance that favored Mike, but a prepared mind and the will that it took to prepare that mind for all eventualities. It's not the same as walking along a sidewalk and spotting a dime on the cement. It is much, much, much more. It is active participation in conducting a search that might prove to be fruitless . . . or that might lead to a basketful of fruit. Mike discovered the watch by crawling laboriously above the black mire, while holding his dive light at an angle and with his facemask nearly touching the swirling ooze, until he saw the glint of gold.

After a boat ride back to the dock, after unloading his equipment, after a five-hour drive home, after a little bit of sleep, after a full day of work, Mike made some time to examine his find. The crystal was missing, and the internal springs, pins, and cogs were a disarticulated pile of parts. But the case was intact and unbroken without dents. He soaked the watch in a fluid chemical solution in an ultrasound cleaner. Almost immediately, corrosion product from the mire in which the watch had lain for 63 years, began to break away from the outer casing of the watch, to reveal the lustrous gold finish that lay underneath.

Mike gently rubbed the casing with soap and a soft toothbrush. With agonizing lethargy an inscription began to appear, as if by magic. Mike did not rush the job. Soon – a character at a time – he was able to read the engraving in old English letters and Arabic numerals:

John Henry Russell Jr.
From His Father
Los Angeles
September 9, 1914

But wait! There's more! Inside the casing there was an inner cover on which was engraved another inscription:

J.N. Russell Jr.
FROM
HIS FATHER
San Francisco, Cal.
June 5, 1884.

Mike then called me and told me about the burnished gold inscriptions on his now prized possession. He called *me* because he knew that I had a copy of the *San Diego's* final crew list, which gave the names of the survivors as well as the names of the six men who perished in the sinking. I quickly found "Russell, J.H. Ensign (T) U.S.N.", thus confirming that he was aboard the *San Diego* on her final fatal cruise.

Russell was a survivor.

Mike displayed the watch in his various homes for the next 34 years, during which time his job took him to Guam and Germany and finally back to the vicinity of DC. The watch was always with him: a fond reminder of day he found it before that portion of the *San Diego* collapsed and both flattened and sealed off the compartment in which it had spent the previous 63 years.

Now I will let Mike tell the rest of the story in his own words:

> As those years passed, technology advanced. Information once nearly impossible to obtain is now readily available at our fingertips. The Internet has revolutionized the way we find and process information. In the case of genealogical research, individuals now have an unprecedented opportunity to trace their family history from the comfort of their own homes.
>
> While researching my own family in March 2015, I decided to take a detour and see what I could learn about John Henry and John Newton Russell Jr. I quickly discovered that "John Russell," along with every possible combination of middle name, was and remains a popular name. I spent many fascinating hours following promising leads that led to dead ends.
>
> I eventually found an actionable reference in a digitized Google Book: "Los Angeles, From The Mountains To The Sea – With Selected Biography Of Actors and Witnesses Of The Period Of Growth And Achievement" written by John Sever McGroarty and published by the American Historical Society in 1921. The book included a brief biography of John Newton Russell Jr., an influential and respected leader in the life insurance industry. On page 421, I found the following paragraph:
>
> "In September, 1893, he married Miss A. Berdella Evans. Their only child is John Henry Russell, who was born at Los Angeles in September 1895. He was educated in the local grammar and high schools, spent one year in the Culver Military Academy in Indiana, and after graduating from Stanford University of California in 1917, entered the special training class of the United States Training Academy at Annapolis. He was graduated in February 1918, and assigned as ensign on the cruiser *San Diego*, which sank. He was then assigned to the destroyer USS *Breese* DD-122, after which he was appointed lieutenant. He was discharged in June, 1919, and then entered the Home Office Agency of the Pacific Mutual Life Insurance Company as secretary."
>
> This information was crucial. Not only did it provide a direct correlation between John Newton Russell Jr., John Henry Russell, and the *San Diego*, it also told me that both men were prominent within the insurance industry. I remembered finding a reference to the annual *John Newton Russell Memorial Award* early on in my research. At the time, however, I couldn't find a connection to John Henry or the *San Diego*. The award was established in 1942

and is given to one outstanding individual each year by the National Association of Insurance and Financial Advisors (NAIFA). I would learn later that John Henry Russell established the award as a tribute to his father who he considered to be a great mentor.

I sent a message to the "Contact Us" link on NAIFA's web site and within minutes received a reply from Jennifer Corcoran, manager of the *John Newton Russell Memorial Award*. I proved her with my contact information and she promised to put me in touch with the Russell Family.

Soon afterwards, I received a phone call from Benton Russell, who lives in Oakland, California. I was amazed to learn that Benton was John Henry Russell's youngest son. John Henry Russell fathered five children: John Lawrence, Newton, and Marcia with his first wife, and Joan and Benton with his second wife. Joan and Benton were born when their father was in his mid-fifties. John Lawrence, an actor who played in numerous movies and starred in the hit TV series "Lawman," died in 1991. Newton, a California State Senator, died in 2013. Marcia, Joan, and Benton are alive and well living in California. Their father, John Henry, died in 1968.

I sensed that Benton was fascinated but perhaps somewhat skeptical. We talked for a few minutes and then he asked me what I planned to do with the watch. I told him that it belonged to his father and it was my intention to return it to the family, preferably in person. I'm not sure which one of us was more excited – Benton for learning about his father's lost watch or me for actually finding a living relative. We set the date for June 20th to coincide with a trip to the west coast my wife and I had already planned.

Over the next several weeks, Benton and I exchanged numerous emails. He sent me pictures of his father in his Navy uniform and a picture taken in 1914 of his father and grandfather standing side by side. That picture clearly shows a pocket watch chain dangling stylishly from his grandfather's vest pocket. Benton didn't know if the picture was taken before or after September 9th, the date of his father's 20th birthday and a day that the watch was presented to him. If the picture had been taken before September 9th, it's possible that the watch in the picture is the same watch that was lost on the *San Diego*.

Benton also sent me a copy of a three-page letter his father wrote less than 48 hours after the sinking. The original letter was written with pencil and paper included in a Red Cross comfort kit Ensign Russell received shortly after arriving in New York. In great form and vivid detail, he recounted his observations, actions, and emotions – all while maintaining a remarkable sense of humor. [The letter is reprinted in its entirety at the end of this chapter.]

Joan and Benton welcomed me at the door. In addition to the box containing the watch, my wife, son, daughter, and granddaughter, Margo, accompanied me. There were about a dozen members of the Russell family and friends also in attendance. After introductions, several glasses of champagne, and a delicious lunch, Joan and Benton shared family stories and numerous documents they had recently discovered from their father's Navy days. One document was a "Claim for Reimbursement for Personal Property Lost in a Marine Disaster." It was a list of personal articles Ensign Russell lost on the

New York - San Diego

San Diego – everything from underwear to a whiskbroom. The watch was the most valuable item on the list. The original value was $175, the approximate time of use was 35 years, and the depreciated value at the time of loss was $75.

With both families gathered in the living room, Joan and Benton asked me to tell the story from the beginning. The unopened box containing the watch sat on a table in front of me. As I told the story, I remembered it as if it had happened yesterday. How excited I was the moment I found the watch and how I wondered about the fate of the man who owned it. Never in my wildest imagination did I ever think I would find the answer. When I finished my story, I opened the box and presented the watch to the Russell family. There were few dry eyes in the room. I cannot think of a better ending.

The Keepsake Locket

After Mike learned how to contact heirs through Internet services, word reached fellow diver Jon Hulburt. Jon had found an engraved gold locket, and he asked Mike to try to find the heirs of another sailor who lost it. The recovery date was April 6, 1980 – more than a year prior to Mike's finding of the watch.

At that time and for years afterward, Jon and I had a routine. We signed up for trips to the *San Diego* at every opportunity that was presented to us. Sometimes we were able to get on two trips back to back: one on Saturday and one on Sunday. In that case we slept on the boat over Saturday night. Our routine went like this . . .

Jon lived in Wilmington, Delaware. On Friday after work he loaded his dive gear into his car and drove to my house in Philly, an hour away. When he arrived, I already had the *San Diego's* deck plans spread across the living room floor. I had a sheet for every deck, plus an inboard and outboard profile. Unrolled, the plans were eleven feet long. Because the wreck lay upside down, we studied the plans upside down – the way the wreck would look to us as we entered through openings and swam through the compartments. We never looked at the plans right-side up; that would lead to confusion.

We always planned to go separate ways in the wreck. In this manner one would not stir the silt and ruin the visibility for the other. After we agreed on what we wanted to do that weekend, we studied the plans together and discussed entry points, emergency exits, and which decks and compartments we planned to explore. In effect, we memorized our routes through the collapsing interior of the hull.

Then we transferred Jon's gear to my Chevy Blazer, and I drove the rest of the way to Freeport, another two hours. We unloaded our gear and transferred it to the boat. We unrolled our sleeping bags on the deck or the engine box cover, then bedded down for the night. That way we didn't have to get up in the morning, but could sleep through all or part of the boat ride, yet another three hours, this time breathing diesel fumes.

This particular day – April 30, 1980 – was momentous for two reasons. One: it was our first dive of the year. Two: it was our first dive on a newly chartered dive boat called the *Ark*. The first of many, I should add. Throughout my career I made more than 150 dives on the *San Diego*. It was my favorite wreck.

Because this was the *Ark's* first trip ever, and word had not yet spread about the boat's availability, Jon and I were the only customers. Owner and skipper Danny Bressette (a long-time friend) brought his two kids along. His girlfriend Joy Meredith was also onboard as mate (in both senses of the word). Danny and Joy were experienced divers, and had dived on the *San Diego* many times before. On subsequent trips, the boat carried six to eight divers. Mike and Lynn Boring were often part of the gang.

According to our plans, I dived in the bow of the wreck, and Jon dived in the stern – and never the twain shall meet. I was working in the dispensary, on a deck that had no outside access or immediate means of escape. I had been there a number of times the previous year. I had to enter the deck below through a gun port, swim aft for fifty feet, then ascend into the deck above through a small opening. I left a strobe light at the opening in case I got disoriented or stirred the silt and created a blackout. The blinking strobe light led me to the only convenient way out of the deck.

Meanwhile, Jon was exploring the officers' quarters and ward rooms some four hundred feet away. That was where he found the locket. I recovered a bunch of medicine bottles and two ceramic jars that day, but Jon's discovery was paramount.

The front of the locket was engraved with overlapping capital letters: "AVJ." On the back of the locket was engraved, "TO MY BELOVED SON VERNON." Armed with this information, after my return home I scanned the crew list – nearly 1,200 names and ranks. My task was made difficult because there was no way to ascertain the order of the initials; that is, which initial referred to the given name, which referred to the middle name, and which referred to the surname. Eventually, I found only one person with the combined initials A and V and J, and the name Vernon. He was Ensign Alfred Vernon Jannotta. The fact that he was an ensign implied that he roomed in the officers' quarters in the stern, where Jon found the locket.

Jannotta was a survivor. He was promoted to Lieutenant Junior Grade before the end of World War One. He worked as a businessman throughout peacetime in the 1920's and 1930's, but remained active in the Navy reserve. By the time the United States entered World War Two after the Japanese bombing of Pearl Harbor, he had risen to the rank of Lieutenant Commander.

He earned the Navy Cross when he was in command of a Landing Craft Infantry flotilla, by first ordering the rescue of survivors after a kamikaze plane flew into a tanker and set it afire, then being the first to board the burning tanker and organize a fire brigade that managed to extinguish the flames and save 50,000 gallons of gasoline.

He also earned a Silver Star, a Bronze Star, and a Purple Heart. He ultimately retired with the rank of rear admiral. He died in 1972.

Jon cleaned and polished the locket, then put it on display in this house. And there the matter rested for thirty-five years.

Mike had less difficulty in tracking Jannotta's heir than he had in tracking Russell's. He quickly found Jannotta's granddaughter, Sharon Covington. She and her husband Barry lived in Potomac, Maryland – a mere two-hour drive from Jon's house. This was also only a two-hour drive in the opposite direction from Mike's house in Chester, Virginia. To make the transfer of the locket, Jon and Mike arranged to meet the Covington's at their centrally located home, along with other relatives who came to witness the family event.

I did not attend the event at which Jon's keepsake from the *San Diego* was presented to the Covingtons, but I sent them three copies of my book, *U.S.S. San Diego: the Last Armored Cruiser*. On page 71, I showed photographs of both sides of the locket. Sharon and Barry sent me a thank-you note – actually, a whole page – from which I would like to pass on a short quote:

Barry wrote: "I had heard of the story of the *San Diego*, but it was just a story. The discovery of the locket and your book help to bring the story alive. I had the pleasure of meeting my wife's grandfather. He was quite a man. Though small in stature, he was huge in his presence and commanded love and loyalty of those who served under him. After the end of WWII, his officers and crew formed a re-union group that got together every other year to pay respect to him for his command and his love for the men with whom he served.

"There are so many stories about my wife's grandfather that one could spend hours telling them. In the context of the story of the *San Diego*, one of my favorite[s] is what he did after the men were rescued and returned to shore. The crew had no money, dry clothes or other necessities, and for some reason the Navy was slow in responding to their needs. Ensign Jannotta contacted his mother who gave him the locket and asked that she wire $2,000 to him so that he could give each sailor $10, regardless of rank. Many years after the war, one of those sailors tracked Admiral Jannotta down to return his $10 and to thank him again. The irony here is that the stories about him never seem to end. Here we are some 40 years after his death and stories still continue to surface."

I am fairly certain that the last word of the quote was not intended as a pun. Yet I cannot help but look back over decades of diving without admiration for the large number of objects that have been recovered from shipwrecks – from the gold of conquistadors to the gold of personal possessions – and whose recovery has added to the sum of human history and knowledge, and brought closure to the families of those who were lost at sea.

Mike and Jon gave up objects that were precious to them – not because of their intrinsic value, for they are wreck-divers and not salvors or treasure hunters who dive for profit. Mike and Jon dive for the love of diving, for the thrill of adventure, and for the joy of finding items that would have remained lost in perpetuity had it not been for their dedication, skill, and keen eyesight. Instead of exploring African veldts or trudging on Arctic wastes, they have found satisfaction in plumbing unexplored depths that lie closer to home. Uncovering relics before they become crushed and buried in a collapsing shipwreck is merely an added fillip to their primary objective of going where few people have ever gone, and seeing what few people have ever seen. To them, the most valuable profits are the memories that they possess and share with others.

We never truly own a material object. We are merely custodians. Eventually we pass them to the next generation, after we leave this mortal coil. What difference if we dispossess ourselves of an historic object a few years before we breathe the final exhale, if it makes others happy?

The Sinking Narrative of Ensign John Henry Russell Jr.

In Benton Russell's possession is a letter that his father wrote to Amy Requa shortly after the loss of the *San Diego*. Benton shared the letter with Mike Boring, who then shared it with me.

My immediate reply to Mike was: "Russell's letter is absolutely awesome. His writing technique was highly descriptive. He should have been an author!"

I asked Mike if he could obtain permission to reprint the letter in this book. Benton replied, "YES! Use the letter." So here it is.

As you will read, Russell wrote the letter in pencil. Years later, his daughter typed the letter in order to make it easier to read. Both the letter and the typescript were kept as family mementoes. With regard to the version that is printed below, I made no changes in the typescript other than to reformat the paragraphs with first-line indents instead of skipped lines, justifying the right margin, and italicizing vessel names. Any misspellings or grammatical errors – and there are a few – were typed that way in the typescript.

July 21, 1918
2:15 A.M.
Dear Amy:

Am aboard the *Maui* and have the mid watch and so an opportunity to write to you. Will contrive to see it mailed as soon as possible.

Please excuse the equipment. It is furnished as part of a red cross comfort kit and is all that is available.

We had quite a trip ashore, Thursday afternoon. As you know from the papers we were struck by a mine or torpedo just abaft mid-ships on the port side and sank in a very few minutes; about 30. The blow came in the engine room, filling it in about five seconds; (Enter I). I was in the chart house (on lower bridge) at the time. The ship shook heavily and at once took a good list to port. There was a heavy explosion, but not very loud. As you know I was assistant navigator of the ship, so stayed on bridge or in chart house. We at once figured out the course and distance to land. It was very interesting being on the bridge. I heard the ordnance, executive, and engineer officer make their reports to the Captain. We kept taking more of a list to port. All hands were ordered along the starboard rail. Meanwhile the six and three inch guns were popping off in great shape – just to lend color to the scene.

The dynamo rooms were flooded very quickly, cutting off current for telephone communication and for the cranes that had to lower the boats. Two boats were caught half-way out, suspended in midair, their crews aboard them. Finally – and to my surprise at the time – "abandon ship" was sounded. In a few seconds hundreds of men were swimming in the water. I remember watching the navigator go over the side with some alacrity. All had life preservers and canteens. I had provided myself with one. I got two out of my stateroom – earlier – one was a special creation mother had given me, the other a regular navy one. I threw mother's in a boat and told them to give it to anyone who would need it. However, I had no idea that we would sink – so I said, "I'll get it when the party is over", – wrong!

On with the story – . Hundreds had left the ship, but all with rafts. Hardly a boat was afloat. A couple of other officers and Henry tried to get a big motor sailor in the water. We tried a slip hook and she dropped about 8 ft. and hit half in the water and half (her bow) on deck. We worked a long time and mighty hard to get her afloat. By now I was convinced she would sink. We were on the top deck (boat deck) and its port water ways were away under water. You can imagine how much she listed. Our boat floated off. It was interesting to watch the great stacks and mast, now over us, come down at us as she listed and sank deeper. A lot of small gear and loose lumber show

New York - San Diego

over and all present looked for a stack "or something" to break up the meeting. These few minutes were very interesting and exciting. The old ship rolling over on us – or at us – and this dern little boat of ours that we fooled with a little too long. I remember my emotions very clearly. I had no doubt that we would get away – or rather – I did not for a second think I would be hurt – but was alarmed about the ship rolling over on us. I merely realized this to be dangerous thing and kept wondering how long before she would come over with a rush; also I wondered if the stacks or mast would break and fall.

As I made a mistake in thinking she would not sink, I made one about her rolling over. Was in hope she would stay up until we could get clear. I yelled (to!) to get out the oars and grabbed one, but it was a warm summer day and they had all decided to go swimming. The whole thing was funny. Just that instant the No. 1. stack struck the stem and I saw the bow crumple up the stack a bit. I saw the boat could not float (#2 stack struck the stern) so I took a hop, skip and a jump into the salt sea water. By now her stacks were well under. I kept thinking about the suction and had one strong conviction – i.e. best to get away from the U.S.S. *San Diego*. I had taken one shoe off while aboard. I rolled over on my back, took it easy so as not to get winded and kicked along nicely with one high power and one lower power leg. In a little way I stopped and took the shoe off and took the shoe off and took a look at six million dollars sink to a gy s bsp bottom. However, my imagination was active and I pictured terrific whirl pools as 18,000 tons in one lump took a final plunge – so overed on me back and made knots to a safe distance and then watched her red bottom with keel and burne gear showing – about like a submarine. Finally there was a roar and a big wave and I looked and, lo – a great ship had disappeared – gone to Davy Jones' locker.

About the next most prominent object was a whale boat 100 ft. from me with my friends of the forsaken motor sailor safely enconched (?) (mon Dieu!) – a "floating palace" it looked – and a _____ (mighty) nice place to be. I made for it, changing my style to the Australian Crawl. I "crept" alongside and floundered aboard with some assistance. It happened that the Executive Officer was aboard – fine man. I manned an oar along with some Jacks and a midship or so. About the first one we picked up was the Captain. I very nobly helped the old gent aboard. We resumed cruising operations "steering various courses and speeds". Went around picking up any in distress and giving orders – f.e. about keeping together, building rafts, etc. We put up sail – as a signal for there was no air at all – smooth sea, sun shining – ideal weather for it all. We sent a dingy ashore (10 miles). A few minutes after the explosion a ship was sighted at about 9000 yards. She was now very plain and we all thought was intending to give us aid. However she made off. An hour or so later we sighted a couple more and we made "all speed" to head them off. Fortunately we were able to. We put the Cap. and exec. on board and an officer and I and a midship and a boatswain mate manned the whale boat and were towed along side by the ship. We eased in among those floating – almost the whole ship's company, cast loose, and started taking them aboard. Great sport I can tell you. We picked out the single ones, and those that were sick or had cramps. I collected a good crew and so graduated to the rate of coxswain. We got several loads and put them aboard one of the three ships standing by. I never saw such a bunch of men. Giving cheer after cheer and singing for hours. They were in the water about four hours. A good part of this time there was nothing in sight and they did not know but that we were 100 miles off shore. Fortunately, I never had to worry a second. I had confidence in my swimming and also knew exactly where we were and knew we were bound to be sighted very shortly. Besides, I was in a boat all except about 20 minutes. But when you consider that almost all the men thought we were a long way out and that a large majority could not swim, the spirit was remarkable. There was no panic and no fright. Instead there was a lot of cheering and singing, constant jokes. Very few cases of selfishness or cowardice. We had our color up, and a sail and the Cap. and Exec. recalling in the stern sheets. We were quite something to look at. We finished them up and came alongside and put them aboard. I was the last to leave the boat and thought I was the last aboard the ship, but there were a couple in a dingy on the other side. We had 708 men and officers aboard this ship, the *Bussum*, a Dutch ship before the board took her over. I went down into the engine room and got thoroughly dried. Later had something hot to eat and then a nap and so the end of a perfect day. We were brought aboard the *Maui* at Pier 2 where we were given Komfort Kits and pajamas by Red Cross and a wonderful meal at about 2:30 AM. Delicious steak and potatoes, salad, and dessert. By time we had received rooms etc., it was 4 AM. The night before I had gotten to bed at 4:15 AM. The navigator had turned in and I had to plot soundings and keep the Captain informed.

A fine lot of sailors. Navy men and officers had abandoned most of their clothing. Pajamas has been the uniform all today. I found one dollar and accepted a proffer of a loan of two, so am well off. Have over a dollar left. First liberty will go to Phi Delt house and get funds and get clean linen. Am fortunate in having a uniform. Have had it cleaned and pressed and sent a boy to get me clean collar, cuff, etcetera, drew some shoes and so am well off. One of the officers tried to buy me a hat but could not.

As for deaths. I don't know of more than half a dozen. We were very, very fortunate. The whole thing was the biggest surprise of my life, first the torpedo and second the fact that we sunk and so very quickly.

Item. Soon after I had sent my only suit ashore to be cleaned, the Captain sent for me. Some object, standing at attention, adorned in a suit of pajamas – talking to the Captain also in pajamas! I happened to be executive officer.

Well Amy – I've been relieved now for over half and hour so will turn in. My address is

    C/O Commander Cruiser Force,
    Steneck Bldg.,
    Hoboken, N.J.

Will inquire at Belmont for letter or telegram from my sweetheart. Have used this entire Red Cross pencil in this letter – so it must wait on reinforcements. Do not know what future holds for me. Matter of weeks before I leave N.Y., I think. All my love, dear, – goodnight.

                                                      J.

Am happy – because this will mean that somehow I am going to see you. Hope you get my telegram. There was an order against them – but I saw two or three communication officers and a few dozen others and at 6:30 A.M. it was sent, and one to the folks.

"Just my luck" to be stuck for the first watch. Love – Am anxious to see you. Plans indefinite now, will write them when I can. 2:15 A.M.

New York - San Diego

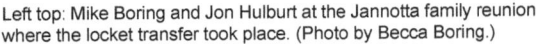

Above: Family photo of son and father Russells, plus a dog.

Left top: Mike Boring and Jon Hulburt at the Jannotta family reunion where the locket transfer took place. (Photo by Becca Boring.)

Left middle: The Jannotta family listening intently while Mike and Jon recount their recovery experiences. (Photo by Becca Boring.)

Above: The watch that Mike Boring rescued from oblivion in 1981. (Photo by Becca Boring.)

Right middle and bottom: The obverse and reverse sides of the locket that Jon Hulburt rescued in 1980.

Lucy Evelyn

Not many people remember the *Lucy Evelyn*. Most folks today never even heard of her. Yet there was a time when this graceful schooner of yesteryear was a well-known tourist attraction on Long Beach Island.

I have seen the *Lucy Evelyn*, and I remember her fondly. At that time, I had no thoughts of becoming a scuba diver, much less a wreck-diver. Even so, I was captivated by her stately hull, tall masts, spread of canvas, sound timbers . . . and low headroom. The latter impressed me the most because I had to duck in order to pass through her crowded cargo hold.

I wish I had taken photographs. But I wasn't a photographer then, either. Or a published author. Like diving, those complimentary careers came later.

From the author's collection.

If all of the above is true, how did I manage to "pass" through her hold, you may ask. That answer is simple: at the time of my "penetration" into the hull, the *Lucy Evelyn* was firmly ensconced on dry land and being operated as a gift shop. The owners were Nat and Betty Ewer.

After purchasing the *Lucy Evelyn*, the Ewers researched the history of the vessel, by obtaining information from the previous owners. They then published their collected knowledge in a 12-page pamphlet which they sold in the store (where the "stores" were kept below deck?). I have supplemented their findings with additional material from other sources.

Let me start by quoting a summary of past and contemporary events: one that was published in 1946, and possibly the source that the Evers used in their pamphlet.

The *Lucy Evelyn* slid down the ways at the height of World War One.

> Owned by the Machias Lumber Company, she [the *Lucy Evelyn*] sailed out of that Maine port year after year, bound south to New York or Norfolk with lumber or potatoes, often taking coal back north. Although never a clipper, she did have a few good passages to her record. On one occasion she left Machias on a Wednesday, and made New York the following Wednesday. She sailed for home the next Sunday, and was at Machias eight days later. At one time in the Sound she was doing twelve knots. Once she took 12 days from Perth Amboy to Hampton roads, although a couple of years later she was only five days en route from Norfolk to New York.
>
> Her worst passage took place in the early '30's, when she left Maine bound for New York with potatoes. Caught in a bad off-shore gale she was swept almost all the way across to the Azores. Fighting her way back, she was nearly to the States when another storm caught her, driving her towards the

West Indies. By this time her cargo had gone bad, and was useless. She had been out for more than three months with nothing to show for it.

Still, she has been a lucky ship. She has weathered gales and storms without too serious damage. Two or three times she has gone ashore in recent years, once losing a rudder, but she always managed to survive. She has been overdue more than once, but that was because she did not get her winds. Well built, she has stood up to the years, even today showing little sign of wear apart from a slight hog that has developed with time.

She was active during the early part of 1939, going south in May with a load of granite from Stonington. In late June she was at Hampton Roads for coal. During the winter she was overhauled. With the dearth of ships, prices soared for anything that would float during the early war years, and the Machias Lumber Company thought it expedient to sell their faithful schooner when they were offered what has been reported to have been $22,000. (A quarter of a century before the schooner is said to have cost $60,000, so she must have paid for herself many times over.)

The new company were known as the Lucy Evelyn Incorporated, and they sent her to the West Indies for a cargo of molasses. On her return north, she fitted out for a voyage to Iceland, but she was caught by a gale while she was attempting to shelter at Vineyard Haven, and, losing both anchors, she was driven ashore, her bottom being badly damaged. Not long after this a group of Cape Verde Islanders saw the schooner; she was what they wanted. After paying $10,000 for her, she was taken to East Boston where another $5,000 was spent repairing her hull and left for New Bedford she was like a new ship.

Her new captain and part owner is John F. Costa, and although he is only 36 years old, he is an old hand at the packet trade. From 1926 to 1931 he sailed with the *Yukon* between Providence and the Cape Verdes. Then he went as mate in the schooner *John R. Manta* out to the islands. The *Manta* was an interesting vessel for when she came into New Bedford harbor on August 20, 1925, with 300 barrels of sperm oil she brought to a close the whaling industry of the ancient port. Captain Costa stayed with her until 1934 when he lost his right arm in an accident. On November 8 of that year the *Manta* sailed for St. Vincent with 13 passengers and a crew of 19; she was never seen again. Later Captain Costa sailed out from Fall River in the big *Burkeland*, and he came back in 1939 in the *Corona*, once a schooner yacht. Then he was first mate of the *Capitana*. Yes, he is a real sailor.

With the *Evelyn* in New Bedford, Captain Costa and a co-owner Augusto Teixeira set about looking for passengers and cargo. Letters from the islands told of the great scarcity of clothing, their supply having been cut off by the war. So trunk loads, crates and bales of clothes were stored in the hold. The islands needed lumber that was short here, too. Still, the owners were able to find some. Then there was cement, furniture, and all sorts of odds and ends. Just before sailing two small trucks and an automobile were tucked away below. And lastly, a number of drums of gasoline and kerosene were lowered down through the hatch; if the fumes should work through the deck under the galley stove perhaps another ship would go missing.

Finding a crew was a problem; there are not many windjammer men left today. Captain Costa finally signed on 12 hands. Some of them had never been to sea, few knew anything about sailing ships, but they would learn on the passage. There was a woman signed on as a stewardess, but she was going chiefly for the trip in sail. Then there were two passengers, one being elderly Mrs. Tereza Neves who was going back to the place of her birth. As the *Evelyn* probably never carried more than seven men all told when she was coasting she was not fitted to carry more. So a house was build amidships, just abaft the main mast, with a double tier of bunks to take the extra men. Another toilet was put in on the main deck on the port side.

Captain Costa complained about the red tape and government inspections that had developed in recent years. He had to get a ship's lifeboat; packets had never carried real lifeboats before, just their yawl boats as a rule. He had to get davits to go with the lifeboat, but only he and Mr. Britto, his mate, noticed that the davits were not strong enough to hoist the boat off the deck; they would have to be strengthened sometime with piping.

In February, before loading, the *Evelyn* had gone up to Newport for dry-docking and inspection. She was found to be in perfect condition. Much new planking had been put into her during her Boston overhaul, and now she was as sound as she was a quarter century before. A tug had towed her to Newport in six hours, but she returned under sail, doing the run in four and a half hours, at times touching 8-1/2 knots.

Sailing date from New Bedford for the islands was set for Friday, May 3, but red tape, passports, visas and the like, put it off to Monday, then Tuesday, and finally Wednesday. Late Wednesday afternoon the Portuguese consulate suddenly discovered that Captain Costa had to sign some seventy papers that were not yet written up!

Thursday the 9th became sailing day. Dawn broke with a blue sky and southwesterly breeze. Shortly after nine in the morning, with the Cuttyhunk Island boat *Alert* as tug, the *Evelyn* backed out of her dock as friends on the wharf waved her away. She swung around, and with the *Alert* out ahead, she moved down the harbor, past wharves that once berthed the whaling fleet, past the ribs of the old tern schooner *Thomas H. Lawrence*, a packet that never did get to the islands but became a wreck in the harbor instead. With the Stars and Stripes flying from the mizzen spreaders, and her *Lucy Evelyn* flag from the fore truck, she brought back memories of the windjammer days.

Soon New Bedford and Fairhaven were in the haze astern. Off to starboard lay Round Hills where the whaler *Charles W. Morgan* used to rest before she was towed west to the Mystic Museum. In Buzzards Bay the *Evelyn* met the first of the ocean swell, her black hull with its white band softly rising and falling. The donkey engine in the forward house puffed as the fore, main, and mizzen gaffs slowly groaned up the masts, the sails, white-gray in color, filling with the wind. The *Evelyn* looked a little naked without her mizzen topmast; she would get one later, perhaps in the islands. This trip she would not set even her fore and main topsails as Captain Costa had no one to go aloft to set them.

Shortly the Hen and Chickens Lightship came into view ahead. Off to port was Cuttyhunk where the whaler *Wanderer* was wrecked years ago. The ghost of the old whaling bark must have stirred as the schooner slipped past for the fore-and-after was using the *Wanderer's* aged taffrail log: it was the only log Captain Costa could find around New Bedford. Many miles it had ticked off in waters round the world in search of whale, and now it was back in service once more.

With the lightship astern, the fore staysail and inner and outer jibs were hoisted. The tow line was slacked, and a moment later the schooner was free, sailing on her own. The *Alert* moved alongside to take off Mr. Teixeira and those who were not making the voyage. Then it was 'Farewell and Bon Voyage'.

The *Lucy Evelyn* pulled ahead, heeling slightly to the breeze. The *Alert* turned, heading for home. The gap between the ships grew greater; waving hands were lost in the distance. Like a mirage from the past, the schooner sailed on, on into the haze. Then she was gone to sight. The *Lucy Evelyn* was outward bound, destination Cape Verde Islands.

Another article, published in 1949, added later contemporary events:

The Maine-built tern *Lucy Evelyn*, which was in the Brava trade following the war, probably brought her sailing days to a close during 1948. In January and February she had worked in the island trade. then, on March 3, she left Fogo for the United States by way of Dakar, where she was to drop two passengers. However, when head winds prevented her from making the African port, Captain John Costa set his course for New Bedford. It was a hard crossing, marked by five gales. A bow seam opened in mid-Atlantic, and the crew had to move some fifty tons of ballast aft in an attempt to lift the leak clear of the water. The pumps had to be worked by hand as there was no gasoline for the donkey engine which normally operated them. Her rigging was in poor shape with two of her booms spliced. On April 12 the three-master slipped past Cuttyhunk, forty days out.

In had not been a profitable voyage; there were no funds to pay off her crew. In June, when the schooner was put up at public auction, she went to N. T. Ewer for $1,550; six years before she had changed hands for $22,000. Her new owner offered to sell her sails, as he planned on hauling the *Lucy Evelyn* ashore to turn her into a store. She was towed to Little Egg Harbor, New Jersey, remaining at anchor there while plans were made to beach her.

Note that "tern" was a local Maine word for a three-masted schooner. Brava was a pleasantly pungent tomato sauce that was especially cherished by Spaniards and American Hispanics.

The Ewers concurred with the ultimate change of hands, but not always with the particulars of the *Lucy Evelyn's* career. Sometimes they had information that was lacking in the articles above. For example, they noted that, in addition to the Machias Lumber Company, one of the part owners was Captain Everett C. Lindsey. The schooner's keel was laid in 1917 along the Harrington River in Harrington, Maine. The vessel was named after Lindsey's two daughters: Lucy and Evelyn. After launching, he commanded the *Lucy Evelyn* for the next twelve years.

Also, the *Lucy Evelyn* "was fully rigged and ready to set sail with a cargo of lumber in her hold, in January 1918, when an unforeseen freeze locked her tight in the harbor, and all efforts to free her were in vain. This was an act of providence, as the winter of 1918 was one of the most severe in history. With the spring thaw, she sailed for New York on her maiden voyage. She left New York for Santo Domingo with a mixed cargo consisting principally of coal, and returned to New York loaded with sugar and molasses. At this time we were still in a war and all shipping was controlled by the Maritime Commission, so the *Lucy Evelyn* could only handle cargo and make such trips as were designated by the Commission. During this time she was almost constantly in the submarine zones along the Atlantic coast, and often encountered wreckage from torpedoed ships. After her release from the Maritime Commission at the end of the war, she cruised all over the Caribbean area, picking up cargo wherever she could find it."

The Ewers provided details of a typical tramp around the world. The *Lucy Evelyn* "was loaded with lumber on her longest voyage which took her from Pensacola, Florida to Santa Cruz, Tenerife, in forty-eight days. Then from Tenerife she sailed to the Barbadoes [sic] in twenty days and loaded the hold with molasses for delivery at St. Johns, New Brunswick. At St. Johns lumber replaced the molasses cargo and she headed across the ocean to Liverpool, England. On the return trip she sailed light, and with strong and favorable winds all the way, she established some sort of a record for a ship of her type covering five thousand miles in twenty days. The entire voyage covered approximately twelve thousand miles."

A donkey boiler provided steam for a windlass. This allowed her to weigh anchor and raise the sails with ease. "With skilled hands, a crew of five men were all that were necessary to handle this ship under sail. Namely, the Captain, Steward, Mate, and two able men. Their quarters were clean and reasonably comfortable, the Captain, Steward and Mate sharing the aft quarters, and the two seamen the fo'c's'le."

The Ewers stated that the *Lucy Evelyn* sprang a leak and "drifted helplessly for three days, until a Coast Guard Patrol picked her up and towed her ashore for repairs. Her crew was in pretty bad shape due to exposure and lack of food and water. During this mishap all of her original records were washed overboard and lost."

She later "ran aground at Boothbay Harbor and lost her rudder. However, she was quickly refloated and repaired. In the spring of that same year she was rammed in the stern by a steamer, during a heavy fog at sea. Her hull was badly damaged and her motor tender was carried away."

After Captain Lindsey yielded command, the *Lucy Evelyn* was being towed downstream when she swung broadside and ran aground "at the Machiasport East Machias bridge, thus blocking traffic, till the next high tide refloated her.

This was but a minor mishap, but her next adventure was far worse. "With a Captain Johnnie Mitchell of New York in command, and a cargo of Maine potatoes in her hold, she set for New York harbor and ran into heavy gales that blew her to the coast of Africa. She worked her way back toward Newfoundland, only to end up in the Barbadoes [sic]. At this port she received the name of 'Rotten Potato Lucy' because her cargo had aged beyond salvage. In desperation, Captain Mitchell, wired Captain Lindsey in Maine to come to his rescue and teach him how to control this vixen. Captain Lindsey, no doubt feeling a smirk of satisfaction, shipped down a freighter, boarded the *Lucy Evelyn*, took command and calmly and safely brought his old girl back to New York, much to Johnnie Mitchell's chagrin. They had finally completed a normal five day passage from Maine to New York in 'record time – one hundred days!"

Legal Tangle

Another misadventure occurred on the night of February 14, 1924. Five days earlier, the *Lucy Evelyn* had docked at Orient Point, Long Island, New York. She remained there for three days while stevedores removed some of the fertilizer in her holds. Then Edwin King – the consignee of the cargo and both president and manager of the Orient Point Wharf Company – directed that the balance of the cargo be unloaded at a nearby dock. King warned the master of the schooner that "there was a dredged channel twelve feet deep at low water reaching in from deep water to the east side of the pier, and that they had dredged off the end of the pier so that boats could turn."

The *Lucy Evelyn* attempted to depart, but due to the states of the wind and tide, after executing the turn "she fetched up, her port side resting against the corner of the pier." A second attempt also failed to let the schooner sail into an east wind away from the dock. A tugboat was available to tow the schooner along the channel into deep water, but the master declined to pay the towing fee. Instead, he decided to wait out the weather. King and his dock hands helped to tie the schooner's lines to the pier.

That night a storm struck the area with fifty-knot winds. Waves and surge lifted and dropped the *Lucy Evelyn* relentlessly. After three hours of pounding, the combined forces of wind, waves, and surge tore the mooring piles from the pier. The helpless schooner was driven ashore, where her hull suffered damage that required expensive repair and replacement of planks.

The Machias Lumber Company – owner of the *Lucy Evelyn* – filed a suit for damages against the Orient Point Wharf Company. Machias claimed that the pier was too frail, that water close the wharf was too shallow, and that the orientation of the wharf and the dredged access channel prevented the schooner from sailing into an east wind. King countered that he warned the master of the *Lucy Evelyn* against the dangers of staying at the wharf, and suggested that he hire a tugboat to tow the schooner away before the weather turned foul. The court sided with Machias.

King appealed, but the superior court also sided with Machias.

In light of today's overcrowded courts and lengthy dockets, the result of Americans' penchant for suing at the drop of a hat if the hat appeared to have been scuffed by being dropped, King appealed to the Supreme Court of the United States . . . and the country's highest court accepted so minor a case.

The Supreme Court reviewed the lower courts' findings and enumerated the facts. It ascertained that King had duly apprised the master of the *Lucy Evelyn* that the schooner could not sail along the channel against the forecasted easterly wind, and that he should hire a tugboat to tow the schooner into deep water in order to avoid becoming trapped. King also apprised the master of the surrounding shallow water, which might make it difficult or impossible to turn the vessel under those conditions. The master ignored King's warning.

King was not a guarantor as the lower courts had proposed. He could not be held liable for the actions of the master.

The Supreme Court: "It was not the condition of the berth or of the pier that caused the damage. There was a perfectly safe exit from the pier at any time provided the vessel used the assistance of a launch or tug. . . .

"It is apparent from the record that: The damage sustained by the vessel was not due to any concealed danger or obstruction in the berth; petitioners furnished a berth in all respects safe for this vessel, except in the one contingency of a storm from the exposed Easterly or Southerly direction which would cause the vessel to pound against the pier; that the dangers and hazards of this exposure were known to the vessel's master and were the subject of discussion between him and petitioners; that a safe exit from the berth could be made by this vessel at any time with the assistance of a small tug, and the schooner could sail away unassisted at any time of high water except under the one particular condition when the wind shifted to an Easterly or Southerly direction and that this was observed by and known to the master; that the petitioners made no representation as to the exact location or extent of the area off the end of the pier where the vessel might turn around, but did warn the master of danger of shoals to the Westerly; that the master had full knowledge of the existence of shoals and the difficulties of turning and sailing away unassisted on an Easterly wind, but made no soundings or other efforts to locate the exact position of deep water or by using his anchors or otherwise to ensure the safety of the manoeuvre [sic] he was about to undertake; that the schooner master observed the shift of the wind to the difficult Easterly quarter but made no efforts to procure assistance; that the type and condition of the pier were observed by and known to the schooner master; that the pier withstood the battering of the weight of the schooner for three hours before the vessel came ashore; that, with the knowledge the master had and in spite of the dangers and hazards all of which were open and apparent, the master accepted and used the wharf without objection, failed to seek any assistance, and returned to and voluntarily remained at the pier after observing weather condition indicating an approaching storm; that the discharge of cargo for that place had been completed before the vessel tried to leave and before any damage was sustained; that no part of the pier gave way until the ship's cavel broke, allowing the vessel to drop back a little and so change the position of the strain."

(A cavel – or kevel, the spelling that is most widely in usage today – is a "stout piece of wood fastened either horizontally or vertically to inside of bulwark stanchions or in a rail for securing or belaying heavier gear, such as topsail halyards, fore sheets, jib-sheets, boom-guys, etc., and warping lines in smaller craft.")

The Supreme Court found that King (representing the Petitioners) was not at fault, and that "the schooner, in such a position, was bound to use reasonable diligence in watching for signs of approaching danger and to take all effective and prompt means and assistance available to get away from the dangerous position."

In short, the schooner master was negligent by not fulfilling his duties as the schooner's master.

The Supreme Court overruled the opinion of the lower courts, and reversed their decisions in the matter of this case. The downside of this lawsuit was that the final decision was not made until May 22, 1929 – a full five years after the complaint was filed for what was equivalent to a fender bender!

For Sale, and Sold

In 1942, the staid and true schooner "was sold to a New York Syndicate known as 'Lucy Evelyn Ship Company Incorporated,' for a reputed $22,000." After one round trip to the West Indies, she was chartered by the U.S. government because another world war was in motion.

During war service she anchored off Vineyard Haven in a hurricane when both anchors were lost. In an attempt to beach her, "she hit the breakwater and pounded a hole in her starboard side. The vessel was abandoned, and, some months later, purchased for $3,500.00 at a United States Marshall's sale, by Dr. Chester L. Glenn."

After extensive repairs, Glenn sold her for $12,000 to Captain John Costa and his uncle Mr. August Teixera [as spelled by the Ewers]. They spent another $10,000 to outfit the schooner for service to the Cape Verde islands. Extra crew bunks were added to the forecastle. A midship house was built for passenger accommodations. Livestock pens were placed on deck.

U.S. Coast Guard historian John Browning noted that on November 15, 1942, "the American schooner *Lucy Evelyn* was reportedly shelled by an enemy submarine. None of the crew of seven was injured. The schooner (no damage indicated) made port at Barranquilla, Columbia." German records do not corroborate such an attack.

The Coast Guard again came to the rescue of the *Lucy Evelyn* after a storm carried away her sails "except the mizzen sail." These Coast Guard rescues were not fortuitous, for the schooner was equipped with a wireless radio. Her initial call sign was JMJV. In 1934, her call letters were changed to KNTT.

"When she reached New Bedford she was a sad sight. Captain Costa rigged her with a complete new set of sails, and patched her masts and booms. She had lost three anchors and practically all of her chain, so it was necessary to find another anchor. Costa was given permission to salvage the anchor and chain from the three-master *Thomas H. Lawrence* which had been sunk in New Bedford Harbor. This salvage operation yielded one large anchor and sixty-five fathoms of chain. These were used aboard the *Lucy Evelyn* till she was beached, and may now be seen at her present location [at Beach Haven, New Jersey]."

The *Lucy Evelyn* made her final commercial voyage beginning in June of 1947. Her destination was the Cape Verde islands. On board were seventeen crewmembers, ten passengers, and a general cargo. On her return passage, unfavorable winds prevented a midway stop at Dakar, so she was forced to proceed directly to New Bedford. The schooner sprang a leak in the bow.

"To raise the forward part of the vessel, the sixty tons of rock ballast in the hold had to be moved aft, by hand, and fast! All hands were ordered to man the pumps when the donkey engine, that normally operated them, ran out of gasoline. The pangs of hunger were felt when the ship's store ran out of flour a week before they reached port, and the last morsel of food was eaten at New Bedford just nine months and nineteen days after she had left, she arrived safe in harbor on April 12th, 1948."

The owners lost money on this voyage. There was no salable cargo, and the crew was owed back wages for nearly ten months of work. As a result, the *Lucy Evelyn* was put up for auction in order to pay her accumulated debts. "The Federal Court in Boston appraised her at $4,500.00 in her present condition. The only bid received on June 2nd, 1948, was for five hundred dollars. This was not sufficient to cover the demands, so the bid was refused.

"Just two days after this, my wife and I happened to be in New Bedford and noticed the ship riding calmly at anchor in the harbor. Being most interested in just such a schooner, we inquired and learned that the *Lucy Evelyn* was to be sold at a final auction on June 9th, 1948."

Sailing the Dunes

The Ewers had the highest bid: $1,550.00. The new owners hired a tug to tow the schooner to Beach Haven via Little Egg Inlet (at Atlantic City) and the Inland Waterway. She was anchored in the bay until October while her landside mooring was being dredged. Soon the *Lucy Evelyn* was run hard aground on a mud bank that had been selected as her final resting place. Dredgers dug a basin into which the schooner was floated on November 2. After bulldozers wrestled the vessel into place, tons of sand and mud were pumped completely around the hull.

The *Lucy Evelyn* was landlocked!

Now the Ewers had a structure to replace the boardwalk gift shop that had been washed away by the hurricane of September 14, 1944. The schooner was aptly christened the Sea Chest.

The donkey engine was removed. The cabins were emptied of all paraphernalia. The interior surfaces of the bulkheads and partitions were sandblasted to a smooth finish and were left natural. A door was cut through the starboard side near the bow in order to facilitate a street level entrance. The deck house was removed and placed on the adjacent ground to be "used as a fisherman's supply depot." The hatchways were converted to skylights. Partitions were removed in order to create larger compartments. The captain's quarters were renovated and converted to a museum.

"Oil head and an air circulating system were placed in the stern of the hold, and the entire ship was wired for electricity. . . . The bow of the hold was fired with shelves made of driftwood and long oars were hung from the beams to act as display fixtures. Large mahogany ships' steering wheels were made into lighting fixtures and hung in each of the hatches. Many old ships' lights that we had collected over a period of years fitted in perfectly with our décor. Other nautical display fixtures including ships' ladders and tables made from the ships' wheels were placed about the hold. Old rope that had been used aboard for many years may be seen decorating the edges of the stock shelves. The hull was painted a shining black with white trim and a bright red waterline."

The Sea Chest opened for business on Memorial Day of 1949. Captain Lindsey and his daughter Evelyn were special guests for the gala event. Thousands of people attended the opening.

The Ewers wrote: "Thus it was that our ship came in."

For the next two decades, the *Lucy Evelyn* served admirably in her new trade: spreading sales instead of sails, and engaging in trade without encountering trade winds. Her lifestyle was pacific but not on the Pacific. In a work of fiction, at this point I would state that my visit to her lumbering remains (or remaining timbers) altered the course of my life, and foretold of the time when I would become a wreck-diver. In this case, however, truth is stranger than fiction. I was unmoved by the *Lucy Evelyn's* graceful if stationary appearance. It was spelunking that caused me to switch from underground exploration to underwater exploration. For details of how this change came about, see

New Jersey - Lucy Evelyn 61

Postcard pictures of the Sea Chest

This is the original Sea Chest when it was located on the beach. It was more of a gift shop than a chandlery. Note the ocean in the background to the right of the building.

The *Lucy Evelyn* after she was permanently dry-docked, and became the new Sea Chest. There was far more space for merchandise in the schooner's cargo hold than there had been in the original building.

The bowsprit and jibboom tower above the adjacent chanties.

In this starboard profile the ground-level doorway is visible slightly forward of the center mast. Those were the days . . .

Lucy Evelyn - New Jersey

Book One of *The Lusitania Controversies*.

Ships are like people. They are born (or launched), live a fruitful life (or career), and eventually expire. The *Lucy Evelyn's* expiration date occurred during the winter of 1972. The cause of her demise was fire.

Despite below freezing temperatures, an oil heater kept the souvenir shop warm, the same as it does in millions of American homes (including my own). Blame for the blaze was placed upon a defective burner switch, which supposedly ignited the pitch that sealed the timbers and planks the way caulking does in a log cabin. The report of smoke alerted local fire fighters. They poured water through the skylights onto the flames inside. The fire was eventually brought under control, but the hull continued to smolder for the next three days.

In typical newspaper fashion, reporters contended that the schooner had burned to the ground. This "observation" was belied by photographs that were taken afterward. The *Lucy Evelyn* certainly was a wreck, but most of her structure yet remained: not repairable to be sure, but still standing high and not level with the ground. Nonetheless, the shipwreck was declared a total loss: her reconstruction was not economically feasible.

Thus did a long-standing icon of Long Beach Island come to an end. Today she exists in the minds of a few as a fond memory of a time when the *Lucy Evelyn* sailed the sands of Beach Haven, where she sold gifts and souvenirs in the grand tradition of a sailor's life at sea.

Today this stately schooner of yore is recalled by a nearby replica building.

Statistics

Built: 1918
Previous names: None
Gross tonnage: 374
Type of vessel: 3-masted schooner
Builder: Harrington, Maine
Owner: Nat and Betty Ewer
Cause of loss: Burned

Lost: February 1972
Depth: on land
Dimensions: 140' x 32' x 11'
Power: Sail

Port of registry: Unregistered
Location: Beach Haven, New Jersey

This photograph plus the picture postcards I found on eBay: a treasure trove in itself. This photo was taken after the devastating fire that destroyed the *Lucy Evelyn*: a sad end to an era that delighted both locals and visitors alike.

Montgomery, alias Max's Wreck?
or, Close But No Cigar?

My New Jersey shipwreck explorers will find this new information interesting – perhaps even fascinating.

No smoking gun, but there is additional circumstantial evidence that Max's Wreck is indeed the *Montgomery*, as I suggested in *Shipwrecks of New Jersey: South*.

Recently, Brandon McWilliams recovered a spoon that was stamped TEAZER. In itself this was no revelation as several years ago Joyce Steinmetz recovered a fork with the same stamp. Kim Dixon brought this recovery to my attention, and she and I brainstormed some speculations about its import.

Meanwhile, Brandon did some research and discovered that the *Montgomery* captured a Confederate blockade runner named *Bat*. The Union navy commissioned the *Bat* for the duration of the Civil War. Afterward, the *Bat* was sold to commercial interests and renamed *Teazer*. Brandon thought that this was too much of a coincidence, and that it provided compelling evidence that Max's Wreck must be the *Montgomery*.

I countered by noting that, although it was indeed a strange coincidence, the *Bat* was not named *Teazer* until a year *after* her capture. So how would *Teazer* silverware get onto the *Montgomery* when the *Teazer* had yet to assume the latter name?

Now Kim provided me with another official record that both she and Brandon discovered independent of each other. They found mention of the *Teazer* in a Senate document that was published in 1870. Here it was noted that the *Teazer* was a British steamer on her first run through the Union blockade when she was captured, and that she was renamed U.S.S. *Bat* when the Union navy purchased the vessel from the prize court, and commissioned her.

If this sounds confusing, let me clarify. In *Shipwrecks of the Chesapeake Bay in Virginia Waters*, I explained in detail how the Confederate raider *Florida* was built in England under the name *Oreto*, and how her name was later changed "on the fly" after being armed as a warship.

A number of Confederate warships were built in England under the guise of merchant vessels as a way to deceive Union observers about their true nature. The Confederates established a straw man (or company) in England. The company was owned and funded by the South for the express purpose of ordering the construction of vessels for the Confederate navy. The Confederates went to great lengths to disguise intended warships as merchant vessels.

On the ways, these vessels were given fictitious names as part of the deception. Decks were secretly reinforced to support the weight of cannons. Magazines were boarded up like secret rooms in a castle. Thus Union inspectors might *believe* that a certain vessel was bound for the Confederacy, but were unable to *prove* it.

Upon completion of construction, the vessels departed under fake papers for foreign ports. Instead of proceeding to their written destinations, they rendezvoused at sea or at an island with a Confederate stores vessel that carried guns and ammunition with which to arm the so-called "merchant" vessel.

Now one can apprehend how *Teazer* silverware found its way onto the *Montgomery*. I theorize that silverware was stamped with the vessel's fictitious name as part of Confederate trickery.

Also in the *Florida* chapter, I went to great lengths to show how the Confederates stole everything of value whenever they captured a Union merchant vessel: food, drink, supplies, and the personal belongings of the passengers and crew. One passenger wrote a multi-page account about how her luggage was rummaged for souvenirs before it was either tossed overboard or burned with the vessel.

One Union vessel that the *Florida* captured was the *Jacob Bell*. When the wreck of the *Florida* was salvaged in the 1980's, divers recovered a spoon that was stamped JACOB BELL.

Which brings us back to the *Montgomery*. Now I speculate that the *Teazer* was outfitted with stamped silverware as a way to dupe Union observers about her intended purpose and ultimate ownership. The *Teazer's* unofficial name was changed at sea to *Bat*, which name was given upon her capture, even though she was registered as the British vessel *Teazer*. Union sailors appropriated some of the stamped silverware. That silverware remained in the galley after the *Montgomery* was sold to commercial interests after the war.

When the *Teazer* alias *Bat* was sold at war's end, the new owner rechristened her with her original name, perhaps because some of the stamped silverware was still on board.

Granted this evidence is still circumstantial – but it's strong circumstantial.

Hats off to Brandon and Kim for pursuing the matter, and for conducting some inspirational research.

If anyone has contrary or confirmatory evidence, please forward such information to me. Constructive criticism is always welcome.

All of the above begs the question: How does this new information fit with Harold Moyers' recovery of a brass tag that was stamped DALLAS? In short, it doesn't. I was never able to find any vessel named *Dallas* that was lost off the eastern seaboard. Thus this contrary evidence remains contrary.

On the other hand, the recovery of a pump that was stamped U.S. NAVY is readily explained as a replacement when the *Montgomery* operated as a Union blockader.

So there you have it. The vote may still be out, but I'm holding onto my prediction that the identity of Max's Wreck is the *Montgomery*.

In the meantime, will someone please recover the ship's bell? Or some other artifact that carries the vessel's name. Then we can put this issue to rest. Permanently.

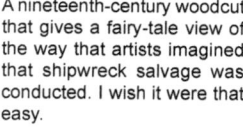
A nineteenth-century woodcut that gives a fairy-tale view of the way that artists imagined that shipwreck salvage was conducted. I wish it were that easy.

Robert J. Walker (alias $25 Wreck)

The identification of the $25 Wreck as the coastal survey vessel *Robert J. Walker* consisted of so much information that it required an entire book to reveal all the relevant facts. I wrote such a book while the present work was in progress: *The $25 Wreck of the Robert J. Walker: Plus NOAA's Antics and Pretensions* (2016). However, I intentionally deleted one part of the story because I did not want to stain the historical aspect of the subject with a personal complaint. So here it is, down and dirty.

In the early 1970's, I saw a rectangular porthole that Joel Entler recovered from the $25 Wreck. At that stage in my diving career, I was fascinated by brass and bronze portholes, and sought to rescue them from oblivion at every opportunity. Joel's porthole was so different, so antique, that I was instantly enamored by it, and wanted to have one for myself.

The wreck was not a popular dive site. Most so-called Jersey divers then and now dived primarily to catch lobsters. Hangovers from the previous decade still speared fish. Only a few were hardcore wreck-divers: that is, those who dived on shipwrecks for the purpose of sheer exploration and penetration of collapsing hulls, and because of historic interest in the wreck. The $25 Wreck was unpopular because it lay in such an advanced state of collapse that there were few holes in which lobsters and black sea bass could hide. Plus, the wreck was unidentified.

Trips to the $25 Wreck were few and far between. They pretty much happened by chance because in those days, destinations for dive trips were not generally prearranged. Like anglers on head boats, most divers didn't care where the boat took them, as long as the site produced lobsters and fish. A charter boat that departed from Atlantic City could go to any one or two of a hundred known snags. Thus the chances were slim that a skipper would choose to go to the $25 Wreck.

In the early 1970's, when the Eastern Divers Association came into prominence, first president Elliot Subervi then subsequent president Tom Roach created schedules that named the destination of each and every trip (weather permitting). Now divers could decide which trips to sign up on based on the boat's destination.

In the mid-1970's, when Bart Malone and I became dive masters for Norman Lichtman's The Dive Shop of New Jersey, and initiated an annual dive schedule, we adopted the EDA system in which destinations were named as a way to entice divers who wanted to dive on specific shipwrecks to sign-up on dive trips. We often put the $25 Wreck on the schedule. Despite my deep and abiding interest in the $25 Wreck, I was not able to get on it. Scheduled trips were either blown out by foul weather or cancelled for other reasons such as mechanical failure.

For the same reasons, it took me thirteen years to get on the World War Two freighter *San Jose*, but on that first dive I made up for all the failed attempts to get there by catching two huge lobsters: a twelve pounder and a thirteen pounder. Both were males, and both were in the same hole: one behind the other. That form of habitation was unheard of, because males always fought each other.

Yet the $25 Wreck eluded me. Forever.

Skip to 2014. The $25 Wreck was identified as the *Robert J. Walker*. With the blessing of the National Oceanic and Atmospheric Association, Dan Lieb and Steve Nagiewicz organized a week-long survey expedition to photograph and measure the layout of the wreck. After the expedition was over, and while I was writing *The $25 Wreck of the Robert J. Walker*, I contacted Lieb in order to obtain information about the survey.

At that time, he claimed that he had sent me an email in which he had extended an invitation for me to participate in the survey. I received no such invitation. I do not believe that any such invitation was extended to me. If Lieb had truly wanted me to participate, he would have called me on the phone after he did not receive a reply from me. Or he would have sent another email. He would have taken some form of additional contact. He did not. Thus the reason that I disbelieved his after-the-fact claim.

Now comes confirmatory evidence. I wanted to include a chapter that detailed the day-to-day operations of the survey, that provided the names and duties of the volunteer participants, and that demonstrated the overall conduct of the survey, including the resulting site plan. Lieb refused to let me have any of that information.

Furthermore, he refused to allow any of the volunteer participants to share their personal experiences with me. When I asked long-time friend Vince Capone for a copy of the side-scan sonar image that he created, he told me that Lieb and Nagiewicz refused to permit him to do so. When I asked Stockton College professor Peter Straub, who oversaw the college students who created side-scan images that Vince Capone processed, and who interpreted the data, if I could have access to that material, he said at first that I could; after all, the purpose of a college is to share information. But after he contacted Lieb and Nagiewicz, he told me that I did not have their permission to view or otherwise access the college's records. Nor would Lieb and Nagiewicz allow me to have access to Herb Segars' underwater photographs. The same was true with regard to my long-time dive buddy Mike Pizzio, who took underwater photos.

The irony of the situation was that Lieb claimed to have wanted me to be part of the expedition, but afterward he did everything he could do to thwart me from learning about the results of the survey. In other words, I was blackballed. Although Lieb and Nagiewicz prevented me from adding a chapter about details of the survey, the real loser was the public for whom I wrote the book. 'Nuff said.

Statistics

Built: 1847
Previous names: None
Gross tonnage: 358
Type of vessel: *Legare*-class iron-hulled steamer
Builder: Joseph Tomlinson, Pittsburgh, Pennsylvania
Owner at time of loss: U.S. Coast Survey
Port of registry: New York, New York
Cause of loss: Collision with schooner *Fanny*
Location: 11 miles southeast of Atlantic City, New Jersey
GPS: 39-13.230

Sunk: July 21, 1860
Depth: 85 feet
Dimensions: 133' x 24' x 9'
Power: Two coal-fired steam engines

74-17.269

United States (and others)

Pennsylvania has shipwrecks? You betcha. But not what you think.

There are shipwrecks in Lake Erie where a projection of Penn's Woods pokes northward to touch freshwater between New York and Ohio. I've done a fair amount of diving in Lake Erie. For prime examples, see *Great Lakes Shipwrecks: a Photographic Odyssey*.

There are shipwrecks in the Delaware River dating back before the Revolution. I even explored one of them. No, I didn't dive on it, for visibility in the river is zilch. Instead, I was part a group of historians who walked through thick mud to a wooden hulk that was exposed at low tide during an extended drought. It was suspected to be the *Alliance*, one of John Paul Jones's commands which was sold out of service, later reduced to a barge, then finally sunk. We took measurement of the length and breadth, and of the thickness of the beams, but our group was unable to substantiate its identity.

The Delaware River also has a number of floating vessels which, although they are not wrecked, have much to show the wreck-diver who is interested in seeing how vessels are constructed and how their interiors are laid out, in order to help them visualize a shipwreck that has collapsed and lost its original shape.

For instance, every spring before the diving season I toured the *Olympia* and studied the deck plans because it strongly resembled the *San Diego*. Next to the *Olympia* floats the World War Two submarine *Becuna*. Not far away floats the *Moshulu*: a 4-masted bark that sailed around the world numerous times after her construction in 1904; she has been converted to a restaurant that specializes in fine-dining.

Opposite Philadelphia's Penn's Landing – where the *Olympia*, *Becuna*, and *Moshulu* reside – Camden hosts the World War Two battleship *New Jersey*, which also served in the Korean War and the Vietnam Conflict, and which now serves the public by providing daily tours.

Less known and not accessible to the public is the 990-foot-long ocean liner *United States*. On her maiden voyage in 1952, cruising at a speed of 35 knots, she crossed the Atlantic Ocean faster than any previous vessel had ever done. This speed record earned her the precious Blue Riband: a record that has yet to be broken. She continued to serve in the passenger service for the next 17 years.

The advent of transatlantic aircraft commuter flights doomed seaborne travel. Ships were slow and expensive; planes were fast and cheap. The only liners that survived this gradual change operated instead as cruise ships. The United States was laid up and, to make a long story short, she has been a white elephant ever since: changing hands multiple times with various plans for renovation for any number of places and purposes.

The $80-million-dollar liner was sold in 1977 for $5 million. She was supposed to become a floating casino and hotel in Atlantic City,

New Jersey, but never even moved from her dock in Newport News, Virginia. In 1984, her furniture, fittings, and interior artwork were sold at public auction.

The empty hull was not only an eyesore of peeling paint and rusting steel, but was made unusable by restrictive OSHA regulations. The Occupational Safety and Health Act required that her asbestos insulation be removed before the vessel could receive an occupancy permit. Asbestos abatement was so expensive in the United States (the country, not the vessel), that it was cheaper to have the hull towed across the Atlantic Ocean to the Ukraine in order to have the asbestos removed, and have her towed back again, than to have the work done domestically. Before asbestos could be removed from buildings (and vessels) that were being demolished, OSHA regulations called for the entire structure to be covered by plastic sheeting to prevent asbestos dust from floating into the atmosphere. And removal workers had to wear protective clothing that resembled spacesuits for a moon walk. Plus, wages were cheaper overseas.

Upon her return in 1994, the white elephant was nothing more than an asbestos-free white elephant: one that was paler but no more desirable. She was docked at unused Pier 82 in Philadelphia, Pennsylvania. She has been there ever since, while plan after plan to inject new life into the hull did not materialize. Owners changed, each with the idea of putting the liner back into service, or using it as a hotel or some kind of housing. None of these plans eventuated. In 2010, then owner Norwegian Cruise Lines decided to scrap the hull for its metal.

The newly created SS United States Conservancy did not have enough money to purchase the idling vessel until rich philanthropist Gerry Lenfest donated nearly $6 million to purchase and preserve the aging liner and make it a self-supporting tourist attraction as part of a waterfront development project, in which the United States would be the centerpiece, much the way the *Queen Mary* serves in Long Beach, California, housing a museum, hotel, restaurants, and offices for local businesses.

The development project foundered. In 2016, Crystal Cruises announced the possibility to convert the liner to a cruise ship. This plan also foundered. The fate of the *United States* is still uncertain. There is talk of scuttling the hull as an artificial reef. This would be a major attraction to wreck-divers.

In the meantime, I present a selection of photographs of artifacts that I found on display at the Windmill Point Restaurant, in Nags Head, North Carolina. Sarah Forbes, owner, bought them at auction and used them to decorate the already elegant eatery. After the restaurant closed for business in 2007, the artifacts were donated to The Mariners' Museum and Christopher Newport University, which lie adjacent to each other in Newport News, Virginia. (Christopher Newport University also houses The Mariners' Museum's library and research records.)

Pennsylvania - *United States* (and others)

Above: Obverse and reverse sides of a matchbook from the Windmill Point Restaurant. Top left: *Olympia*. Left: *Moshulu* and downtown Philadelphia skyline. Bottom: *New Jersey*. Not shown are *Becuna* and *Gazela Primeiro* (a Portuguese fishing vessel that was stopped by the German U-boat *U-701* during World War Two, but which was released because she was registered to a neutral nation.

United States (and others) - Pennsylvania

Above: An entire bar from the *United States*, including the stools and glasses. Top right: Ship's bell. Right: Life preserver. Below: Dining room tables, chairs, and settings. Note the bell and model in the background. The entire upstairs dining room of the restaurant was furnished with tables, chairs, glassware, and silverware from the *United States*. Except for the lack of motion, I felt as if I were standing in the ship's dining room. The pumpkins below the bell were decorations for Halloween.

Pennsylvania - United States (and others) 71

Above is another view of the bar from a different angle. The windows look out over Pamlico Sound. Note that the tabletop in the foreground has a raised lip on the perimeter in order to prevent dishes and glassware from sliding over the edge.

At left is a true blast from the past: a juke box with records from the 1950's and 1960's. Young generation readers should note that before compact discs and before cassette tapes there were records: plastic discs that played music by dragging a needle across a groove in the surface. Note the tall ashtray and bar stools to the left.

The walls on both floors of the restaurant were covered with pictures, paintings, and display cabinets: the latter filled with china, cutlery, and hundreds of items too numerous to show or describe. See some on the next page.

United States (and others) ~ Pennsylvania

Shipwreck Discovery Twofer
Amazing Grace and Pilgrim's Progress

"Twofer" is a slang word that means "two for one." Thus the title of this chapter means "two shipwreck discoveries for one trip."

Not many divers can claim to have discovered two shipwrecks on a one-day trip. Enter the dive boat RV *Explorer*.

During the summer of 2016, the *Explorer* departed from her dock in Cape May, New Jersey with five people on board: owners and skippers Rusty Cassway and Brian Sullivan, plus divers Stephen Lagreca, Bart Malone, and Tim Terrey. Their mission: to check out deep-water hang numbers offshore of the *India Arrow*.

One might suspect that they were lucky to find even one shipwreck, much less two. Luck had nothing to do with the research that went into unearthing hang numbers from a list of hundreds. Luck did not make the members decline to sleep late that weekend, and instead arise in the wee hours of the morning and drive to the New Jersey shore, where the boat was docked at Cape May. Luck did not force the team to decide to check the validity of dubious hang numbers.

No. It wasn't luck that steered the boat to GPS coordinates of an unknown nature instead of going to a well-known and often-dived shipwreck. It was conscious will and determination that sent these divers to locations that could have proved to be nothing more than a reef, a ledge, or a pile of rocks – as is usually the case with unidentified hang numbers.

The hang-log name of the first set of numbers was Amazing Grace. The nomenclature did not necessarily have any meaning. Hangs have been given names for a number of reasons – and sometimes without reason. For example, a hang may be named for the skipper who hooked his dredge on the hang, or for the boat that lost its gear. A hang could be called after an event that occurred when the site was discovered, such as the Broken Scissors. (For "discovered," read "when the gear was hung or lost.") A hang might be named after the boat's mascot: a dog, a cat, or a canary; or the cat *and* the canary – no, that was a movie title.

The *Gloria & Doris* was named after two women who happened to be aboard the charter fishing boat when it anchored into a snag. The Magnolia Wreck was named after bars of brand-name anti-friction metal that were recovered from the site. The Offshore Piece was named after . . . well, you get the idea.

Amazing Grace

The Amazing Grace hang was named after a scallop boat that disappeared with all hands in the vicinity. The cognomen was applied because the scalloper's hull was painted maroon, and subsequent scallopers found maroon paint on their gear when they hauled in their nets after contacting the hang.

In this case, the wreck that the *Explorer* hooked into on the sandy seafloor actually *was* the *Amazing Grace*. Who would have thought? The depth of the wreck was recorded as 253 feet.

Although the discoverers didn't know it at the time, the loss of the *Amazing Grace* was historically significant as a turning point in the history of safety at sea.

In the 1980's, uninspected fishing vessels were sinking at an alarming rate. The boats were worked hard, and there was little time between offshore trips for maintenance and repairs. As a result, the hulls of many boats suffered extensive wear and tear that received only jury-rigged upkeep, in order to keep the boat at sea and hauling in biomass in the form of fish, scallops, crabs, lobsters, and shrimp.

A hull that might look and feel sound might present only a façade of worthiness. Sometimes, a well-kept boat was caught offshore in a squall or storm that overwhelmed the fishing vessel despite the skill of the skipper and the courage of the crew.

What happened to cause the *Amazing Grace* to sink will never be known.

According to the abstract of the Marine Accident Report of the National Transportation Safety Board, "About November 14, 1984, the 86-foot-long uninspected U.S. fishing vessel *Amazing Grace* sank while on a fishing trip for scallops about 80 miles east of Cape Henlopen, Delaware; there probably were seven crewmembers aboard. A 16-day search by the U.S. Coast Guard resulted in finding only one of the two liferafts on [sic] the vessel. The liferaft was empty. The crewmembers are missing and presumed dead. As of the date of this report [July 9, 1985], the *Amazing Grace* has not been located. The vessel's estimated value was $500,000.

"The National Transportation Safety Board is unable to determine the probable cause of the loss of the *Amazing Grace*."

Facts concerning the *Amazing Grace* on the day of her departure were few. Although the Report neglected to name the vessel's crewmembers – in fact, it claimed not to know the exact number of crewmembers – newspaper accounts provided the information. Paul Robles was the skipper; the crew consisted of Jimmy Bowers, John Davis, Don Hancock, Darrio Perez, James Raynor, and David Ruffin.

The last known person to see the *Amazing Grace's* skipper and crew alive was Paul Robles' brother, who was the skipper of the *Amazing Grace's* sister ship, *Atlantic Pride*, and who worked for the same company. This was on the morning of November 7, when the *Amazing Grace* departed for a 17-day "fishing trip for scallops off the Virginia, Maryland, Delaware, and New Jersey coasts."

The next day, Robles radioed his unnamed brother on the *Atlantic Pride* "requesting 200 scallop bags, which are used to store the scallops after shucking, and some cleaning supplies for delivery to the *Amazing Grace*. Before the captain of the *Atlantic Pride* left Hampton [Virginia] on November 8, a member of the owner's family asked him to buy some spare 'V' belts for the freshwater pumps on the *Amazing Grace* and to deliver them to the *Amazing Grace*.

"Sometime between 0100 and 0600 on November 14, the mate on the *Amazing Grace* and the mate on the *Atlantic Pride* were in radio contact to arrange a meeting to transfer supplies. . . . The captain of the *Atlantic Pride* said that, at the time of the radio conversation, the winds were blowing from the northwest about 40 mph (35 knots) and the seas were about 10 feet high. He told his mate to head toward the *Amazing Grace* to deliver the supplies."

At that time the two scallopers were ten miles apart.

"About 0720, the captain of the *Atlantic Pride* contacted his brother via radio, and his brother reported that the *Amazing Grace* had taken a wave over its bow, that there was water on the after deck, that the crew was to open the freeing ports, and that he was going below in the engineroom to pump out the fish hold. The captain of the *At-*

lantic Pride testified that his brother did not express any sense of concern or that there was a problem."

The rendezvous was called off because of inclement weather. That was the last that anyone heard of the *Amazing Grace*.

Further radio calls failed to elicit a response. Robles' brother tried to call the Coast Guard but "was unsuccessful, so he asked the captain of the *Carolina Princess*, another fishing vessel in the area, to call the USCG." He was successful in making contact. He gave Coast Guard the approximate position, and described the vessel's length and color scheme.

The search for the missing crewmembers was massive. The Coast Guard started by contacting all the local harbors where the *Amazing Grace* might have docked in an emergency. The Coast Guard then broadcast an urgent message to all vessels in the area to be on the lookout for an 80-foot trawler with a maroon hull and white superstructure.

When none of these measures helped to find the *Amazing Grace*, the Coast Guard deployed search and rescue craft: initially a jet-propelled fixed-wing Falcon, two turbine-powered Sikorsky helicopters, the 95-foot cutter *Cape Starr*, and the 82-foot cutter *Point Bataan*: all within two hours of receipt of the SOS from the *Carolina Princess*.

Five hours later, the *Cape Starr* and *Point Bataan* were recalled because "they were not considered to be effective search platforms in the 8- to 10-foot seas." They were replaced by the 216-foot cutter *Chilula*.

After nightfall, the Coast Guard dispatched a C-130 aircraft to search the dark ocean for flares.

To ascertain the probable drift and speed of a life raft or a person in the water, the Coast Guard employed a system called CASP, for Computer Assisted Search Planning. This system took into account the current, tide, and wind in order to project the most likely locations of drifting objects with different characteristics of motion: a partially submerged boat, a person in the water, a life raft with and without a drogue.

Search craft then followed this track from the last reported position of the *Amazing Grace*, and based their search patterns on the computer's predictions.

Both the *Atlantic Pride* and the *Carolina Lady* ceased scalloping operations in order to join in the search for survivors from the *Amazing Grace*.

On November 16, three Coast Guard and two Navy aircraft combed the area that had an 86-percent probability of finding the *Amazing Grace* or her survivors.

At eight o'clock that night, the fishing vessel *Capt Lis* "sighted three flares about 22 nautical miles to the northwest of the last reported position of the *Amazing Grace*." All the fishing vessels converged on that area while an aircraft searched from the air. They searched all day of November 17.

"On November 18, "five USCG and one USN aircraft searched 19,200 square nautical miles."

These concentrated search efforts continued until November 20, when the search was provisionally terminated, but then it was extended for one more day.

On November 21, the "561-foot-long Danish containership *Clifford Maersk* recovered a Givens liferaft." The serial number matched one of those on the *Amazing Grace*. "The liferaft was found near the portion of the planned search area that was not completed because the aircraft ran low on fuel. On November 21, the USCG had searched areas to the north and to the south of the location where the liferaft was found."

Again the search was extended so that aircraft could examine the area in which the life raft was found. "The USCG also requested the USAF to conduct a photographic reconnaissance flight in the area and the USAF agreed, although this was not a normal procedure." This resulted in the capture of an image in which an orange object was detected.

The search was continued. Over the next several days, the search located "several pieces of debris, including a 14-foot-long open boat" on November 26, and another open boat on the following day, but no orange life raft." An unidentified "object" was also photographed.

On November 30, the USCG's active search again was suspended. "The 16-day search had covered 192,146 square nautical miles. There had been 106 aircraft sorties resulting in 564 hours of aircraft search time. The estimated cost to the USCG and U.S. Department of Defense units involved in the search effort was $2.1 million; the two USAF reconnaissance fights cost an additional $10 million. The USCG Chief of Search and Rescue in New York stated that this search was the largest search effort he had ever been involved with during his 18 years in USCG search and rescue assignments."

One might wonder how a vessel could disappear with all hands, and nothing was found but an empty life raft. In the 1970's, Lloyd's of London reported that every year an average of fifty vessels were lost without a trace – and these were not small fishing vessels but large-size freighters and tankers that were manned by large crews, and were equipped with radios and multiple life boats and rafts: they departed normally but never reached their destinations, and no distress signal was ever heard by radio. It makes one wonder how a huge commercial vessel could sink or be swamped so fast that the skipper, radio operator, or helmsman did not have time to transmit and SOS. But it happened, and on the average of fifty vessels per year.

In the present case, the NTSB did not have much information to study. Investigators examined the history of the skipper and crew; in the absence of construction plans they studied photographs of the boat; they scanned the vessel's accident record, which included three groundings "without significant damage;" they interviewed the people who spoke the *Amazing Grace* by radio; they read the most recent marine survey report of the vessel's then current condition, maintenance, and gear replacements and installations, which also described her safety paraphernalia; they scrutinized the repair invoices; they reviewed the meteorological situation; and they talked with the vessel's owners, the Daniels family, about the readiness and seaworthiness of the boat.

A former skipper of the *Amazing Grace* stated, "Kenny Daniels never cut me short on no gear, no equipment, nothing . . . [ellipses in the original report] I worked with the best boats." This skipper testified, "I was never denied anything for the crew's welfare that I asked for."

So what went wrong?

Hypothetical calculations that took into account such factors as the vessels approximated weight based upon scallop catch assumptions, the amount of seawater on the deck and in the fish holds, the state of the sea, whether or not the freeing ports had been open for drainage, and stability characteristics under all possible circumstances, and the clam dredge overturning moment. These theoretical speculations resulted in some nice looking formulas and graphs but, lacking any kind of factual information,

Sister ship of the *Amazing Grace*. (Courtesy of Rusty Cassway.)

were nothing more than speculations.

Understand that these speculations were necessary not so much to ascertain why the *Amazing Grace* foundered, but how such situations could be avoided in the future.

A Coast Guard study showed that between 1970 and 1982, some 185 fishing vessels were lost *each year*! This equates to some 2,400 fishing vessels sunk during the thirteen-year period of the survey. "An average of 70 fishing vessels were lost because of capsizing, flooding, or foundering."

This same study showed "that there were an average of 43 lives lost each year due to the total loss of vessels and that an average of 30 lives are lost each year due to the capsizing or foundering of vessels. USCG statistics for 1983 show that of the 250 vessels lost, 102 were lost as the result of capsizing, flooding, or foundering, and resulted in 111 deaths. The above data do not include State-registered fishing vessels."

In the big picture, the loss of the *Amazing Grace* was not an unusual event.

Worse yet, "USCG statistics show that the death rate for commercial fishermen is seven times the national average for all industry groups (twice that for miners)."

Perhaps most alarming was the fact that, according to the USCG Proceedings of the Marine Safety Council, "the number of deaths relative to the number of vessels seems to be rising."

Of the three broad categories of the reasons for vessel losses – "human failure, vessel related, or environment" – "human failure stands out. These failures include: a. Poor watchkeeping practices. b. Navigational errors and rules of the road violations. c. Lack of understanding of the various forces acting on the vessel, especially as concerns the stability; i.e., failure to load and operate the vessel according to its stability chart, modification of the vessel without consideration of possible change in stability characteristics, operation of the vessel in weather conditions which overwhelm the vessel, etc. Furthermore, the human factor often plays a role in those casualties where the direct cause was failure of some vessel component."

In other words, a moment's inattention or the failure to anticipate or recognize an oncoming event, was a likely cause of many vessels' foundering or capsizing. This was especially true of draggers and trawlers due to the weight of nets that were filled to near capacity when the nets were raised high out of the water while the vessel was wallowing sideways in a trough in heavy seas and high wind.

The combination of large waves and a momentary increase in metacentric height can roll over a vessel without a moment's notice. One second the crew could be laboring with the net, and the next they could be either dragged under water with the boat or swimming for their lives.

More than one dragger or trawler pulled itself under water backwards by the strength of its winch when the bottom gear hung on an obstruction.

Most "hangs" are sites of catastrophe, the least of which is the loss of the gear, and the most of which is the loss of the vessel.

I have dived on many shipwrecks on which a haul net was clearly visible; sometimes more than one. The location of many shipwrecks was ascertained by commercial anglers who lost expensive gear.

All of the above has to do with the loss of a boat. But what about a crew whose boat sank and they are left drifting in the waves?

The most obvious survival expedient is an inflatable raft, especially when a boat is sinking so fast that there is no time to launch a lifeboat. The *Amazing Grace* was equipped with two six-person, self-inflating Givens life rafts. One of them was spotted by the Danish containership *Clifford Maersk* on November 21, seven days after the *Amazing Grace* was presumed to have sunk. The vessel stopped, recovered the raft, and introduced a mystery.

The message that the *Clifford Maersk* transmitted stated, in part, "Passed orange coloured [British spelling] half blown inflatable rubber liferaft. Stopped to investigate and found raft has been used but empty."

The preponderant word in this message was "used."

According to the NTSB report, "The two six-person liferafts were mounted in gimballed cylindrical cradles secured with hydrostatic release systems and were located on either side of the aft pilothouse deck."

These rafts were designed to release automatically and self-inflate upon submergence to a pre-set depth. The rafts were supposed to contain ten ounces of water per person, "three hand-held red flares in addition to its survival equipment package."

"According to the *Clifford Maersk's* crew, the liferaft was found with the two main chambers fully inflated. The three canopy chambers were deflated partially Both the sea anchor and heaving line were deployed fully, and there were no provisions aboard. The blade of the line-cutting knife was extended, and the knife was found stowed in its canopy storage packet on the liferaft. After photographing the liferaft, the crew destroyed the liferaft by cutting it into small pieces and throwing the pieces overboard."

These facts imply that some crewmembers survived the sinking of the fishing vessel.

Noticeably missing from survival gear on the raft were the three flares with which it was supposed to have been equipped. Recall that the *Capt Lis* observed three ignited flares on the night of November 16, in an area where Coast Guard Search and Rescue aircraft subsequently patrolled after receiving word of the sighting.

This is another implication that some of the crewmembers were alive and awaiting rescue after four days alone on the wide, wide sea.

Requiescat in pace. RIP.

As a result of these dire events, the National Transportation Safety Board charged the U.S. Coast Guard with making recommendations for reducing such avoidable loss of life. Subsequently, the Coast Guard conducted an exhaustive investigation into the manner in which the search for the *Amazing Grace* and potentially drifting survivors was conducted, in order to ascertain possible flaws in the system.

No system is flawless, but search efforts proved to be as effective as conceivable in light of available manpower and rescue craft, both air and sea. However, the Coast Guard did find deficiencies in the way in which commercial fishing vessels were equipped and handled.

The Coast Guard noted, "The typical fishing vessel captain has had no formal training in vessel safety and has learned navigation, radio procedures, first aid, and the use of lifesaving equipment from on-the-job training or by attending fishing industry expositions. Most fishing captains do not know all the factors that affect the stability of their vessels."

Crewmembers were often hired off the docks at the last minute prior to departure. They sometimes possessed little or no experience in life at sea. They were taught to handle fishing gear on the spot, but were not familiarized with boating operations or emergency procedures. In this regard, crewmembers were equivalent to early flight attendants, who were little more than flying waitresses.

As the NTSB noted in its report, "Since there was no crew list left ashore, and the Safety Board as of the date of this report has not found anyone who saw the vessel depart from port, the identities and number of persons aboard is uncertain, except for the captain and the mate, both of whom spoke on the radio later to another fishing vessel."

In the commercial fishing business, a crew list was seldom if ever compiled and submitted to someone in authority. The Coast Guard recommended that fishing vessels be required to do so.

"Fishing vessel captains normally do not have any scheduled communications with shore. Some captains are reluctant to broadcast their position and the amount of their catch in order to prevent their competition from finding their fishing area. Other captains do not want to let other fishing vessels know when they are returning to port because the time of their arrival at the processing facility will affect the price offered from their catch."

In addition to all of the above, the single most important factor that the Coast Guard found lacking in commercial fishing vessels was an EPIRB.

EPIRB is the acronym for Emergency Position Indicating Radio Beacon. The Class A top-of-the-line device is one that is designed to float off a sinking vessel and to switch itself on upon contact with seawater. The device then transmits a homing signal on a specific frequency. The transmission alerts rescue vessels and directs them to the location of the floating EPIRB.

An investment in the amount of $200 to $300 could have saved the lives of the crew of the *Amazing Grace*.

A Class B EPIRB does not float free off a sinking vessel nor activate automatically. It is waterproof, but must be activated by means of a switch.

A Class C EPIRB is waterproof but has a short range. It is used for coastwise or lake operation.

The loss of the *Amazing Grace* and her six- or seven-man crew was – to coin a cliché – the straw that broke the camel's back.

In 1978, the Coast Guard had already made such a recommendation: "We believe that increased use of EPIRBs is desirable from a search and rescue (SAR) point of view. On 21 November 1978 we issued Commandant Notice 2370 on the use of EPIRBs by fishing vessels. This notice explicitly directed Coast Guard District Commanders to use such means as are practicable within their districts to encourage fishing vessels (those going more than twenty miles offshore) to carry EPIRBs."

"Encourage" was all the Coast Guard could do. It was not authorized to "demand" the use of EPIRB's. To do so required legislative action.

In 1980, he NTSB had already sought "authority to require the carriage of emergency position indicating radio beacons (EPIRB) on documented U.S. fishing vessels and, in the interim period, pursue all available means to encourage their use."

Despite the alarming number of fishing vessel losses and fatalities, and the combined efforts of the Coast Guard and the National Transportation Safety Board, legislators were slow to act.

After the NTSB's 1980 memorandum, the Coast Guard took the long view: "The Coast Guard intends to seek legislative authority to require the satellite EPIRB on U.S. vessels, including fishing vessels. The Coast Guard does not intend to seek legislation authority to require the present EPIRB system on fishing vessels since the satellite system could be ready for implementation in the *four or five year period* [my italics] that would be needed to obtain the enabling legislation to get the final regulations in effect. The satellite system is expected to render the present system obsolete, so there would be no reason to pursue its mandatory carriage on fishing vessels. By seeking legislative authority now for the satellite system while it is still under development, the Coast Guard will be prepared to implement the system with a minimum of delay as soon as it is operational."

The Coast Guard reiterated its stance in February of 1982: "When an acceptable operational satellite system comes into being, we will seek legislation to provide us with the necessary authority to require satellite EPIRBS on U.S. vessels."

Six months later, the NTSB issued this statement: "The international satellite system project, COSPAS-SARSAT, which began in 1982 is now in its demonstration and operational phase. . . . According to available information, the system has provided alert and location data in 112 marine and aviation distress incidents worldwide involving 333 persons and resulting in the rescue of 289 survivors. Among these distress incidents were 12 involving fishing vessels from which 87 persons were rescued."

Drafted legislation included an exception from the requirement to carry an EPIRB "on coastwise vessels carrying passengers for hire that carry radiotelephone communication equipment that complies with Federal Communications Commission requirements." Due to the investigation of the sinking of the charter fishing vessel (head boat) *Joan la Rie III*, on February 4, 1984, this exemption was eliminated. This meant that regardless of the type of radio that a vessel kept on board, vessels were required to carry an EPIRB.

The Coast Guard concurred in part. Its objection pertained to the type of EPIRB that should be carried, in particular the Class S. This EPIRB was similar to the Class B except that it floated: a feature that made it more useful for life rafts than an EPIRB that would sink if dropped accidentally.

NTSB: "Since the loss of the *Amazing Grace*, the Daniels family and other fishing

Delaware - Amazing Grace 81

companies in the Hampton Roads area have provided their vessels with Class A EPIRB's. The owner of the *Amazing Grace* testified that he was not aware of the existence of EPIRB's until the loss of the *Amazing Grace*."

Nonetheless, most fishing vessel owners would not voluntarily go the expense of an EPIRB. As with seatbelts in automobiles, they needed to be forced to purchase and use them.

Because the *Amazing Grace* had transmitted a message which stated that the boat "had taken a wave over its bow and there was water on its after deck," the NTSB concluded, "The loss of the *Amazing Grace* without any distress message being received or any survivors or bodies being found indicated a sudden and rapid sinking of the vessel."

Despite a catastrophic sinking, an automatic EPIRB would have notified nearby vessels of her loss, and would have continued to transmit signals to search and rescue vessels. The NTSB stated it this way: "If the vessel had been equipped with an EPIRB, its sinking might have been detected earlier, and the search effort could have been confined to a smaller area."

Worse yet was this epitaph: "In the 5 years since the Safety Board made Safety Recommendation M-80-23, about 1,000 fishing vessels and more than 200 lives have been lost in accidents."

Finally, "Although the USCG actively has promoted voluntary installations of EPIRB's on fishing vessels, most fishing vessels still do not carry them. The cost of providing the approximately 33,000 documented U.S. fishing vessels with EPIRB's is estimated at less than $10 million. The search for the *Amazing Grace* alone cost about $12 million. Because the date for implementation of a full satellite system is still indefinite, and many issues are yet to be resolved, the Safety Board believes that there is no justification for the USCG to delay requiring EPIRB's on U.S. fishing vessels. The USCG has indicated that legislative authority is necessary to require EPIRB's; if this is the case, the Safety Board believes that the USCG should seek the appropriate legislative authority immediately so that regulations requiring U.S. fishing vessels to be equipped with current EPIRB's can be promulgated without further delay."

And so it was done.

In 2007, Class A, B, and S EPIRB's became prohibited. Vessels carrying such devices had to replace them with units that could be tracked by satellite. Personal Locator Beacons (PLB) also communicated via satellite.

The Coast Guard also initiated a program to study fishing vessel design with regard to stability under a variety of conditions.

Furthermore, the Coast Guard successfully lobbied for legislation that required skippers to be licensed. Licensing required passing a test on a wide range of subjects, such as navigation, Rules of the Road, signal recognition, and so on.

Thus the loss of the *Amazing Grace* was a legacy that has saved countless lives ever since.

In several of my books and in some of my workshops, I stressed the problems of "going adrift at sea," and what to do about it. That's because I held the record for drifting away from the boat or having the boat leave me behind on a wreck. The feeling was always uncomfortable. My purpose was to prepare people for such an eventuality, and to offer advice on what to do if such a situation occurred; and what paraphernalia to carry: paraphernalia that would help rescuers to find missing divers. I always related one such incident that I related in *Andrea Doria: Dive to an Era.*

My strategy worked, especially on offshore trips, and particularly on the *Andrea Doria*. Divers started to carry strobes, flares, dye markers, day-glow stripes on hoods, and so on. But one diver topped it all. After reading my books and hearing my lectures, he was so concerned about being lost at sea that he showed up for a *Doria* trip with an EPIRB in a plastic waterproof container. He even had a candy bar inside the container. The model he had bought was equipped with a manual switch.

The *Doria* lies in an area that is known to produce exceptionally strong currents. He figured that if he got blown off the wreck, or drifted away from the boat – both scenarios had a history of recurring – he could open the container on the surface and switch on the unit, thus enabling the Coast Guard to home-in on the signal. The concept caught on among wreck divers.

Due to mass production after Coast Guard regulations required EPIRBS for boats, the unit cost was reduced drastically, to the point at which it was affordable for an individual to buy one for occasional use. Additionally, technological breakthroughs enabled manufacturers to produce units that were smaller and lighter in weight than they used to be. Satellite pick-up is worldwide.

As long as I am telling EPIRB stories, here's another one. Two thieves stole a boat and trailer from the owner's driveway. After stashing them in a hidden location, they fiddled with the onboard equipment, in the process of which they triggered the switch on the EPIRB. They switched it off immediately, but the signal had already been transmitted. The Coast Guard intercepted the momentary satellite signal, and triangulated the transmission as being located nowhere near the water.

They notified the local police, who went to the GPS coordinates, and promptly arrested the thieves. It doesn't get any better than that. Or does it?

Pilgrim's Progress

Having one feather in their cap did not prevent the *Explorer's* skippers and crewmembers from checking out another set of GPS numbers. This time they found and dived on a wreck that proved to be the fishing vessel *Pilgrim's Progress*. Perhaps the loss of the *Pilgrim's Progress* was not as historically meaningful as that of *Amazing Grace*, but her skipper and crew lived to tell the travails of the boat's final moments and their dramatic rescue.

The skipper of the *Pilgrim's Progress* was Captain R. S. Meekins, Jr., of Wanchese, North Carolina. Thanks to his remarkable memory of events, I can relate her story in exacting detail.

The *Pilgrim's Progress* was built by Nupert & Wallace in Thomaston, Maine. She was launched in 1952 as the *Kennebec* (after a river in Maine). Her hull and timber frames were made of oak, and the outer planking was made of long-leaf pine. The design of the hull was like that of a schooner but with a sailing yacht stern, which made her a double-ender. Originally she was ketch-rigged.

The *Kennebec* was built for Maine Products (of Portland, Maine) to be employed as a sardine carrier. She was subsequently sold and converted to a dragger. Later she was bought by Dagbard Larson. At first he used her for swordfishing, but then he switched over to dragging. She had two masts for retrieving nets.

Pilgrim's Progress in better days. (Courtesy of Rusty Cassway.)

After Meekins bought the boat from Larson, he renamed her *Pilgrim's Progress*, and had her remasted so that the after mast was taller than the foremast. She was now schooner-rigged. The canvas on the after mast acted as a righting or studding sail, which helped to stabilize the boat's roll in high winds.

Meekins mostly net-fished for flounder and lobster, which used the same gear. When he fished for shrimp in the sound, he used outriggers. The outriggers were removed whenever he went to sea. Eight hundred thousand pounds (400 tons) of catch could be stowed in the boat's capacious holds. For keeping the catch cold, he carried 15 tons of ice in the winter, 26 tons in the summer.

On what proved to be the final voyage of the *Pilgrim's Progress*, the crew consisted of four men: Captain R. S. Meekins, Jr., master; Wiley Montague, cook; and deck hands Orville Daniels and Terry Hoffman.

January 7, 1995 found them returning to Wanchese after a fairly successful fishing trip to the Wilmington Canyon (known colloquially to commercial anglers as the Northern Bite) off Atlantic City, New Jersey. They planned to do a little more fishing in the Baltimore Canyon (alias the Southern Bight) off Cape May, New Jersey; and then the Washington Canyon (alias the Portegue Hole) at the Maryland/Virginia border. At this point the wind was blowing 30 knots from the southwest.

When the high-water alarm sounded around midnight, Meekins went below to investigate. The boat was equipped with three inch-and-a-half pumps that operated individually; they did not operate through a common manifold: the usual set-up on most boats. Instead, each pump operated on separate discharge and suction systems.

Two primary pumps were driven by belts on the diesel engine; one auxiliary pump was belted to the 24-horsepower Lister generator. Meekins cleaned the strainer on the automatic pump, then tried to start it manually. The pump spurted one time, then quit.

Meekins cleaned the strainers, but still none of the pumps would suck water. Ironically, when he switched the deck wash hose to bilge suction, he could not get it to pump. In other words, the pump worked as a deck wash but not as bilge suction.

By some strange fluke of happenstance, the auxiliary pump would not start either. Meekins cleaned all three strainers, and kept trying to get the pumps to start. He worked on the systems for a couple of hours as the boat headed slowly on its southward course.

Soon the water rose to an alarming depth.

About two o'clock in the morning, Meekins radioed the Coast Guard and alerted them of his predicament. The Coast Guard from the Cape May, New Jersey station dispatched a helicopter to his location.

Meanwhile, the crew started a bucket brigade as a way to keep the water down until help arrived. They opened part of the flooring in the engine room so they could dip a five-gallon bucket into the bilge. One man stood on the ladder that rose up out of the engine room. Another opened the back door in the after cabin. The man on the ladder dumped the water onto the deck, which then ran overboard through the scuppers.

By working hard, they managed to hold their own. Nonetheless, in case of the need for an emergency evacuation, the life raft was put over the side and tied to the gunwale with a small line. When the helicopter arrived, Meekins took the engine out of gear and let it idle, so the helicopter did not have to chase after the boat.

Under some circumstances, the Coast Guard helicopter was equipped to lower a high-pressure pump to a vessel in distress. Rough seas prevented such deployment.

At this time, the crew and Meekins donned their survival suits. Meekins, reading the fear on the crewmember's faces, radioed the helicopter to forget about the pump and rescue the crew. Meekins planned to stay on board and work on his own pumps again and attempt to get them sucking water.

The Coast Guard, being short of space, dumped the floatable pump overboard to assure room for the survivors.

Meanwhile, the wind had dropped to around 10 knots. While standing on deck waiting for the Coast Guard swimmer to be lowered, Meekins and the crew heard the roar of a large sea. They turned and looked behind them and saw white water on top of a sea estimated at 20 to 25 feet high.

The rogue wave pooped the boat. Water crashed over the transom, poured through the aft cabin doorway, and into the engine room waist high. The batteries, elevated in the lazaret, were not flooded in the sudden inundation.

When the engine room flooded, the floorboards were lifted on the rising water. As the water sloshed back and forth, one floating floorboard hit the gear shift lever on the clutch in the engine room. This put the engine into gear. As the boat surged ahead suddenly, the safety line snapped, and the raft went adrift, lost in the darkness abaft the boat.

Meekins rushed below and shut off the engine.

The electrical circuits shorted soon thereafter. The lights flickered out. Now the only way to see was by the helicopter's floodlights. Without power of any kind the *Pilgrim's Progress* was doomed. Because of the lack of radio communication with the Coast Guard, there was nothing left to do but for the crew to abandon ship.

The Coast Guard chopper was prepared for this. I have witnessed rescues in which a basket was lowered to the deck of a boat so that a stricken diver could be hoisted into the air and whisked away inside the fuselage. But dive boats were different from fishing boats.

Draggers and trawlers were equipped with outriggers in order to spread nets. In Alaska, where fishing vessel tragedies were all too common, the basket or the lowering cable sometimes got entangled in a boat's outriggers or net lines, threatening to drag the chopper down if the boat sank abruptly. As a result of too many close calls, the Coast Guard protocol no longer allowed for lowering a basket to the deck of a fishing vessel, even if it did not have outriggers.

Instead, a Coast Guard swimmer either jumped from the chopper into the water at least a hundred feet away from the vessel in distress; or he was placed in a harness or basket and lowered to the surface of the sea. These hardy rescuers are known as Helicopter Rescue Swimmers, or Aviation Survival Technicians. In addition to a rigorous six-month physical training course they are also taught advanced first aid. In essence, they are swimming Emergency Medical Technicians.

The Coast Guard helicopter maintained its position above the *Pilgrim's Progress*, and continued to illuminate the area by means of powerful searchlights. Meekins and the crew wore suits. A survival suit is like a diver's drysuit except it is not equipped with an inflation device, and it was made to fit loosely. The crew had no difficulty in donning their suits, but Meekins could not get the zipper to close over his stomach.

These suits are not meant for swimming; only for floating. They are not equipped with fins. One by one, the men jumped overboard into the arms of the rescue swimmer, who then towed his charge away from the boat. The chopper hovered overhead and lowered a basket or stretcher. The swimmer helped his charge into the basket, which was then hauled up and into the chopper.

Meekins was the last man to abandon ship. When he hit the water, his partially-open emergency suit flooded with ice-cold seawater. He suffered from cold as the rescue swimmer towed him to safety. Meekins kept going in and out of unconsciousness due to swallowing large amounts of seawater. The rescue swimmer was having a hard time towing a nearly dead weight – both Meekins and the water in his flooded survival suit – and was getting out of breath despite his staunch physical condition. When they finally reached the basket, which was elongated like a stretcher, the swimmer was not able to get Meekins to crawl into it lengthwise, the way he was supposed to do it.

The pair of them struggled in the water. Eventually, the swimmer managed to get Meekins on the basket sideways: athwart, as it were, from one side to the other, on top of the basket instead of inside it, with his legs hanging over the railing's edge. In this manner he was hauled up to the hovering helicopter. The Coast Guard flight crew cut the survival suit off of Meekins, so he could breathe better and sustain consciousness.

The rescue swimmer waited alone in the dark until the basket was lowered to him. Although he was wearing thermal protection, he must have been freezing after spending so much time in January water. After he was brought onboard, the helicopter headed for home – Cape May, New Jersey – where it arrived just as the sun appeared over the horizon.

Thus ended a dramatic nighttime rescue operation at the hands of the Coast Guard who were in all ways dependable: from the efficient organization and training programs, to the onsite individuals: pilot, copilot, flight crew, and rescue swimmer. Certainly there is no better rescue establishment anywhere in the world. It is due to these dedicated men and women that Americans feel safe on voyages at sea.

Meekins had owned and operated the *Pilgrim's Progress* for twenty-four years. Her sinking represented more than a financial loss. I could tell from his voice as we discussed her loss that he missed her sorely. The *Pilgrim's Progress* was not just a work boat, like a vehicle that a person drives to work every day. She was almost part of his family. Any hull is replaceable, but no one can replace the sentiment that grows over decades of loving care.

Amazing Grace statistics

Built: 1978
Previous names: None
Gross tonnage: 145
Type of vessel: Steel-hulled fishing vessel
Builder: Deep Sea Boat Builders, Bayou LaBatre, Alabama
Owner: Ironside Trawling Company, Wanchese, North Carolina
Port of registry: Wanchese, North Carolina
Cause of sinking: Unknown

Sunk: November 14, 1984 ?
Depth: 253 feet
Dimensions: 86' x 22' x 11'
Power: Diesel engine

Location withheld by Rusty Cassway

Pilgrim's Progress statistics

Built: 1952
Previous names: *Kennebec*
Gross tonnage: 62
Type of vessel: Wooden-hulled fishing vessel
Builder: Nupert & Wallace, Thomaston, Maine
Owner: R. S. Meekins, Jr., Wanchese, North Carolina
Port of registry: Wanchese, North Carolina
Cause of sinking: Foundered

Sunk: January 7, 1995
Depth: 190 feet
Dimensions: 86' x 18' x 8'
Power: Diesel engine

Location withheld by Rusty Cassway

Rusty Cassway took this picture as Brian Sullivan shone his light on a depth-charge next to the *Northern Pac*.

Northern Pacific

Known familiarly to wreck-divers as the "Northern Pac," this 509-foot-long ocean liner has never been visited as much as it should have been. The potential for exploration is almost unlimited. The vast interior of the upside down hull offers wonderful opportunities for long penetrations.

When I first dived on and inside this wreck in the 1970's, I made one dive on which I found a seabed opening some 75 feet forward of fantail. I squeezed through the crack into a cathedral-like room with an overhead about 20 feet above me. I could clearly see a broad lighted area at the stern, so I entered and worked my way aft, grabbing an 8-pound lobster on the way. The enormous space spanned from port to starboard so that I felt as if I were swimming through a 4-lane turnpike tunnel.

The fantail was buried under the sand. The hull plates had fallen off, leaving only the vertical beams to support the structure above me. From inside looking out, and vice versa, the appearance was that of a building that had been framed with studs but not yet sheetrocked. The sight was awesome.

Sadly, in later years the stern collapsed and sealed off the huge compartment that was once so voluminous. Today, the hull is sagging or flattening as the port and starboard beams are bending. The so-called "big crack" on the port side is wide and inviting. The starboard side – called the "dark side" because the hull used to present a solid, impenetrable wall – is now open because many of the steel plates have been shed. Penetration is now easier than ever.

Rusty Cassway told me that "there are hundreds of fire bricks inside that look like stacks of gold bars." These bricks are boiler bricks that reflected heat back to the boiler, and kept the boiler room slightly cooler than it would be without the heat-resistant wall.

Perhaps the most startling discovery was a depth-charge on the outer perimeter: proof that the wreck had been mistaken for a German U-boat in World War Two. Rusty's photograph on the opposite page leaves no doubt.

This postcard picture shows the *Northern Pacific* passing through the Panama Canal.

Cuyahoga

No text here, just photos that I discovered in the U.S. Coast Guard Historian's Office after publication of *Shipwrecks of Virginia*. The cutter was sunk in the Chesapeake bay after a collision with a freighter, then raised and scuttled in the ocean. Note the collision hole in the bottom picture. Deck plans are shown on the opposite page.

Virginia - *Cuyahoga*

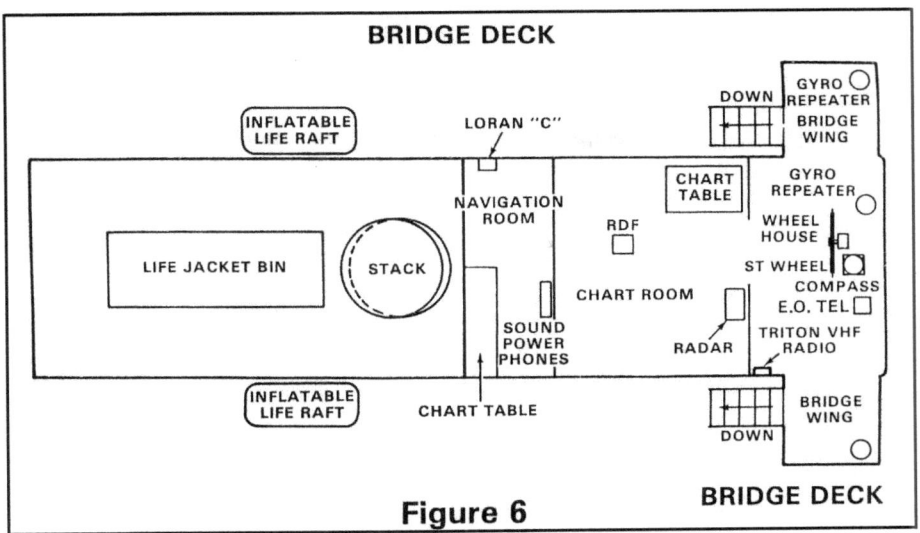

Figure 6

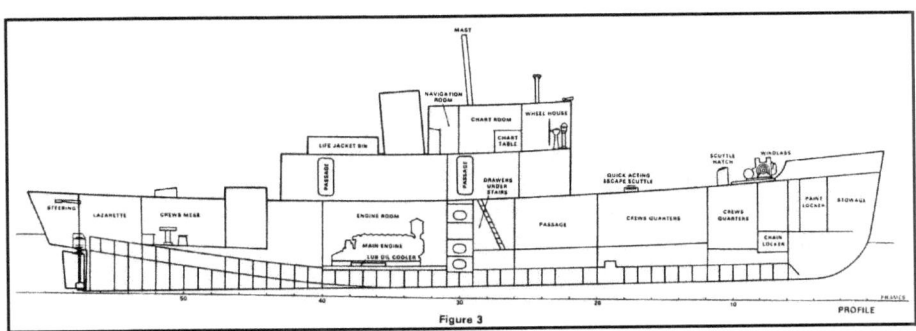

Figure 3

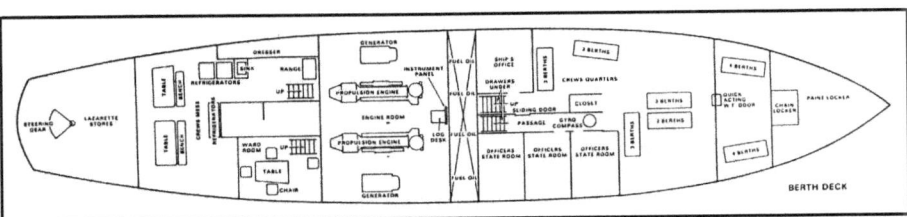

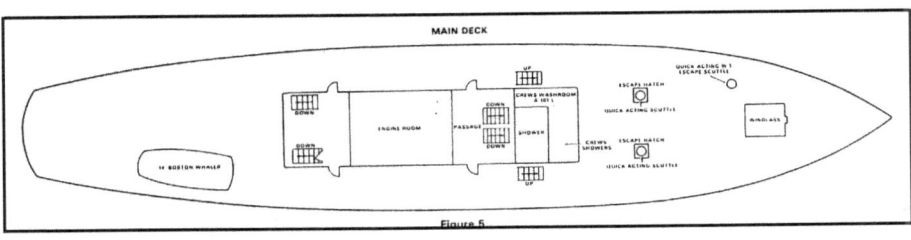

Figure 5

Despatch

Nowadays the *Despatch* is practically forgotten, but for seventeen years in the eighteenth century she was the most famous vessel in the United States. That was because she served as the Presidential yacht: equivalent to today's Airforce One. I can do no better to annotate her career than to reprint an 1891 lyrical eulogy that preceded her demise by seven months:

That "Peace hath her victories no less renowned than war," is evidenced by the serious regret felt throughout the navy at the news of the condemnation of the *Despatch*. Almost every month chronicles the death and burial of one of the old vessels, and as each passes from the active list it carries with it a momentary regret or a reminiscent heartthrob on the part of the officers whom, in its earlier and stronger years, the good ship carried safely into foreign waters. Nothing could be more natural than this sense of reverence for the man-of-war upon whose timbers reliance has been placed surely and securely in moments of peril.

But the rapid retirement of the wooden fleet, while punctuating history with the passage of an old and the advent of a new era, does not affect the little *Despatch*, whose service has been of a different sort from that of her larger and more formidable sisters, and whose years have been fewer than theirs. Her duty has been that of standard-bearer to the Executive, and while her small hull and spindle spars may not have been imposing in the presence of the fleet, there floated from her masthead an emblem that made her more conspicuous than they – the blue flag with its crescent, its coat of arms, and its thirteen stars, signifying the presence of the President of the United States.

Seventeen years ago George Steers built the two-hundred-and-fifty-thousand-dollar yacht *Americus* for Henry C. Smith, a wealthy broker of this city [New York], who forthwith became the owner of the largest, the fastest, and the most elaborately-equipped steam yacht in the world. For three years the stately pleasure craft held her own among the private vessels, visiting all ports and impressing all marine architects with her beauty of design and equipment. Then financial reverses came upon Mr. Smith and he was reluctantly forced to part with his floating palace at a sacrifice. He sold his yacht to the wealthiest purchaser in the land – the Government – for $90,000, and the *Americus* became the *Despatch*.

For a year after her purchase by the Government the *Despatch* cruised intermittently on the home station, and in 1878 she was sent to Europe as a dispatch vessel to serve the needs of the United States Minister at Constantinople during the Russo-Turkish war. There she remained a year, returning to the United States in 1879 with the invalid seamen of the American squadron. At Norfolk [Virginia] that year she was put out of commission and subjected to extensive repairs. October 17, 1880, the trim little craft, looking very sleek and natty after her rehabilitation, was again put into commission and became the President's yacht, being the first Government vessel to hoist the Executive's distinguishing flag. Since that time it has been her proud boast

Virginia - *Despatch* 91

The *Despatch* in her glory days. (Courtesy of the Library of Congress.)

among her sisters that she has carried more distinguished persons than any ship of the navy. President Garfield, President Arthur, President Cleveland and President Harrison have successively trodden her decks while making their official excursions.

New Yorkers will remember the *Despatch* as she lay in the harbor in her capacity as President Harrison's yacht at the time of the centennial celebration of the inauguration of President Washington, which occurred in April, 1889, in this city. That was the first official trip President Harrison took on board his yacht, although she had been in use upon other occasions in the course of his Administration. Besides Cabinet officers, Senators and Representatives in Congress, and officers of the army and navy, the *Despatch* has carried a number of crowned heads and other prominent foreigners, among them being the late King Kalakaua, Queen Kapiolani, Dom Pedro, ex-Emperor of Brazil; the Compte de Paris, and Lord Chief Justice Coleridge.

The dignified service that has thus lent a charm to the President's yacht is by no means confined to her frame, her timbers, her decks, or her spars. Included within the province of her honored personality, if the word may be used, are her boats, five in number, each of which contributes its own little chapter to the volume of the parent's history. The barge, or President's gig, which hangs from the stern davits, carries at its bows the decorated device of the Navy Department. The first flag to fly from this boat was the tawny emblem of Queen Kapiolani of Hawaii, and the first official to sit upon its thwarts was the Queen herself. For these reasons the gig has always been called "Queen Kapiolani" – Phoebus! what a name for a jaunty little gig made up of graceful curves and pretty colors! But the boat is a creature of circumstance, as is the parent craft, and the former, like the latter, bears a name that serves as an indelible imprint of distinguished service.

The whaleboats of the *Despatch* have another history. They formerly belonged to the *Bear* and the *Thetis*, the vessels employed by the relief expedition that went to the Arctic in 1883 to search for General Greely and his unfortunate party. One of them is named the *Dorothy* in honor of the little daughter of Mr. William C. Whitney, ex-Secretary of the Navy.

While the *Despatch* has been honored with many a salute in recognition of her distinguished passengers, it is doubtful if she ever received a volley of greater and more peculiar interest than that accorded her one summer day in the Chesapeake several years ago. The old frigate *Constellation*, commanded by Captain N. H. Farquhar had just returned from a summer cruise with the midshipmen from the Naval Academy. One afternoon, as the practice ship lay at anchor at Lynn Haven Bay, the Quartermaster espied a vessel rounding the point. When it drew nearer he recognized the *Despatch*, flying, to his astonishment, the flag of President Arthur. The Quartermaster was so overcome that he was several minutes in getting his senses. Finally he hastened to the Captain's cabin with the news, and that officer, alive to the emergency, ordered all hands to quarters.

Few, if any, of the midshipmen knew what it was all about. They obeyed the summons to "Cast loose and provide," half suspecting that it was only a false alarm, and it was several minutes before the gun captains were able to report their guns ready for firing. Their surprise when the order came back "Commence firing" was only equaled by the surprise and indignation of Captain Farquhar himself, when, in response to his order, there belched forth from the guns such an indiscriminate, irregular and altogether erratic fire as never

A more prosaic photograph of the *Dispatch*. Note that the name is misspelled. The number that follows the name is not a date, but a negative number. (Courtesy of the National Archives.)

before was heard in the annals of the salute. Instead of the precise, three-minute guns, fired in regular order fore and aft as the code provides, President Arthur was honored by an intermittent series of jumbled explosions that shook the foundations of the historic old bay and caused the yellow-faced fishermen on the shore to open their eyes in terror and dismay.

    First one gun was fired, then three or four, followed by a long pause, after which came a rattling broadside without any meaning whatever, the whole punctuated here and there with the shouts of gun captains, the creaking of tackles, and the indignant roars of remonstrance from the captain. Finally, by dint of sheer lung power, he calmed the troubled spirits of the guns and stopped the racket, but meanwhile the *Despatch*, with its honored passenger, had steamed hastily away. Doubtless the President had been frightened into a speedy retreat. Instead of receiving, as he had expected, the national salute of twenty-one guns, he had been honored with something like fifty – a compliment such as no figure in the world's history ever earned by deeds of valor or royalty. But, as Captain Farquhar learned to his great mortification in the investigation that followed, there is no law, and no navy regulation, human or divine, that holds sway over the impulses of a couple of hundred midshipmen when the youngsters are in the throes of a bad case of "rattle."

    In the above quotation, I must call attention to the disparity of dates with regard to the year of construction and the length of time that Smith owned the *Americus*. Seventeen from 1891 is 1874. Supposedly, this simple subtraction yields the latter number as the date of construction. Yet this date conflicts with dates that are given in two official records that I obtained from the Naval Historical Center. Unfortunately, instead of providing clarification, official Navy records make matters worse by contradicting each other.

    For example, one official document states that the *Despatch* was "purchased in November, 1873," while another official document states that the *Despatch* was "purchased at New York, N.Y. in 1874." These dates ignore the length of time that Smith supposedly owned the luxurious yacht.

    To complicate matters even more, *Merchant Vessels of the United States* claims that the *Despatch* was built in 1873, then "purchased in 1874 from H.C. Smith, New York."

    I see no way out of this quagmire of too much data. If I had seen only one of these three documents, I would have had no reason to disbelieve it. As the saying goes, the person with two watches is never sure of the time. It is likely that Smith's ownership of the *Americus* was shorter than the time that was given in the article. Moving on . . .

    . . . to another contradiction. One official Navy record states that the *Despatch's* speed was 12 knots, while another states that it was 16 knots. This is another knotty Navy issue. Today, U.S. Navy historians are attempting to take control of 26,000 wrecks worldwide. They can't even get simple history straight on a single vessel, much less manage 26,000 lost and submerged wrecks. For additional details about the Navy's proposed takeover, see *The Great Navy Wreck Scam*. Moving on again . . .

    Long before the *Despatch* became the official Presidential yacht, and before she was commissioned as a Navy vessel, her first job for the government involved the *Vir-*

ginius Affair (which see elsewhere in this volume, and in more detail in *Shipwrecks of North Carolina: South*). The *Despatch* transported Captain Whiting to Cuba where he took command of the *Virginius* after Spain surrendered the blockade runner following her illegal capture. When the engine of the *Virginius* broke down, the *Despatch* towed the *Virginius* to the Dry Tortugas, where the tow was taken over by the USS *Ossipee*. The *Despatch* then served as a dispatch boat, transporting soldiers and sailors for what was expected to be a war between the United States and Spain – twenty-five years before the Spanish-American War. Moving on yet again . . .

Another interesting connection: the commander of the *Despatch* from 1882 to 1884 was Lieutenant Samuel Dana Greene, who was executive officer on the Civil War ironclad *Monitor* for her entire career.

Note, too, that the above article neglected the mention that the first President to have use of the *Despatch* was Rutherford Hayes.

The ultimate demise of the *Despatch*, which occurred on October 10, 1891 – is best portrayed in the following in-depth contemporary article, which I reprint in full:

> The United States steamer *Despatch*, which for the last nine years had been practically the official yacht of the President and the Secretary of the Navy, has ceased to exist.
>
> What remains of her lies on the shoals off Assateague Island in an almost shapeless mass.
>
> Her timbers parted, and her rigging all awry, every wave that breaks over the *Despatch* adds to her ruin, and as it recedes carries away one more portion of this once famous yacht in the form of driftwood.
>
> It is a matter of congratulation, or rather of thankfulness to a divine Providence, that all her officers and every member of her crew succeeded in getting off in safety.
>
> The wreck of the *Despatch* is a singular illustration of the oft-repeated truth, "Man's extremity is God's opportunity."
>
> The *Despatch* was on her way from Brooklyn to Washington, where she was to take on board the President, Secretary Tracy, and some officers of the navy, and convey them to the naval proving grounds, down the Potomac, to witness experiments in testing some of the armor place for use in the armament of the new vessels.
>
> The night of Friday, October 9th, she was off the coast of Virginia. The weather was heavy and dirty, and the commander of the vessel, Lieutenant Cowles, was on deck looking out for the lighthouse that marks the treacherous Assateague shoals.
>
> Assateague Island lies off the western portion of that promontory which divides the Atlantic from Chesapeake Bay, and at the foot of which is Cape Charles. It is well off the coast. Between it and the mainland lie first the wide and shallow Chincoteague Bay, then the long and barren Chincoteague Island, and then the tortuous and almost impassable Assateague Channel. The island is one of the most inhospitable-looking places on the Atlantic coast. it fronts the sea for nearly thirty miles and has hardly an inhabitant. Along the shore rises a line of high sand-hills, which overlook the sea, and from which can be

From *Harper's Weekly*.

seen a long line of breakers and great tracts of low-lying marsh and meadow. In the middle of the island, which has an average breadth of about one and a half miles, rises the great lighthouse and a little further down is the life-saving station; these, with a few fishermen's huts, constitute the only human habitations on the island.

The light on the island is marked on the charts as a white light, but it is a well-known fact to mariners that on certain foggy nights what is really a white light appears to be of an orange tint – almost red. And this is how it seems to have appeared to Lieutenant Cowles, who evidently mistook it from the light on the *Winterquarters Shoals* lightship, at least a mile and a half from the Assateague lighthouse, which carries a red light.

At any rate, at three o'clock on the morning of Saturday, October 10th, when most of the crew of the *Despatch* were down below and she was going at about eight knots an hour, she suddenly struck. Here she went ashore, and how she happened to be a mile and a half out of her course Lieutenant Cowles thus explains:

The light on Assateague Island, which, as has already been stated, is on the charts as a white light, did not, he states, "burn as a white light on Saturday morning. It was red." After he found where he was, he adds, there was no way of getting out. As to how she struck, all he can say is, she struck where she did, and there she stayed. "I never," he continues, "saw worse surf. After much trouble I got out an anchor, which prevented her threshing around. Then she gradually was forced in-shore. I knew no power on earth could save her. Water poured into the engine-room, and the ship was shattered from stem to stern. I was reluctant to get out and leave the ship, but it had to be done, and we escaped in our own boats and in that of the life-saving crew."

It has long been common talk that the machinery of the *Despatch* was out of order, and Lieutenant Cowles when asked if she were seaworthy, replied:

"All I shall say is that the *Despatch*, I believe, could have got out of the pocket she was in and off the shoals if it had not been for her weak machinery. Her boilers were nearly played out. Why, when I was at Cuba, away back during the *Virginius* trouble, the *Despatch* was carrying despatches between Havana and Key West. She was a fifteen-knot boat then. But she was so nearly worn out lately that her speed was down to less than nine knots, and was constantly diminishing."

The officers and crew had a narrow escape from death, but as it were by a miracle, and through the great bravery of Captain James T. Tracy and his crew of the Assateague Life-Saving Station, succeeded in getting off alive.

The *Despatch* was a wooden, schooner-rigged steamship, which had been a sort of official yacht since President Arthur's time, when she took the place of the old *Tallapoosa*. She had a tonnage of 730 tons, and a displacement of 500 tons. She was 174 feet in length, 25 feet in breadth, and had a mean draught of 12 feet 4 inches. Her speed when her machinery was in good order was fifteen knots. The vessel was originally a yacht. She was built in 1873 for Henry C. Smith, the well-known broker, by George Steers, at a cost of $200,000. Smith's orders to Steers were for the "largest and handsomest yacht." Smith owned the vessel about three years. Then he had reverses. The vessel was sold at auction and was bought by the Government for $90,000.

In 1877, during the Russian-Turkish war, she was sent to Europe to be used as a dispatch boat by the United States Minister at Constantinople. She returned in about a year, and was refitted with new boilers and otherwise repaired.

From *The Illustrated American*.

Virginia - Despatch

Early in the year 1880 the *Despatch* was transferred to the Navy Department, and was used for Presidential sailing tours and navy-yard inspection jaunts. She carried General Sheridan in his last illness from Washington to Nonquitt. A year ago or so Chief Naval Constructor Wilson reported that unless extensive repairs were made the *Despatch* would not last much longer. Last summer Secretary Tracy made a tour of inspection of the various navy yards on her.

She had on board at the time she was wrecked a crew of sixty-eight men. Her officers were:

Lieutenant – York Noel.
Lieutenant (junior grade) – Richard T. Mulligan.
Assistant Paymaster – S. Lawrence Heap
Passed Assistant Engineer – Julien S. Ogden.

All sailors may be said to be ex-officio superstitious, and the crew of the *Despatch* are no less so than their fellow-tars. As they waited on the desolate island for a vessel to take them off, they recalled the fact, that a strange black cat – an omen of evil – jumped on to the deck of the steamer as they were leaving New York Harbor. This cat was the only living object left on board all the day after the wreck. Poor pussy, with an air of dejection, sat on the highest joint she could get. She waited for the end and was apparently resigned to her fate. It came sometime during the night, and the cat was found on the beach on the Monday morning.

The unfortunate men had a hard time of it on the island. Suffering from exposure to a terrible storm, with no clothing except that in which they reached the shore, and drenched to the skin, they were compelled to eat and sleep, and get what little shelter they could, in a place not fit for dogs. Many of the poor fellows had no shoes. But naval routing and discipline were observed just as on board ship, and the men never grumbled, although they were sorely in need for some time of supplies. All that had been saved from the pantry were several boxes of bread, and all that was saved from the medicine chests was a small bottle of brandy, which did not last long among seventy-three men continually exposed to a cold and driving storm on a lee shore day and night.

Captain Tracy and his crew, of the life-saving station, received a note of thanks for the hospitality they had extended to the men.

And last but not least, another article which furnished information that was deficient in the previous one.

The wreck of the United States steamship *Despatch*, or "the President's private yacht," as she has been unofficially titled for many years, seems, in the absence of any statement from her officers, to have been the unfortunate result of bad seamanship. That the boat was to have been condemned in the very near future has nothing to do with it. She might have been an entirely new cruiser, with the paint fresh on her sides. It may be, however, that the Court of Inquiry will clear Lieutenant Cowles, whose record so far has been an excellent one, and prove that some one has not blundered. The boat went on the shoals off Assateague Island at three o'clock last Saturday morning. the crew of the Assateague Life-saving Station answered her signals for assistance in one hour and a half, having to pull their life-boat to her over two miles of sandy beach, with the water for the greater part of the time up to their armpits. J. S. Tracy, the keeper of the station, sent his boat out ten times, and succeeded in landing all of the 74 persons on board in safety. Nothing was saved from the steamer except those articles which were later washed upon the shore. Even the silver plate of the ship, which is valued at several thousands of dollars, is reported lost. The crew of the *Despatch* behaved remarkably well, and showed the excellence of their past training and discipline. It was six hours before they were all landed, and in that time, although the water was washing over the decks, the men were as orderly and undismayed as though on parade on shore, and not hanging to a boat that was going to pieces under their feet. The brightest part of this disaster is the prompt and able work of the life-saving crew, whose quarters on this almost desolate coast are rough and insufficient to a degree. their willingness to help the government's servants is a lesson for the government to help them, her stanchest [sic] servants, and after they have been given the life-saving medal, for which all life-savers hope, Congress should appropriate enough money to make their quarters not barely habitable, but free from all discomfort.

The *Despatch* had already been condemned as unfit for service before she made her final voyage. Now that the hulk was being torn apart by the surf, there was no need to consider whether or not to replace her worn and inefficient machinery. Therefore, eighteen days after running aground, the Navy made an unusually quick decision to sell what was left of the derelict, "as is, where is."

"The *Despatch* will be sold to the party offering the highest price in cash for her. Each proposal must be accompanied by a cash deposit or certified check for the full amount of such offer or proposal. All deposits with proposals not accepted will be returned to the bidder or bidders within seven days after the opening of the proposals. The bids will be decided by the Secretary of the Navy, by lot. The *Despatch*, a complete wreck, lies on the beach near Assateague light-house, Virginia. Proposals must be for her as she is or may be found when taken possession of by the purchaser."

The sealed bids were opened on November 10, 1891. There were four bidders. The lowest bid was $25. The next highest was $36. The penultimate highest was $75. The winning high bidder was G. W. Schultz & Company, of 308 Walnut Street, Philadelphia, Pennsylvania. He paid the princely sum of $160 for the remains of the Presidential yacht. Considering that the Navy spent $32.96 for advertising the auction, the net profit amounted to $127.04. Schultz's salvage efforts went unrecorded.

In 1997, a treasure hunter outfit called Sea Hunt discovered the wreck of the *Despatch*. Sea Hunt was not searching for the *Despatch*; she was searching for the Spanish frigate *Juno* (which see), which sank off the coast of Virginia in 1802, with great loss of life and with her holds filled with stolen gold, silver, and jewels. (For details of her loss, see *Shipwrecks of Virginia*.)

Sea Hunt was checking hang numbers from commercial anglers in search for the *Juno* when a towed magnetometer accidentally passed over the site of the *Despatch*.

Virginia - Despatch

This wasn't the only shipwreck that Benson discovered during his search for the *Juno*: he found nearly a dozen others, yet unidentified.

Ben Benson, Sea Hunt's owner, said, "I think we're going to find some really interesting artifacts, perhaps gifts from heads of state, a compass, a steering wheel. I'm not seeing scattered pieces. It's lying largely in one mass." He added, "I'd like to do some more work on it and raise some artifacts from it, depending on what the government tells me I can do."

The last part of the previous sentence refers to the State of Virginia, with which Benson had a salvage permit that not only guaranteed that Virginia would receive 25% of Benson's profits, but which let the State to keep any artifacts that the State – not Benson or his archaeologists – deemed were historic: which could mean all or none, but in any case to the State's benefit and not to Benson's.

As far as I have been able to determine, Benson's dream to salvage the *Despatch* . . . is still a dream.

The next person to show any interest in the *Despatch* was Clive Cussler, author of Dirk Pitt thrillers and founder of the National Underwater and Marine Agency. In 2012, Ellsworth Boyd – long-time shipwreck writer and editor of NUMA's newsletter – posted a sincere request under the NUMA heading for volunteers to help in organizing a new search for the Presidential yacht. Several people showed interest but an expedition never materialized.

As long as I mentioned Cussler, I would like to take this opportunity to segue to his character, and to inform my readers about the kind of person he is in real life.

In the mid-1990's, when I was writing *Shipwrecks of New York* (1996), I wrote to Cussler because I knew that he had discovered the wreck of the *Lexington*, in Long Island Sound. I planned to give him credit for discovery. I asked him for any details about the search for and condition of the wreck, and anything else he thought might be important. A few weeks later I received a thick packet that had been sent by ordinary mail. The packet contained his entire *Lexington* folder, including original documents. I was flabbergasted.

I would never have entrusted such valuable material to the United States Postal Service. It might have been irretrievably lost. And he sent it to someone he did not even know! Cussler was way too trusting.

I photocopied every document before I returned his originals via Federal Express. If the packet went astray, at least I could make another set of photocopies for him. The packet was delivered safely. If you want to know more about his character, and about his dedication to shipwreck research and discovery, read his two volumes titled *The Sea Hunters*. You won't be disappointed.

Statistics

Built: 1873
Previous names: *Americus*
Gross tonnage: 730
Type of vessel: Wooden-hulled yacht
Builder: George Steers, New York, NY
Owner: U. S. Navy
Cause of loss: Ran aground

Sunk: October 10, 1891
Depth: 22 feet
Dimensions: 174' x 25' x 12'
Power: Coal-fired steam
Armament: Three 20-pounders
Purpose: Dispatch boat and Presidential yacht
Location: Assateague Island

Francis E. Powell

This 20-year-old tanker was blown to pieces by a German U-boat in 1942. The hull separated into three sections. The midship section sank fairly soon; so far it has not been found or identified. This is a shame because wheelhouse contains the navigational equipment. The attack position noted in the log of the *U-130* was 38.05 North and 74.53 West. The nautical chart shows a wreck symbol 3 miles east of there, with a least depth of 8-1/4 fathoms (50 feet) in 12 fathoms (72 feet) of water.

The bow and stern sections remained afloat and drifted away from the position of the torpedoing.

The location of the stern was supposedly confirmed by the Coast Guard cutter *Gentian*, first by lowering a submersible camera to the wreck, then by putting divers on the bottom. It is a popular dive site today. Perhaps. In *Shipwrecks of Virginia*, I gave the loran coordinates as 27038.0 / 41766.3, and the depth as 90 feet. However, Ted Green states that the wreck at that site is not the *Francis E. Powell*. (At the time that I wrote *Shipwrecks of Virginia*, I had not yet dived on the wreck site in question. I relied upon local wisdom for identification.)

Green provided GPS numbers for that location: 37-32.078 / 75-13.769. As that wreck is definitely not the *Francis E. Powell*, then the stern section remains lost or unidentified. For information about the wreck at that location, see the chapter about unidentified Virginia wrecks, specifically the section titled Steel Vessel Barge (alias False Powell).

The location of the bow section has been another bone of contention. During the war, the Navy believed that it lay 15 miles off Parramore Island . . . which it does; but the Navy got the wreck confused with another wreck that lay 5 miles away. Thus it has come down through history that the site of some other wreck was instead given as the bow of the *Francis E. Powell*.

Ted Green knew the true location of the bow, and he took me there. I went as crewmember on one of his regularly scheduled charters aboard the *O.C. Diver*. The customers did not want to dive on the wreck because it was not very good for finding lobsters or spearing fish. Therefore, he dropped me alone on the wreck – literally.

He did not grapnel into the hull. Instead, after I got fully dressed in my dive gear, and stood by the stern waiting to jump into the water, he cruised over the wreck until he saw it on the depth recorder, took the transmission out of gear, and shouted, "Go!"

I went.

I made myself heavy, turned head down, and kicked for the bottom. I landed atop the upside down hull; which means that I landed on the flat bottom of the hull. The depth was 77 feet. The steel plates were beautifully overgrown with colorful coral, sponges, and sea anemones. I circumnavigated the topside of the wreck; it was half the size of a football field and, except for the marine encrustation and a bilge keel, practically as smooth.

I then dropped over the side and sank to the seabed at a depth of 100 feet. My hand went wrist-deep into the soft muddy bottom. I rose above the seabed and swam around the wreck through large schools of sea bass and some tautog. I spotted two holes less than a foot from the stem and about four feet off the seabed. The lower hole was circular and measured 6 inches in diameter. The other hole measured some 6 inches by 12 to

15 inches: shaped like an oval or lozenge. I took these holes to have been made by shells that had been fired by the Coast Guard cutter *General Green* in her effort to sink the bow section by letting trapped air out of the pocket in the forward compartment. I also spotted the hawse pipes with no anchors in evidence.

The blunt end of the bow section was sheared off nearly straight across, with jagged edges of metal protruding aft. Inside I saw an interior bulkhead still in excellent condition; this watertight bulkhead must have been responsible for preventing the wreck from sinking. I entered along the right side which, as the wreck lay upside down, was port instead of starboard. The interior crossthwart bulkhead stopped me from penetrating more than half a dozen feet.

I ascended slowly, looking upward along the beam of my light in anticipation of finding a layer of black oil as I did years before on an inverted barge in search of the *Menominee* (which see for details). It was there, just as it had been on the barge. I avoided farther ascent and instead exited the wreck.

I did a short free-hanging drift decompression before rising to the surface and waving for Ted to come and pick me up. There was no doubt in my mind that this was the bow of the *Francis E. Powell*.

Green gave me the GPS numbers for publication (as he did with the rest of the GPS numbers in the Virginia section): 37-29.064 / 75-17.146.

The top view of the *Francis E. Powell* is cutaway plan that is known as an inboard profile. It shows the broadside as if the outer hull were peeled away, exposing the arrangement of the various compartments deck by deck. The bottom plan is an overhead view of the Upper Deck as if the top plates were invisible. According to my estimated length of the bow section, the hull must have sheared off immediately forward of the wheelhouse.

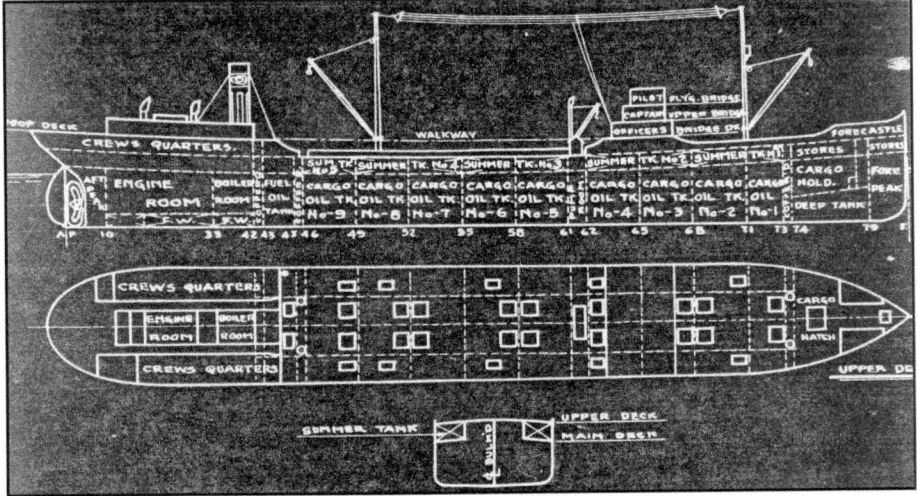

Gere

The *Gere's* end is succinctly told in this contemporary newspaper article (copied verbatim, complete with misspellings, grammatical errors, and poor typography):

> Eight men were drowned and seven had a narrow escape from death by the foundering of the Norwegian steamer *Gere*, Saturday, six miles from the *Winterquarter* lightship, 50 miles south of the Delaware Capes. The seven men who were saved arrived this afternoon on the British S. S. *Aroyo*, which took them from the lightship before reported as having the shipwrecked seamen aboard. The men saved are Julius Meyer, the captain, and six seamen. They are now in the care of the Norwegian consul in this city [Philadelphia, Pennsylvania].
>
> The men tell a thrilling story of shipwreck in which every one was for himself, in english that could scarcely be understood they said the *Gere*, which left here Friday with a crew of fifteen and a cargo of coal for Sagua la Grande, Cuba, encountered rough weather after passing out of the Delaware capes. Off the *Winterquarter* lightship, when only three men on deck an unusually heavy sea struck the steamer which keeled over at a dangerous angle. She was struck by high seas and finally went over on her side.
>
> Meantime the other members of the crew came on deck and taking in the situation obtained life belts. Nothing could be done to right the vessel, and as she was rapidly settling the crew looked about for safety. The only boat had been swept from the davits and was floating away. There was nothing for the men to do but jump into the sea.
>
> Some of them jumped and others slid down the side into rough water. All of them managed to find timber of other floating objects. The ship went to the bottom within three minutes and the stronger swimmers struck out for the boat which was floating bottom up. After a trying time the little craft was righted and an attempt was made to clear it of water. After two hours' struggle enough water was gotten out to put two men aboard and with the aid of their hands and a pair of marine glasses they scooped enough water out to permit others to climb in.
>
> All the time this was going on the crew was fighting a losing battle with death. The weakest of the swimmers and two that could not swim, went down one by one. One of the men who could not swim appealed to Alexander Henderson to save him. The latter struggled to keep his head above water told him he could not, and that it was every man for himself. When the water was finally out of the boat the last remaining man clinging to it was hauled in and it was found that seven were missing.
>
> The weather was still rough and the tossing craft with its load threatened to capsize with every wave. A small mast with sail attached which was recognized as having belonged to one of the crew, was spied floating near and one of the men jumped overboard and towed it to the boat. It was erected and with this mast the boat floated before the wind until 4:30 p. m., when the survivors sighted the *Winterquarter* lightship.

Virginia - Gere

The writer certainly did not earn any gold stars for literacy. But the story he told was one of desperate and heroic proportions.

The *Lloyd's Register* spelled the skipper's name as Mayer. Other sources spell the name of the vessel that took the survivors off the lightship and transported them to safety as *Arroyo*.

Another newspaper added this bit: "The rapidity with which the *Gere* sank is believed to have been due to an unusually heavy load of coal. It was commented upon as the *Gere* passed down the Delaware river that she had only about nine inches of free board."

Yet another noted: "Members of the crew say the captain and chief engineer, H. H. Neilsen, a Norwegian, were the last to leave the ship. The engineer was drowned."

Additional information was published later: "The ore laden steamer *Arroyo*, from Santiago Cuba for Philadelphia passed Marcus Hook Deld [sic] yesterday with the captain, first officer, and five seamen of the *Gere*, who were rescued and taken aboard the lightship at Cape Henlopen. While passing the Cape the *Arroyo* was signaled and she hove to and took the survivors of the wreck off the lightship. The *Gere* formerly ran to this port as a fruiter from the West Indies.

The position of the *Gere* at the time of her loss was given inconsistently as 9 miles east-northeast of the *Winter Quarter Shoal* lightship, and 6 miles from the lightship.

The questions that these positions beg are these: Is there a known wreck in the vicinity of those positions, and does it fit the description of the *Gere*? The unfortunate answer is: Close but no cigar.

The closest contender lies 6 miles *south* of the *Winter Quarter Shoal* lightship. It is variously called the Sub Wreck, alias the Bottle Wreck, alias the Pipe Wreck, alias the Norwegian Freighter. The last alias implies that commercial anglers thought that this was the wreck of the *Gere*: information that was likely handed down from the time of the freighter's loss. But is it true? Or were they referring to the other Norwegian freighter: the *Hermod*? I would like to think that this wreck site is that of the *Gere*. It has several positive attributes that conform to the *Gere* with regard to timeframe . . . but one damning piece of evidence that knocks the *Gere* out of the ring.

Read the description of the Sub Wreck in the chapter on Unidentified Wrecks off Virginia. You'll find that it has a compound engine – that is, an engine that possesses two cylinders – whereas the *Gere* was propelled by a triple expansion reciprocating steam engine. Oh, well . . .

Statistics

Built: 1903
Previous names: None
Gross tonnage: 754
Type of vessel: Steel-hulled freighter
Builder: Chantiers Navals Anversois, Hoboken, Norway
Owner: Joh. E. v. d. Ohe & Lund
Cause of loss: Foundered
Location: 6 miles from the *Winter Quarter Shoal* lightship; or 9 miles east-northeast of the lightship

Sunk: September 25, 1909
Depth: Unknown
Dimensions: 190' x 29' x 14'
Power: Coal-fired steam
Port of Registry: Bergen, Norway

Hermod

In 1918 a war was raging in Europe: the Great War, as it was called at the time. When the Great War was superseded by a greater war which went by the name World War Two or the Second World War, the Great War was retroactively renamed World War One or the First World War.

Although the fighting in Europe had been ongoing since 1914, the United States did not enter the war on the side of the Allies against the Axis powers until April 6, 1917. Troops and materiel were sent "over there" in large numbers and huge quantities, but the U.S. homeland was a safe place to be. Germany did not send U-boats to the American eastern seaboard until 1918. The first attack occurred on May 25.

By that time, the *Hermod* had already run aground on Winter Quarter Shoals. She was on her way to Philadelphia, Pennsylvania with a cargo of sugar when, "It is supposed the captain [G. Kirsebom] lost his bearings and steered his ship on to the shoal." The date was April 15, 1918.

At that time, vessel losses did not receive much media attention because war correspondents captured the headlines. The *Hermod* garnered no more than a couple of paragraphs that were repeated in small hometown newspapers. One article stated that the *Hermod* was originally an ore carrier. The most detailed information about the catastrophe was printed in *The New York Maritime Register*:

Apr 15 – Str *Hermod* (Nor), with sugar for Philadelphia, was wrecked Saturday near Winter Quarter Shoal. The captain, his wife and 24 members of the crew were taken off the wrecked ship by the Assateague (Va) Coast Guard. Two of the crew are reported to have been drowned. The shipwrecked crew were afterward transferred to a government vessel, which proceeded southward. The *Hermod* is a total loss, together with her cargo. At the time of the disaster a high wind prevailed and the weather was very foggy."

Perhaps the fog explains why the skipper did not see the *Winter Quarter Shoal* lightship, which was stationed offshore of the submerged reef.

Two weeks later, the NYMR reported: "The keeper of Assateague Coast Guard station reports visited the wreck of str *Hermod* (Nor), before reported, with a government engineer and diver and found the steamer broken in two, bow end in three fathoms of water, stern fallen away and in four fathoms; seas breaking across forward part between bow and bridge; bow highest out of water, forward hatch just out of water, anchors and chains hanging from hawsers; been stripped of everything of value, which have been carried away by unknown persons; brought up few bags quite empty; thinks some cargo may be saved if conditions remain right and work started promptly."

I don't know if any bags of sugar were salvaged, but I can confirm that none of the sugar remains today to sweeten the wreck site.

A handwritten sheet of paper that I found at the National Archives stated that the *Celtic* was the vessel to which the *Hermod's* survivors were transferred." It also stated that the Coast Guard cutter was attached to "Station # 150."

When I shared this information with Ted Green, he told me that he frequently dived on a wreck that straddled the Winter Quarter Shoal, and that, in the absence of any other wrecks nearby, it must therefore be the *Hermod*. Or, as Sherlock Holmes averred in "The Beryl Coronet," "It is an old maxim of mine that when you have excluded the

Virginia - Hermod

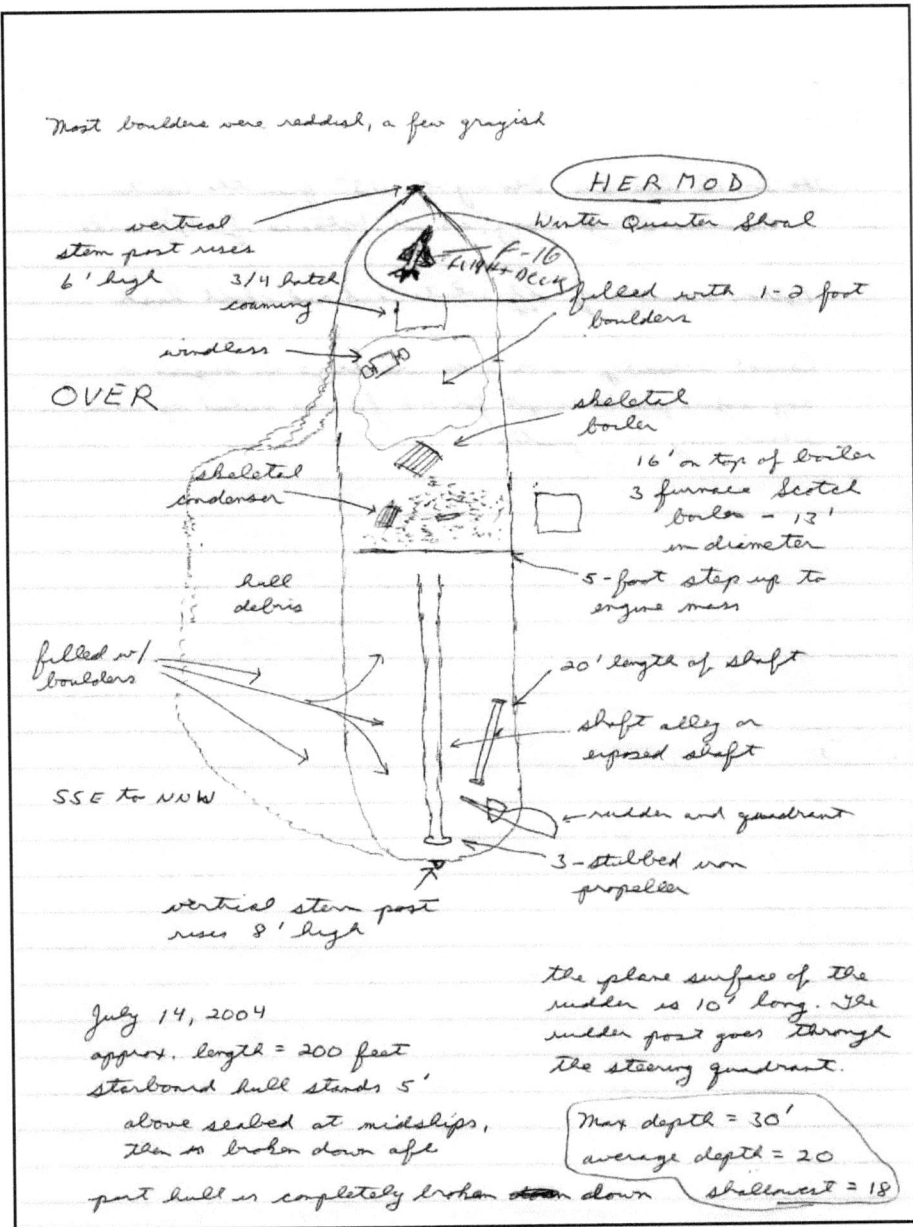

Above is one of my typical shipwreck survey drawings. I generally draw the rough draft on a slate underwater, then transcribe the image onto paper after returning to the boat, at which time I add notes from memory while they are still fresh in my mind. On the back of the sheet I add expanded descriptions, which can be seen bleeding through the paper in reverse. (I will paraphrase from these descriptions on the following page.) When I was not looking, Richie Burr took the opportunity to pull the paper out of my briefcase and draw a fighter plane on the bow, and write "F-16 flight deck." If an F-16 was actually secured to the bow of the wreck, I overlooked it.

impossible, whatever remains, however improbable, must be the truth."

Green went one better. He measured the boilers and found that their dimensions were large enough to provide sufficient steam for a vessel of the *Hermod's* size. He remembers when a person could stand on the boiler and have his head and shoulders out of the water. Nowadays, the depth at the top of the boiler is six feet. Nonetheless, boat skippers should take heed and approach the wreck cautiously, especially during extreme low tides and when big rollers are running, or you might be feeding at the trough.

The bottom consists of off-white sand and shell hash.

Initially, I wrote on my survey transcript, "Cannot actually see or even visualize an engine or any engine parts except for one ferrous metal cylinder which may be a piston." However, on a subsequent dive, hovered 10 feet above the wreck and scanned the wreckage. By doing so, and concentrating my gaze on the engine location, I was able to visualize the engine and most of its parts. The engine had collapsed so that the pistons, rods, and other assemblies were strewn apart like pieces of a puzzle that has not yet been assembled.

The *Hermod* is a fun wreck to explore. The shallow depth affords ample time to swim from stem to stern again and again, and to observe the distinctive features that the site has to offer. The hull is nearly contiguous so there is little to no chance of getting lost. The average depth is 20 feet, although washouts go as deep as 30 feet.

Statistics

Built: 1903
Previous names: None
Gross tonnage: 2995
Type of vessel: Steel-hulled freighter
Builder: J. L. Thompson & Sons, Sunderland, England
Owner: Bruusgard, Kiosteruds Dampkibs. Akties, Norway
Port of Registry: Drammen, Norway
Cause of loss: Ran aground on Winter Quarter Shoal
GPS: 37-58.230 / 75-08.808

Sunk: April 15, 1918
Depth: 20 to 30 feet
Dimensions: 325' x 48' x 21'
Power: Coal-fired steam

Loran: 42067.7 / 27061.8

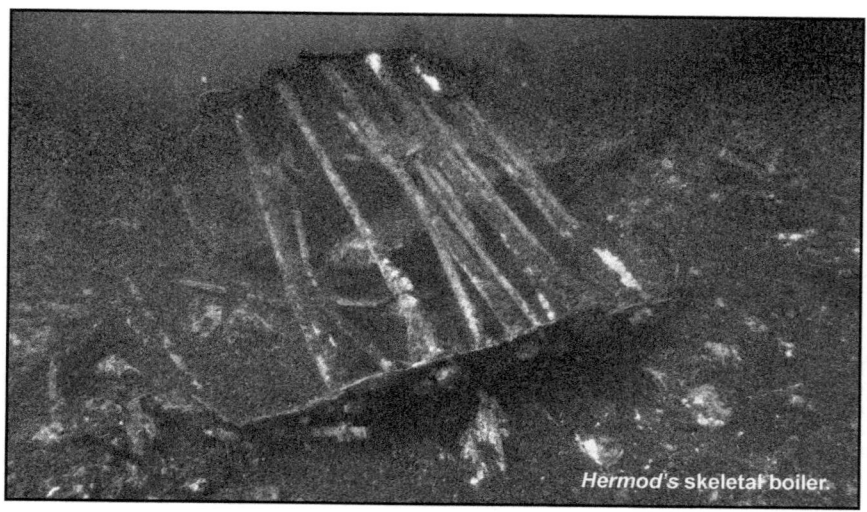
Hermod's skeletal boiler.

Juno (and Galga)

It goes without saying that whenever treasure is found, there are people who do everything in their power to take it away from the finder. There has not been a shipwreck treasure discovery in the history of the world that did not become entangled in lawsuits that continued for years . . . or decades. The *Juno* is a typical case in point.

Let's start this chapter with a parable. Suppose a person robs a bank and gets away with a fortune. Before he can spend his ill-gotten gain, he is forced by circumstances to secrete the money. The bank robber then dies. Generations later, an unrelated person finds where the stolen money was cached. He thinks that he has struck it rich. But an heir of the bank robber intercedes, and claims that the purloined loot belongs to him (or her) because his ancestor was the one who stole it. The case goes to court, and the judge finds that the hornbook law of "finders, keepers; losers, weepers" no longer applies. Despite the fact that the finder spent millions of dollars and years of his life in searching for the missing bank money, the court awards the proceeds of the costly salvage operation to the heir, who had no financial risk in searching for the money, and who spent nothing on recovering it. Case closed.

This is not only the way of the *Juno*; it is the way of nearly every modern shipwreck treasure find. The new law is "finders, weepers; losers, keepers."

The *Juno* was a frigate that foundered in 1802. Lost with her were 425 men, women, and children. Also lost with her was "much wealth" that was described as two million pesos in silver, and a million pesos' worth of "valuables."

At the time I published *Shipwrecks of Virginia* (1992), salvage operations had not yet gotten underway. In fact, no actual wreck site had yet been identified. Five years later, Quicksilver International started showing video footage of a "site" that lay at a depth of 180 feet. This site consisted of a rectangular ridge of sand that rose a foot or so above the outboard seabed. Potential investors were led to believe that this was the suspected site of the *Juno*. Yet the site produced no artifacts that could positively identify it as the *Juno* – or even as a shipwreck.

Underwater work was apparently suspended for another five years. In 1992, I was temporarily involved with Quicksilver's operation. This came about due to my association with Peter Hess. After eight years of dogged legal wrangling, he and I had finally prevailed in our suit against NOAA over public access to the Civil War ironclad *Monitor*. (For details of the saga, see *Ironclad Legacy: Battles of the USS Monitor* (1993)). Peter was doing legal work for Quicksilver, so he got me involved with diving on a suspected *Juno* site. Also on the dive team were Barb Lander and Brian Skerry.

For orientation, a Quicksilver executive showed us a video clip that presented the rise of sand around the site. I scoffed, and told the exec that I saw nothing in the footage to indicate that a wreck lay buried under the smooth level rise of sand. I commented that the low rise could have been a natural feature that resulted from a trick of the current. In addition, wreck sites are never smooth and level, but rugged and bumpy.

He agreed with me, then admitted that this was the video that he showed to potential investors as a way of getting them to venture some capital in the company. At least he was honest with *us*.

The four of us spent two days in diving on a site: one that did not have a one-foot rise surrounding it. We dived in two teams of two. The depth that I recorded was 178 feet. The first day we carried hand-held magnetometers. One person passed the magnetometer's hoop over the sand; the other placed a flag on a "hit" that the mag indicated. We were getting hits left and right. It seemed as if the entire site was a pile of magnetic anomalies. The exec retuned the magnetometers in order to make them less sensitive. Nonetheless, we kept getting more hits than I thought possible on a wooden-hulled vessel.

The next day we dug holes with diver propulsion vehicles. Usually a DPV is used to pull a diver forward by means of a propeller that was rotated by a battery-operated motor. To dig, I let air out of my drysuit to make myself heavy, jammed my knees into the sand, pulled the nose of the underwater scooter into my belly, and pressed the on-switch. The propeller wash blew away sand with phenomenal speed. I could dig a hole that was one-foot deep in only a minute or so. We dug holes under every flag, several feet across and a foot or two in depth, and never found anything but more sand. Altogether we moved enough seabed to completely expose a good-sized shipwreck. The salvage operation was a total bust.

Another handful of years passed in Quicksilver's ongoing five-year plan. Like Russia's five-year plan, this one did not work either. According to the Association of Underwater Explorers, in 1997, "Divers, submersibles, and remotely operated vehicles surveyed the site and recovered various artifacts. Yet, the identity continued to avoid them."

Worse yet, again according to AUE, the following year one of Quicksilver's divers – Tai Wilkerson – "experienced complications and became unconscious. Attempting to get Tai to the surface, his dive partner inflated his drysuit, rocketing him upwards from 180'. Though surface personnel worked furiously to revive him, his traumatic and rapid ascent thwarted their attempts; the coroner's report indicated massive embolisms in the spine and brain."

After this tragic event, Quicksilver's long-time connection with the *Juno* faded from existence.

Next on the scene was Sea Hunt, Incorporated. Sea Hunt was owned by Ben Benson, an entrepreneur who came to believe that the *Juno* lay close to shore off Assateague Island. There is nothing in the historical record to reject such a scenario – or any scenario for that matter.

Quicksilver chose to search offshore because an ancient ship's bell had been hauled to the surface in a dragger's net from 180 feet of water, and was viewed as a possible connection with the *Juno*.

Benson based his premise on the location of an eighteenth-century anchor that a commercial angler had snagged in his net. The anchor could conceivably be of Spanish origin. On the other hand, it is logical to presume that if the *Juno* had run aground on a barrier island, at least some of the 425 fatalities should have made it to shore alive.

Be that as it may, Benson obtained hang numbers from local skippers, and set his course on exploring the area with the hope that one of the hangs might turn out to be the long lost *Juno*. In this manner he accidentally discovered the Presidential yacht *Despatch* (which see). More to the point of the instant chapter, and cutting to the chase, after conducting research at the Accomack County Courthouse and obtaining a search permit from both the Virginia Marine Resources Commission and the Army Corps of Engineers, Benson found and recovered, among other things, a Spanish coin dated

Virginia - *Juno* (and *Galga*)

1799. Granted that a single coin did not establish proof of identity, at least it was indicative that a shipwreck might lie under the sand nearby, a mile north of Chincoteague Inlet and one quarter mile from shore.

Benson also obtained a permit for another Spanish shipwreck, the *Galga*, which sank in 1750. In all three cases (*Juno, Despatch,* and *Galga*), the State of Virginia stood to gain a hefty 25% of the proceeds of any and all artifacts that Benson sold, plus the State got to keep any individual artifacts that it believed merited State possession.

Both Spanish wrecks were held responsible for occasional coins that beachcombers found in the adjacent dunes.

Benson's researches paid off in spades and shovels. He learned that when Leon Rose dragged up the anchor noted above, adhered to it was a pewter plate. Bob Payne bought the anchor and plate for display in his shanty where he sold marine and nautical memorabilia. Etched on the plate were barely distinct letters that could have spelled "Juno," "Jane," or "Jolle." A contemporary article claimed, "According to an expert in London, the plate was made between 1770 and 1790."

By means of side-scan sonar, Benson discovered the intact hull of a ship that was buried in the near-shore sand. Now he enlarged his operation by employing a prop-wash deflector: a shallow-water device that diverted the propeller wash of a solidly moored vessel so that instead of blowing water aft, an elbow conduit blew the water downward. The result was a powerful leaf blower that loosened the sand to let it drift away with the current, effectively digging a hole in the seabed to expose whatever lay underneath.

At this point Benson put on hold all work on the *Galga* and the *Despatch*: the *Galga* because the site consisted of a long and disarticulated scatter field, the *Despatch* because the wreck's relics possessed great historic interest but little commercial value. He concentrated his efforts on the *Juno*.

Lest these few paragraphs make treasure salvage seem inexpensive and effortless, the reader should understand that by this time in Benson's all-consuming endeavor, he had already spent at least half a million dollars, and he was still counting. As he noted wryly, "Most treasure hunters pour more money into the sea than they ever take out."

Nonetheless, his enthusiasm was not waning for his expensive personal project: one that was yet only a year and a half old.

Soon, however, the clear calm waters got muddy, muddled, and murky: not the ocean waters but the legal waters, where even angels fear to tread. There were individuals and government agencies that did not want Benson to succeed in his quest to work the three wreck sites, for which he had already been given official sanction. Or, if he succeeded in identifying the wrecks, they wanted him to fail in his ultimate endeavor; that is – the way it is phrased in Admiralty law – to return lost merchandise to the stream of commerce. Benson's worst enemies were the kind of man-eating predators known as land sharks.

Benson's dream quest now became a nightmare.

The contrary initiative against Benson was instigated by the National Park Service. The NPS has a long and sordid history of disservice to American and foreign visitors to the parks and monuments that it "manages." (For "manages" read "controls.") On more than one occasion I have personally been a target of NPS mismanagement and sting operations that were purposely designed to extort money from unsuspecting citizens, so I know how vicious park rangers can be under their innocuous-looking Smokey-the-Bear hats.

One incident occurred when I was diving in Dry Tortugas National Park. Next to the wharf where the dive boat docked lay many years' worth of trash that people had dumped overboard. I asked a ranger if I could collect some of the discarded bottles. He gave me the go-ahead, then left. I swam along the bottom and collected those bottles that appealed to me. When I surfaced and swam to the boat, Billy Deans gave me the low sign. I let go of my mesh back before I climbed up the ladder. A different ranger appeared suddenly and walked off in a huff.

The rangers were running a scam. One gave me permission to recover the bottles while the other lurked in the bushes. One of my dive buddies (I don't remember who) spotted the other ranger where he was crouched behind a bush. When my buddy asked the ranger what he was doing, the ranger told him that he was waiting for me to surface with a bagful of bottles so he could give me a citation in the amount of several hundred dollars. It is illegal to disturb or collect rocks, plants, or archaeological objects in National Parks.

The irony of the situation was that I could have been cited for throwing a bottle overboard (littering), then cited again for recovering it along with other trash. Also – now that the statute of limitations has expired – I can relate that after the boat was moved to a mooring in the harbor, Billy "drove" to the dock under the cover of darkness, recovered my mesh back, and drove his DPV back to the boat. We had the last laugh on the park rangers.

Another time I was canoeing down the Rio Grande in Big Ben National Park. After the five-day trip, Cheryl Novak and I planned on spending the night in the campground. When we arrived, we saw that the rangers had closed half of the campsites. The other half was filled. At 5 o'clock, a horde of rangers left the office in park vehicles. We followed them out of the area, and watched them dispersing onto nearby dirt roads. Camping is allowed only in the campground. Camping is *not* allowed anywhere else in the hundreds of square miles of outlying desert.

We found a good spot for dinner. As we broke out our camp stove and freeze-dried meals, a ranger sneaked into a position where he could observe our activity through binoculars. I sensed the scam right away. Big Ben lay in an area so remote that the nearest town lay 50 miles away. By closing half the campground, visitors who wanted to explore the park for several days were left with two choices: make a hundred-mile round trip to town and return in the morning, or find a secluded spot and camp illegally.

We took our time in cooking and eating our dinner: activities that were not illegal. Not until we pitched a tent or unrolled sleeping bags could the ranger swoop down and hit us with a fat fine. An hour later, as the sun sat on the horizon, we packed our gear, drove away, went to town, rented a motel room, and left the ranger fuming and empty-handed. We did not return, but continued on our way to explore other natural features (like descending into Carlsbad Caverns and climbing Guadalupe Peak).

On my 1990 *Monitor* expedition, non-uniformed female rangers played undercover cops by sidling up to my dive buddies after hours, in order to ask questions about our conduct on the wreck: did we touch anything, move anything, or recover anything? After a while, the questioning became so obvious that my buddies refused to talk with the women. Meanwhile, a uniformed male ranger harassed me at the dock by making accusations about my right to dive on the wreck and about the damage that I could do by swimming around it. They all then reported their observations to the NOAA observer, who then called the Marine Police (another NOAA agency) and arranged to have an agent harass us at the wreck site the following day during diving operations.

In his exuberance to create trouble, the police boat ran me over while I was decompressing. Fortunately, I was deep enough to avoid the screws, and getting screwed.

After returning from a three-day backpacking trek in Glacier National Park, I was talking with a ranger who casually told me that if the NPS had its way, visitors would be banned from all national parks. The so-called Service believed that its purpose was to preserve the parks in their natural state. The NPS suffered visitors only because Congress demanded that it do so.

On the other hand, rangers belonging to the Bureau of Land Management have always welcomed me with open arms, were happy to have me backpack on BLM property, and went so far as to suggest routes to take and places to camp. A person may camp anywhere on BLM property, but only in tiny designated spots that were miles apart in national parks. I wish the NPS would be dissolved, and management of the parks transferred to the BLM. If only it would happen . . .

In short, the attitude of the NPS is definitely anti-people. The NPS hated visitors because they got in the way by exercising their right to visit national parks.

Thus it came as no surprise to me that the NPS did everything in its power to balk Benson's legitimate salvage operation. The NPS came into play because Assateague Island is a strictly controlled national seashore, with rules and regulations so onerous that it is difficult for visitors to enjoy their stay. Rangers prowl the premises in hopes of finding the most miniscule violations for which they can cite people with large fines. Rangers use binoculars to spy on beachcombers. They used the same method to keep their eyes on Benson when his boat was moored over the putative *Juno* site.

Because the park boundary ends at the low water line, the NPS had no jurisdiction over Benson's activities, either searching or salvaging. Nonetheless, the NPS confronted the State of Virginia and tried to get it to revoke Benson's license, claiming that his operations disturbed visitors on the sandy beach a quarter mile away. The Virginia Department of Historic Resources sided with the Virginia Marine Resources Commission and the Army Corps of Engineers in approving Benson's permit. In accordance with the Abandoned Shipwreck Act of 1987, Virginia owned all shipwrecks within the three-mile territorial limit. Virginia did not tell the NPS how to manage (or control) Assateague Island National Seashore, and Virginia did not want the NPS to tell the State how to manage its offshore bottomlands.

Still, the NPS was adamant in its attitude that the Spanish wrecks should be left to rot instead of being salvaged so that people the world over could see and enjoy the aged artifacts that Benson might recover. I should interject at this point that the NPS did not permit people to search for shipwrecks or archaeological material on property that it controlled, especially Assateague Island. People found searching on the island's beaches or dunes could be arrested and either fined or jailed, or both. Park rangers actively patrolled the grounds (or sands) for violators.

As Peter Hess noted, "The *Juno* was an unknown wreck. Fishing boats were getting caught on it, ripping up pieces of it, coins washing ashore. How can they [the NPS] argue that somehow it was protected in the state that it was in is just ridiculous."

As one of Benson's attorneys, Hess was stretching a point because none of the three wrecks that Benson found had been positively identified. Benson had nothing but strong suspicions; the greatest strength of those suspicions was his willingness to believe.

Anyway, Hess's statement is a valid argument which archaeologists refuse to acknowledge, despite the fact that they can see it for themselves. If a shipwreck was so-well preserved on the bottom of the ocean, then it would look exactly the same as it looked when it slid down the ways. The fact that it looks like wreckage or a pile of debris is mute testimony that shipwrecks are in no way protected under water. But I am preaching to the choir. Marine archaeologists are so far in denial that they cannot see the difference between a ship on the briny deep and one on or under the seabed. Their attitude is equivalent to claiming that a new-built house and one that has burned to the ground are one and the same.

Be that as it may, the NPS found another way to interfere with Benson's operation. If it could not get a State to stop Benson, it went for a sovereign nation: the country of Spain, which had abandoned the wrecks to their fate. Spain's lack of interest in Spanish galleons has a long history that goes all the way back to 1687, when William Phipps salvaged the *Conception* off the coast of Hispaniola; or when Burt Webber reworked the wreck in 1978. Nor did Spain give a hoot in the 1950's, when Robert Weller found and worked the Spanish wrecks of the 1715 fleet on Florida's eastern seaboard. Spain totally ignored Mel Fisher's 1985 discovery of the mother lode of the *Atocha*.

Be that as it may (again), the NPS used the United States Justice Department as a cat's-paw to induce Spain into interceding on the behalf of totalitarianism. As Anthony Troy, another one of Benson's attorneys, remarked, "It is inconceivable that the Justice Department would side with a foreign government against the legitimate interests of the Commonwealth of Virginia." Inconceivable or not, Spain bowed down at the insistence of the Justice Department, and agreed to enter the contest as intervenor.

Keep in mind that the NPS was not so much *for* Spain as it was *against* American citizens in general, treasure salvors in particular, and Ben Benson specifically. This action of the NPS made me wonder what motivated a government agency, and the individuals within that agency, to go to such great lengths to ruin a person with a bona fide interest in saving history from destruction, especially when the NPS had no stake in the matter. I usually call it bureaucratic territoriality, but this situation goes much deeper than that.

Spain was not the only adversary. One Richard Cook got into the act by claiming that Benson had used some of his research material to locate the *Galga*. Even if the claim were true, as it probably was, the claim was putting the cart before the horse, to coin a cliché, because the wreck that Benson found had not yet been identified. For that matter, neither had the other two wrecks been identified. All this legal action was based on pure speculation. Cook sought recourse for copyright infringement of his research in the amount of a quarter of a million dollars – and that was before the validity of the claim of identification had been made. Cook's case was summarily dismissed, in part because Benson testified that he found the *Galga* by conducting "a 400-hour magnetometer survey that took two months to complete."

It seems that it did not occur to anyone involved in the case that none of the wrecks

Virginia – *Juno* (and *Galga*)

had yet been identified. In fact, it was the court itself – in the name of Judge Calvitt Clarke – who brought this to the attention of the arbiters in general (again) and the lawyer for the Justice Department in particular. (By the way, Clarke was the same judge who presided over my *Lusitania* case. For details, see *The Lusitania Controversies*.) This was another case of putting the cart before the horse.

Clarke dismissed the case, and suggested that Spain intervene on its own recognizance. At this point in the contretemps, Spain retained its own attorney and staff, and filed its own motion to intervene, while the Justice Department acted as amicus curiae (Latin for friend of the court, but in this context a friend of Spain). Now came exchanges of briefs, rebuttals, rebriefs, and debriefs, all of which are too many and too lengthy for me to repeat in a chapter.

The full story would require a whole book. In fact, it did take a whole book: *The Golden Galleon* (2007), by John Amrhein Jr., who believed that he had already found the *Galga* under the beach, but was not permitted by the NPS to excavate it. I heartily recommend the tome to anyone who is interested in the nitty-gritty details of the machinations, manipulations, and legal prestidigitations that resulted from Benson's reported findings of the *Juno* and the *Galga*. Here is my CliffsNotes version (with many thanks to John Amrhein for his encyclopedic knowledge of events, his dedicated research, and his great attention to detail):

Despite the lack of verifiable evidence, the court awarded the *Juno* site to Spain and the *Galga* site to Virginia.

In light of Benson's investment of one million dollars, he sued Spain for a salvage award.

Spain countered by claiming, "Sea Hunt has provided no credible information identifying the actual site of the *Juno*." This leads me to wonder: if Spain did not believe that the site that Benson was working was the *Juno*, why did it claim the site as Spanish property? And why did Spain claim that the site was a military graveyard.

Don't worry yet about the obvious contradictions. They get worse.

Siding with Spain, the Justice Department noted, "Sea Hunt is still unable to assert with certainty that it has found the remains of *Juno* and saved any of its contents from loss. Although Sea Hunt has recovered a number of items listed in the attached inventory, it has not identified any of them as associated with the *Juno*." I repeat: if the wreck was not the *Juno*, why did Spain fight so hard to take it away from Benson?

The Commonwealth of Virginia pointed out this gross conflict of reason and rationality: "Until such time as this court has established a discrete location of the *Juno* wreckage, recovery of historic artifacts under the Virginia Marine Resources Commission Permits No. 97-0498 and No. 97-0163 (the permits) should be allowed to continue freely in the areas covered by the Permits."

Sea Hunt argued that "should the vessels be proved to be non-Spanish vessels the court would have no further jurisdiction over Spanish claims to non-Spanish vessels."

Again, despite the lack of verifiable evidence that Benson's site was the *Juno*, and despite Spain's claim that Benson's wreck site was *not* the *Juno*, the court denied Benson's salvage award yet ordered him to give to Spain the artifacts that Benson had so far recovered.

I hope my readers see the exquisite irony of this ruling.

Upon appeal, the 4th Circuit court ruled that both wreck sites belonged to Spain, and that therefore Benson was obligated to give his recovered artifacts to Spain.

Spain reiterated: "Sea Hunt has not located the *Juno* or otherwise achieved success that could merit a salvage award."

To which Virginia argued: "Sea Hunt also has an obligation to the Commonwealth *not* to turn over to any third party – including Spain – any artifact recovered under a Virginia-issued permit if that artifact came from *any source other* than one of those two ships. . . . Thus, the fact that Sea Hunt recovered an artifact under a Virginia permit does not mean that the artifact came from either *La Galga* or *Juno*. . . . The obligation is not, however, an obligation to turn over to Spain all artifacts from the two specific ships. If Spain claims that Sea Hunt has failed to abide by this obligation, it should identify the particular artifact(s) that gives rise to its concern and to prove the origin of such artifact(s). By asking this court, in effect, to presume the origin of all artifacts and to shift to Sea Hunt the burden of proof, Spain is not acting in keeping with the Court's previous order or with basic principle governing the burden of proof. . . . Spain has never agreed that the recovered artifacts came from their ships. . . . An item-by-item inquiry is needed, with Spain bearing the burden of proof as to the origin of any item that it claims. . . . All other artifacts recovered by Sea Hunt belong to the Commonwealth."

This beautifully articulated reasoning put Spain on a spot. The issue begs the question: How could Spain claim that the recovered artifacts belonged to Spain if Spain denied that the wrecks were the *Galga* and *Juno*?

If Virginia nailed the unassailable truth, Sea Hunt hammered it in even deeper: "The parties and the Court relied on supposition, conjecture, and speculation when referring to the unidentified vessels as the *Juno* and *La Galga*. . . . This court cannot and should not adjudicate *in rem* claims of an intervening claimant as to a vessel which the intervener contends has not been found. This is hornbook principle of admiralty law and plain common sense. . . . Sea Hunt has requested counsel for Spain to verify which artifacts came from the *La Galga* and the *Juno*, so that those artifacts can be turned over to Spain. Spain, through counsel, has refused."

Spain: "Apart from Sea Hunt's own representations to the Court that it had located the vessels and was recovering artifacts from them, the artifacts include Spanish coins dated 1734, 1740, 1741 and 1799, all of which match the 1750 sinking of *La Galga* and the 1802 sinking [of the *Juno*]. For all of its evasion and obfuscation, Sea Hunt has never as much as hinted that there is any other Spanish vessel in the area it examined."

Despite the truth of this statement, Spain ignored the well-known fact that Spanish coinage was an accepted coin of the land in the 1700's, and was in common usage in British colonies. Thus those coins could have been found on any shipwreck whose loss post-dated the minting date. Furthermore, all four coins were recovered from the *Juno* site, so that they had no relation to the *Galga* site in spite of Spain's overreaching allusion.

In 2001, the judge made this statement: "The court is faced with a problem that, in reading through this very thick file, that there is really no – been any statement by Sea Hunt positively this stuff came from *Juno* or these artifacts came from *Juno* or *La Galga*. We believe they are, but that's as far as they've gone, in my opinion."

With an opinion based on supposition, speculation, allegation, surmise, and con-

Virginia – *Juno* (and *Galga*)

jecture, the court ordered Sea Hunt to give the recovered artifacts to Spain – which country, as noted above, did not believe that the *Juno* site was the *Juno* or that the *Galga* site was the *Galga*. The rendered opinion sounds more like the Salem witch trials than a modern legal opinion. At least Benson did not spend a million dollars to get hanged or burned at the stake.

Case closed. Again.

Now guess who got to keep and display the artifacts at its visitors center? The National Park Service! The NPS told visitors affirmatively that the artifacts were recovered from the *Juno* and the *Galga*!

What a miscarriage of justice.

Oh, and what about the parable at the beginning of this chapter? I have never heard it said nor seen it mentioned in print that all the gold and jewels that Spain transported from the Americas to the homeland, over the course of three hundred years, *was stolen*. That's right. Spain robbed the Mayans, Aztecs, Incas, and other indigenous peoples, while murdering and enslaving them in the process, and now claims to be heirs to their long "lost" fortune.

According to local legend, the ponies that live and graze on Assateague Island were stranded there when the *Galga* ran ashore on the lonely strand. Assateague Island is still a lonely strand: one which stretches for thirty-seven miles from Ocean City, Maryland to Chincoteague Island, Virginia. The feral ponies still thrive on the barrier island. Every they are rounded up and made to swim across the channel to Chincoteague Island, where some are sold at auction. The proceeds support the Chincoteague Volunteer Fire Department. "Pony Penning" day takes place on the last Wednesday of July.

Menominee

I wrote about the tugboat *Menominee* and her three barges in *Shipwrecks of Virginia* (1992). They were shelled by a German U-boat during World War Two. The tug and two barges sank. The wrecks had not been located at the time of publication. For years I had the *Menominee* at the top of my search list. The *Menominee* was also at the top of Trueman Seamans' search list.

In 1991, prior to publication, Seamans proposed a dedicated trip to search for the tugboat's remains. I was ecstatic about the idea because I wanted to describe the wreckage in the book, and to publish the location so that interested divers could see the wreck for themselves. Trueman and his wife Andronike ran the dive charter boat *Sundowner* out of Virginia Beach, Virginia. They figured on making the trip pay for itself by having other divers meet us at the dock on Chincoteague Island.

The three of us – Trueman, Nike, and I – drove the boat from Virginia Beach to Onancock. Every day for a week we searched in the historical location and dived on nearby wrecks, none of which I had ever explored. Despite our commitment to the primary objective, we never found the wreck. But we had fun exploring the other wrecks and sharing the good times with our fellow divers.

My most memorable dive was on the *Winter Quarter* lightship (as we knew it at the time, before Ted Green identified it as the *Hermod*). I saw lobster claws under a steel overhang. I shot my hand into the hole . . . and snagged the sleeve of my drysuit on a sharp-edged projection. I didn't get cut, but the rusty metal sliced through my sleeve. Water immediately started pouring into the arm. I forgot the lobster and raced for the anchor line. Too late! By the time I reached the surface, my drysuit was flooded all the way to the toes.

Another interesting dive was on an unidentified steel barge that rested upside down on the sandy bottom, much like an inverted bathtub. After circumnavigating the outside perimeter I determined that the wreck was of recent origin. The hull plates were firmly secured in position, so there were no holes or hideaways in which lobsters could hide.

One end of the barge was open from keel to seabed: as if the hull had been sliced by a giant knife. Obviously this gross damage accounted for the reason that the barge sank. I entered from sand level, and penetrated some 20 feet or more, playing my light from side to side. There were not even any fish inside.

Slowly I rose, shining my light upward. The relief of the barge was at least 15 feet. The overhead was so black that it completely absorbed the beam from my light. I paused, and wondered why the inside of the bottom was perfectly smooth. Suddenly I realized the truth of the matter: The totality of blackness was oil! The oil that had not escaped from the compartments when the barge sank was now trapped inside the wreck. I narrowly averted the disaster of poking my head into the viscous substance and having it coat my hood, mask, and regulator.

For years afterward, Trueman and I shared woes over not finding the wreck where it was supposed to be.

Fourteen years after my trip with Trueman and Nike, Ted Green approached me with the same idea: a week-long exploratory trip with the primary objective of searching for the *Menominee*. He ran the dive charter boat *O.C. Diver* out of Ocean City, Maryland. (Although Trueman still grieved over the *Menominee*, by then the Seamans had moved to Florida and were out of the tugboat picture.) Ted had obtained coordinates from some local commercial anglers who fished in the vicinity of the tug's historic location. He wanted to check them out.,

He fleshed out the boat with dive buddies of ours; I went along as crew. We started the trip on August 8, 2005. This time we hit pay dirt. And not only that, we also found the *Barnegat*.

The tugboat's highest point of relief is the rounded stern, which rises eight feet above the white sandy bottom and shell hash. This isolated section measures some fifteen to twenty feet in length. A twenty-foot gap separates the stern from the main part of the wreck. Along the port side, several isolated chunks of steel (which comprise the vertical hull) provide stepping-stones.

The aft end of the main part of the wreck consists of interwoven debris: beams, plates, and unidentifiable chunks of metal. There is no sign of an engine: either it was salvaged or it collapsed and is so encrusted that it is not discernible. Steam pipes and fittings litter the area. A steam condenser on the port side measures twelve feet in length and four feet in diameter.

The two boilers dominate the area forward of the engine space. These boilers lie side by side about eighteen inches apart. Each boiler measures twelve feet in length and twelve feet in diameter; half of each boiler is buried.

The vertical rise of the port hull stands three feet high, and extends from the aft end of the steam condenser to the forward end of the boiler. No vertical hull exists on the starboard side; the starboard side of the starboard boiler curves into the seabed, with no wreckage exposed farther to starboard.

The wreck essentially ends at the forward end of the boilers. However, about fifty feet farther forward and along the centerline, a chunk of wreckage stands about three feet out of the sand: much like a small rudder on the longitudinal axis. Thirty feet forward of that, three isolated chunks of steel stand three feet out of the sand, extending perpendicular to the centerline. This eighty feet of area is essentially nothing but sand that is punctuated by these four chunks of metal.

The only part of the barge that remains is the lower hull structure: cross beams and planking that comprise a huge area of wood. The beams are thick and fairly solid, but the planks are rotten and can be broken apart by hand. The wreck rises three to four feet along the perimeter, and as high as six feet along the centerline.

I nicknamed the *Barnegat* the Flounder Wreck. Flounder lay shoulder to shoulder and tip to tail on the surrounding seabed and inside the wreck. I did not see any flounder that measured less than two feet in length, and only a few that measured less than two and a half feet.

No coal was in evidence, leading me to speculate that, although the wreck lies in the approximate position given in contemporary official reports, it might not be the *Barnegat*. The flounder could care less.

MENOMINEE   depth=60 feet
    GPS: 37-32.047 / 75-26.025   Loran: 27094.0 / 41746.8

BARNEGAT   depth=75 feet
    GPS: 37-31.879 / 75-26.504   Loran: 27096.0 / 41744.1

Olinda

With regard to the location of the freighter *Olinda*, which was torpedoed by a German U-boat in World War Two, in *Shipwrecks of Virginia* I wrote, "A thorough examination of archival documents indicated general disagreement of where she actually went down. The *Olinda's* chief officer and second mate placed the sinking at 37-30N/74-10W; both were on watch during the initial attack. The army plane that spotted the flaming vessel reported her position as 37-55N/74-00W; it was flying a dead reckoning course out of Mitchell Field. The plane from Langley Field gave the burning ship's position as 37-38N/74-00W; he also reported seeing three lifeboats with approximately ten men in each. The *Dallas* picked up one lifeboat at 37-40N/74-13W, the second at 37-40N/74-23W, and in her combat report backtracked their drift to a probable sinking location of 37-30N/75-00W. (This position is also verified by German records.) The final ONI (Office of Naval Intelligence) report summarized that attack position as 37-30N/74-00W, with the caveat, 'Last sighted afire on 100-fathom curve. Presumed to have drifted to sea before sinking.'

"The distance between the inshore position and the offshore position is about sixty miles, the difference north to south some thirty miles, the difference in depth about 5,000. That is a pretty big triangle for a search grid."

If we ignore the backtracked location – which is 55 miles from the closest of the other three locations, and which lies inshore in 90 feet of water, and assume that the longitude is a typographical error – we have a smaller, isosceles triangle that extends 26 miles north to south, and 8 miles east to west at the base.

Ted Green thinks he knows the actual location. He was trading wreck numbers with a commercial angler when the angler offered him a set of coordinates that he and his fellow anglers called the Olinda. How they assigned such an associational nomenclature to a hot fishing spot that lies nearly within the boundaries noted above is lost to history. They don't know and don't care about the identity of the site; they just know that it produces large quantities of large fish to keep their customers happy.

Two kinds of commercial anglers are familiar with the site: those who troll the surface for pelagic fish such as marlin and tuna, which are known to frequent the area;

Black sea bass hiding inside a shipwreck.

Virginia - Olinda

and those who bottom fish on the wreck for black sea bass and tautog. The wreck has nothing to do with attracting pelagic fish; it just happens to lie in an area where those fish already abound: a mere coincidence. The Delaware tournament blue marlin record was caught near the *Olinda*.

On the other hand, the wreck has everything to do with attracting bottom dwellers. Bass and tog live on, around, and inside shipwrecks because the collapsing hulls provide shelter and places to dart and hide from predators. Fluke and flounder often congregate on the seabed that surrounds shipwrecks. After sinking, a vessel quickly becomes a habitat or artificial reef: an oasis in a watery desert environment.

Green's newly acquired location lies slightly outside of the triangle: a bit westward of the left leg, and near the northern very acute angle.

He took his boat – the *O.C. Diver* – to check out the numbers and located the wreck without difficulty. He then ran over the wreck from several directions in order to estimate its size from the depth-recorder readings. As close as he could tell, the wreck at that location approximated the length of the *Olinda*.

He insisted that I publish the GPS numbers in order to encourage technical divers to check out the wreck. The GPS numbers are 37-47.268 / 74-11.873.

Before you grab your gear and rush out to dive on a virgin wreck, know that the depth is 400 feet.

An oddity of this location is that the so-called Olinda wreck lies only three miles from the historical sinking location of the *U-111* (also covered in *Shipwrecks of Virginia*). The *U-111* measures 235 feet in length, compared to the *Olinda's* 359 feet.

This makes me wonder: Could the so-called *Olinda* instead be the German U-boat? Or, alternatively, do the anglers have a nearby hang that might be the site of the long lost *U-111* (which would not be the last U-boat, nor even the penultimate U-boat)? Those are posers that I hope to see solved.

Green assured me that the wreck is not a U-boat. The signature is too large in both length and breadth, and it rises higher than the height of a U-boat: 20 to 25 feet above the seabed. The hull appears to have collapsed outward: a happy circumstance which broadens the wreck's width, and which provides more structure for fish to inhabit. The high relief also attracts mid-depth fish such as cod and pollock.

The dolphin is another species of highly sought pelagic fish.

S. G. WILDER
(plus BRUNSWICK and WHITEHAVEN)

Built: 1887
Previous names: None
Gross tonnage: 604
Type of vessel: Wooden-hulled barge
Builder: Hall Brothers, Port Blakely, Washington
Owner: Brooks-Scanlon Corporation, Foley, Florida
Port of registry: Jacksonville, Florida
Cause of sinking: Foundered
Location: The Middle Ground north of Winter Quarter Shoal

Sunk: July 3, 1933
Depth: 80 feet
Dimensions: 166' x 37' x 14'
Power: None

The *S.G. Wilder* started her long career as a barkentine. When windjammers become uneconomical in comparison with their steam driven counterparts, she became one of the many thousands of sailing vessels to be dismasted and converted to a barge. On June 28, 1933 the tug *Kaleen* left Charleston, South Carolina, with the *S.G. Wilder* in tow. Aboard the barge were three men, Captain Ben Knowles in command. One account claims that five men were onboard, but this seems unlikely.

Tug and tow pulled into Norfolk, Virginia and picked up two more unrigged barges, the *Whitehaven* and the *Brunswick*. It was a common sight along the eastern seaboard to see a tug and a covey of barges working their way from port to port. On this voyage the *S.G. Wilder* carried lumber, the *Whitehaven* carried 2,197 tons of coal, and the *Brunswick* carried box shooks. (A shook was a set of parts for assembling a barrel or packing box.)

Soon after reaching the open ocean the weather turned for the worse. As the *Kaleen* battled her way north, to New York, her tows became unmanageable. Soon a full blown gale was unleashed upon them. Seventy- to eighty-mile-per-hour winds whipped the sea to froth, and rain fell thick upon heaving waves. By the time they passed the *Winter Quarter* Lightship, it was time for action.

Standard practice under such circumstances called for each barge skipper to take control of his own vessel, cast off the lines, and drop anchor. The barge could then ride out the storm with its head into the sea. All three barges acted in accordance with accepted protocol.

The *Kaleen* then swung around and approached each of her charges. Amid the tempest, the three men on the *Whitehaven* gladly abandoned ship for the security of the tug. Likewise, the three men on the *Brunswick* boarded the *Kaleen*.

The men on the *S.G. Wilder* were in dire straits. Their barge was taking on water. Captain Knowles signaled for assistance while the crew worked the pumps. Two Coast Guard cutters and the steamship *A.L. Kent* hove to in order to render aid. By that time no vessel could get close to the barge without putting herself in danger. Mountainous seas would have thrown the two vessels together, possibly sinking both.

The men abandoned the *S.G. Wilder* in a dory, and not a moment too soon, for the barge quickly succumbed to the ravages of the sea. So, too, did the dory, taking three men with her, including Captain Knowles, Pop Lewis, and a man named Frank but

Virginia - *S.G. Wilder* (plus *Brunswick* and *Whitehaven*)

whose surname the official records gave as "last name unknown."

Later that night both the *Brunswick* and *Whitehaven* foundered as well. Three valuable cargoes were lost in addition to three precious lives. In the eternal contest of men against the sea, the night of July 3-4 was won by the sea. The *S.G. Wilder* was valued at $13,700, her cargo at $14,600; neither vessel nor cargo was insured. According to the Record of Wreck Reports, part of the wreckage was found and destroyed by a Coast Guard cutter on or about July 9, 1933.

Modern charts are marked with many wrecks and obstructions in the area where the *S.G. Wilder* went down. Some of these sites have names attached to them in the records that back up the charted symbols. One such site is labeled *S.G. Wilbur*. No such vessel is listed in the *Lloyd's Register*, so I suspect that it is a typographical error intended to be the *S.G. Wilder*. According to a 1949 wreck report, the wreck called the *S.G. Wilbur* was located at 38° 13.37' north latitude, 74° 45.38' west longitude, and was wire-dragged to a least depth of 72 feet.

There are two wreck sites in that immediate vicinity, called the Twin Wrecks. Both sites consist of metal hulls that I have identified as the *Saetia* and the *Oklahoma*. (For details, see *Shipwrecks of Delaware and Maryland*, by this author.) Since the *S.G. Wilder* was constructed of wood, it could not possibly be either of the Twin Wrecks.

On the other hand, three wooden wrecks are grouped fairly close together in an area known as the Middle Ground. (According to one report, the *Whitehaven* went down about five miles north-northeast of the *Winter Quarter Shoals* lightship.) The barge *Gordon C. Cooke* was sunk in that vicinity on April 12, 1947, but that vessel was constructed of steel and is easily distinguishable. (For details, see *Shipwrecks of Delaware and Maryland*.) It is unlikely at this time that any definite determination of identity can be made among the three wooden wrecks – if indeed any of them constitute the remains of the three wooden barges that went down on July 3, 1933.

This photograph of the *S.G. Wilder* shows her before she was dismasted and converted to a barge. She is shown fully rigged with her sails capturing the wind that once propelled the barkentine across the world's oceans. (From the author's collection.)

Saginaw

Built: 1883
Previous names: *Benison, Saginaw, Benison*
Gross tonnage: 1,835
Type of vessel: Iron-hulled screw steamer
Builder: Caird Purdie & Co., Barrow, England
Owner: Clyde Steam Ship Company, New York, NY
Port of registry: New York, NY
Cause of sinking: Collision with SS *Hamilton*
Location: Three to five miles south or southeast of the *Winter Quarter Shoals* lightship

Sunk: May 5, 1903
Depth: Unknown
Dimensions: 245' x 34' x 24'
Power: Coal-fired steam

    The Clyde liner *Saginaw* had two major mishaps during her twenty-year career. The first was when she ran aground off the New Jersey coast, on March 23, 1897, during a heavy gale, while bound for New York from Haitian ports. "The crew and one passenger aboard were rescued by life savers. The ship was badly pounded, but was eventually salved."

    The *Saginaw's* second mishap was getting in the way of the self-styled ship rammer *Hamilton*. The Old Dominion liner had already done in a much larger vessel: the freighter *Macedonia*. (For particulars, see *Shipwrecks of New Jersey: North*, by this author.) Related in *Shipwrecks of Virginia* is the woeful tale of the loss of the *Asenath A. Shaw*, also sunk by the *Hamilton*. In the present case, perhaps, some of the blame can be laid on a clinging nighttime fog.

    The *Hamilton* was southbound from New York City to Norfolk, Virginia. The *Saginaw* was northbound, Norfolk to Philadelphia, Pennsylvania. On board the *Saginaw* were eighteen passengers and a crew of twenty-six, plus a general cargo worth some $100,000. Both vessels sounded their foghorns, and the watches of each heard the deep, bass tone of the other. The fog was so thick that lookouts could see no farther than a ship's length. The *Hamilton* crept along at eight knots, the *Saginaw* at nine.

    When the liners approached within sight of each other, the sum of their closing speeds gave them less then seven seconds in which to avoid a collision. Both vessels maneuvered to avert disaster. The sharp bow of the *Hamilton* sliced through the stern quarter of the *Saginaw*, sheering it off completely. A few seconds later, both ships were no longer in each other's view.

    The *Hamilton* suffered a crumpled bow but was in no danger of sinking. She reversed engines, circled back, and lowered lifeboats.

    The *Saginaw* immediately commenced to settle by the stern. Passengers who were awakened by the crash rushed on deck and scrambled for the bow. Lifeboats were launched while the liner took on a definite list. The first boat swamped when it hit the water, drowning all fifteen women who had been placed on board. Only the Second Officer swam for his life. During the ten minutes that it took the *Saginaw* to sink, two other lifeboats and one raft were launched successfully.

    Not everyone had gotten off before "the rush of water into the bow of the *Saginaw* had caused the decks to burst from their fastenings with a roar like the report of big guns, and tons of freight of all description soon littered the sea." Clinging to the still-visible topmasts were several men, including Captain J. S. Tunnell, master.

The *Hamilton's* lifeboats charged into the flotsam of cargo and struggling humanity, and plucked people from the sea. Rescue operations continued frantically for an hour, until no more living souls could be found. Lost with the *Saginaw* were fifteen (or twenty; accounts differ) human lives and a valuable cargo of resin, sheeting, turpentine, tobacco, yarn, and naval stores. Captain Tunnel survived, but he was "badly injured about the head and internally; two ribs broken."

Captain R. B. Roaz, master of the *Hamilton*, gave his version of the collision to eager reporters. "It was clear when we left New York yesterday afternoon but we ran into a fog bank four miles north of Egg Harbor [New Jersey], the fog lasting until we reached Cape Charles [Virginia] this morning. It was about 4:40 this morning that we were proceeding at about nine knots an hour. We had been under reduced speed since encountering the fog. We could not see a ship's length ahead when we heard a whistle on the starboard bow two points ahead. We stopped the *Hamilton*, and then I heard another whistle. Suddenly the *Saginaw* loomed up three points on the bow, and the *Saginaw* attempted to run across the *Hamilton's* bow. We backed at full speed, but struck the *Saginaw* on the port quarter. In a very short time she went down. When the *Hamilton* backed off she was settling. We lowered two boats, but meanwhile the *Saginaw* had lowered her boats, and a raft. I picked up two of these boats and a raft. The third probably was sunk."

One passenger of the *Saginaw* gave his personal perspective as well. E. B. Cole "placed $700 and a diamond ring beneath his pillow before retiring. When the crash came all thought of valuables was forgotten, and he sought safety on deck. Then he remembered the money and started below, but was driven back by the waters. Describing the collision, Mr. Cole declared it was so sudden that one could scarcely realize what had happened. Mr. Cole grasped a piece of wreckage and managed to reach one of the topmasts of the sunken ship, from which he was taken by a boat from the *Hamilton*."

On board the *Hamilton*, the daughter of Rear Admiral William Schley took up a collection for the newly destitute passengers and crew of the *Saginaw*. She quickly raised $95 to distribute among the needy survivors.

Initially, considerable confusion existed with respect to the location of the wreck. According to one source, the collision occurred somewhere between the lightships marking the shoals off Winter Quarter and Fenwick Island – a rather broad swath of sea that extends some thirty miles in length.

Three other sources that I unearthed claimed that the two ships collided "off Hog Island, Delaware Coast," "off Hog Island, Maryland," and "off Hog Island, Va." Clearly, two correspondents did not have a clue about the location of Hog Island, which is located in Virginia waters more than forty miles south of the Maryland border, and is not anywhere near Delaware. Yet even the report that placed Hog Island in the correct State of the Union was wrong about the wreck's location by placing it too far south.

A preponderance of evidence was published in *The New York Maritime Register* on May 13, 1903: "Steamer *Manna Hata*, at Baltimore May 7 from New York, reported that on May 6 passed sunken steamer *Saginaw* about two miles SE of *Winter Quarter* lightship in thirteen fathoms of water. Also passed a large quantity of wreckage, containing part of a roof of deck house, lot of joiner boards, spool twine and small driftwood. Did not see any dead bodies. The wreck was very dangerous, as it lay in the track of the coasting trade. United States Collier *Lebanon*, which arrived at New London May 7 with coal, passed through wreckage from str *Saginaw* on the way up the Jersey coast, and picked up several barrels of oil and other freight from the sunken steamer. No dead bodies were seen. Str *Mokta* (Br), at Portland May 8, from Baltimore, reported passing the wreck of the *Saginaw* off the Virginia coast on the 5th, and when about five miles south of Winter Quarter shoal lightship large quantities of wreckage was passed."

At first blush the *Lebanon's* sighting is not credible. However, I think the phrase "on the way up the Jersey coast" was a matter of either inaccurate reporting or poor descriptive technique. The *Lebanon* was probably northbound along the eastern seaboard when she spotted the *Saginaw's* wreckage, and gave a global description that declined precision but that could not be misinterpreted. The locations given by the *Manna Hata* and the *Mokta* corroborate each other fairly well. Furthermore, the depth given by the *Manna Hata* (thirteen fathoms) is strikingly close to the depth given by the *Saginaw's* engineer, whose name was listed as Selzer. He stated that the ship lay "in fifteen fathoms of water." These two depth reports (78 feet versus 90 feet) represent a difference in depth of only 12 feet.

Originally, I placed an abbreviated chapter about the *Saginaw* in the first edition of *Shipwrecks of Delaware and Maryland*. After I obtained additional information that placed the wreck off the coast of Virginia, I deleted the *Saginaw* from the revised edition of 2002. In the first incarnation, I wrote, "Although the Hydrographic Office charted the wreck as a hazard to navigation, records still extant make no mention of the *Saginaw* or its location. It either lies waiting to be discovered and identified, or it was blasted apart and is no longer recognizable as the ship it once was."

Researchers should note that the *Saginaw* was propelled by a compound engine whose cylinders measured respectively thirty inches and fifty-five inches in diameter. She was equipped with two Scotch boilers. The engine and boilers were built by Westray Copeland & Company, of Barrow, England.

While the *Saginaw* may be fished and dived regularly, the wreck has yet to be positively identified. I would like to suggest the possibility that the *Saginaw* may be the Sub Wreck, alias the Bottle Wreck, alias the Pipe Wreck, alias the Norwegian Freighter. Several facts bolster my conjecture.

The Sub Wreck is the remains of a nineteenth-century steamship. It stands upright at a depth of 85 feet – nearly identical with the average of the two reported depths. The highest point of relief is the top of the compound engine, which stands nearly 20 feet tall. Forward of the engine lies a pair of boilers, side by side. Each boiler measures fourteen feet in diameter and twelve feet in length. A donkey boiler lies forward of the boilers, on the centerline. What appears to be a condenser lies on its end adjacent to the starboard side of the starboard boiler.

The rest of the wreck is considerably broken down. Most of the hull has fallen outboard so that the machinery area is surrounded by a large field of low-lying debris in the shape of a lozenge that exceeds two hundred feet in length. The only other major recognizable feature is a section of propeller shaft midway between the engine and the propeller. Two blades of the propeller are exposed, protruding upward like Mickey Mouse's ears.

Although this meager description makes the wreck sound less than exciting, the

Virginia - Saginaw

site holds a continuing fascination for divers because of the artifacts that have been recovered, such as clay pipes and lead linotype.

Danny Fisher showed me some of the linotype that he recovered. The lead facing was partially corroded so the fine print was difficult to read. Also, the type was reversed. I held one in front of a mirror and saw that the heading was *The Admirable Crichton*. I let out a yelp when I deciphered the title because it has always been my favorite play. I had read it in high school. James Barrie, the author of *Peter Pan*, wrote this classic piece of literature in 1902.

Scott Jenkins found a V nickel that was dated 1902. These finds indicate that a sinking date of 1903 is within the bounds of reason.

Part of the cargo that has withstood the ravages of time consisted of peanuts! Joyce Steinmetz had some samples analyzed, and learned that they were a Virginia hybrid. This implies that the vessel was outbound from the Chesapeake Bay when it sank.

However, one fact that refutes my speculation is Doug Buckley's recovery of several Coke bottles that were stamped with a date of 1909. He told me that these Coke bottles were not loosely scattered about the wreck – as they would have been had they been tossed overboard by later day salvors or anglers – but were buried and stored in their original wooden case. I can offer no resolution for this apparent anachronism.

But Ted Green can. He would not be surprised if Buckley misremembered where he found these bottles. Because Buckley used to dive an awful lot on the *Monroe*, Green suspects that Buckley found the bottles there, then got confused about their origin.

The recovery of a diamond ring would not only constitute a valuable find, but would provide a very definite clue to the wreck's identity – especially if it were found beneath a pillow.

Sub Wreck location:
GPS: 37-52.065 / 75-03.432
Loran: 27075.1 / 42519.0

Right: I have enlarged and reversed a photograph of the linotype so that the title is readable. The linotype is not as legible as it should be due to corrosion from the chemical bath in which it was submerged for so many years.

Below: A rough drawing of the *Saginaw* as the *Benison*. (From the author's collection.)

Unidentified Wrecks Off Virginia

160 Wood Wreck (alias Fourth of July)

GPS: 37-53.241 / 74-38.495   Loran: 26902.9 / 42051.8
Wooden hull, low relief   Depth: 155 feet

    The central core of this low-lying wooden wreck is small, but it is surrounded by scattered and noncontiguous pieces that make the wreck interesting to explore. The central mass measures less than one hundred feet in length. A keelson is in evidence for most of this distance. There is no discernible stem, but off the forward end lies a pile of anchor chain whose links measure six inches in length. Off to port lies a chunk of wreckage which possesses a hawse pipe with chain going through it. This chain connects to the chain pile. Off to starboard lies a Navy-style folding anchor.

    Abaft the hawse pipe chunk and to the port side of the central core lie two scallop dredges. Between the dredges and the central core there is an unrecognizable rectangular metal chunk. At this frame point but off the starboard side of the central core, an iron propeller lies flat on the sand. The center of the propeller has a hole where the shaft would go. My best guess is that the propeller was carried as cargo.

    Farther aft and off the starboard side lies an object that looks like a capstan cover: it is dishlike and has a curved lip. The bottom of this cover is rubbed smooth, right down to the bare metal. I suspect that it is a turtle rub. (A turtle rub is a place where sea turtles lodge themselves in order to sleep, to avoid being buffeted about by current or tide or deep ground swells.) Abaft and diagonally away from the central core is a large piece of wooden wreckage.

    To port of amidships lies a large donkey boiler that measures ten feet in length and five feet in diameter. Rusting of the outer shell has exposed some of the tubes. No propulsion machinery is in evidence, nor are valves or steam pipes. Halfway between this boiler and the anchor chain pile lies a massive windlass that lies on its side.

    The sternpost is obvious, as is the taper of the hull. A small piece of wreckage lies off the starboard side, while the disarticulated rudder lies off the port side. The rudderpost measures twenty feet in length, and lies across a jagged metal band. Two pintles lie flush with the sand. The blade of the rudder measures four feet in length.

    Farther off the starboard stern lies a rectangular section of wood that looks like part of the upper deck, ripped off the hull. This section of wood has the appearance of a small barge. Ropes are entangled in this section, and float above the bottom. Farther yet off the starboard stern lies another piece of wreckage that is long and narrow.

    This wreck is full of incongruities. The hull is obviously extremely old and worm-eaten. The folding Navy anchor is an anachronism, being too new in design for the age of the wreck. The windlass is oversized, and no winches were in evidence. The donkey boiler is larger than most auxiliary boilers that were employed in sailing vessels as a means of generating steam to operate winches and the windlass. Yet the boiler is smaller than one that would be employed to generate steam for propulsion machinery, of which none is in evidence. The loose propeller is located near the bow, notwithstanding the lack of an engine and a shaft assembly. The plane surface of the rudder appears inordinately small for the size of the wreck.

    Of only one thing I am certain: the resident turtle cares nothing about the identity of the wreck.

Ammunition Wreck (alias Barrel Wreck)

GPS: 37-44.422 / 74-59.937   Loran: 26994.0 / 41925.3
Wooden hull, medium relief   Depth: 110 feet

I do not know the origination of the name Ammunition Wreck, but Ted Green prefers to call it the Barrel Wreck, for obvious reasons. The centerpiece of this wreck is a large cargo area that is packed with barrels of what appear to be concrete. These barrels are nestled together like corn on a cob, and lay in rows side by side. These barrels occupy an area that measures twenty feet across by more than thirty feet in length. Thick wooden frames and planks are exposed beneath the barrels. Isolated lumps of wreckage exist fore and aft of this central clump, and to either side. In decent visibility, one can skip from one clump to another – but it is easy to get disoriented, so divers beware if return to the anchor line is desirable or essential.

Beyond one end of the barrel clump stands a thickly encrusted lump that rises eight feet above the surrounding debris. One vertical member is tall, narrow, and rounded on top – much like an aircraft propeller blade. A horizontal member offers the same aspect. Although these blades do not look like typical vessel propeller blades, they could very well be two blades of a four-bladed propeller that was turned by auxiliary diesel power. In addition, the barrels could be exposed because we are seeing the bottom of an upside down hull. These observations fit well with the supposition that the wreck is the *Madrugada* (which see for details *Shipwrecks of Virginia* (1992) and *The Kaiser's U-boats in American Waters* (2010).

I did not recognize anything that could be construed as a diesel engine, but several of the nearby lumps fit the dimensions of an engine (or engines), and could be covered with debris that disguises their true form. A large metal section that is bowlike in appearance lies off and to one side of the end of the wreck that is opposite the propeller. Granular sand, which is the off-white color of eggshell, surrounds and intersperses the wreckage.

This wreck lies four miles from the historic position given in Navy records for the location of the *Madrugada*.

Bone Wreck

GPS: 37-45.735 / 75-11.823   Loran 27053.0 / 41922.8
Metal hull, high relief   Depth: 70 feet

According to local lore, the Bone Wreck was given its name because of the presence of bones – not human bones, but animal bones, probably those of domestic grazers. Today, these bones are no longer in evidence. Later, the wreck was given an alternative name: the USS Bone. This was because of the recovery of portholes that were stamped "USNYW 1867", the implication being that the wreck was once a Navy vessel. These portholes are the same as those found on the *Nina* (see *Shipwrecks of Delaware and Maryland*, by this author) except that the backing plates are hexagonal.

The wreck measures approximately two hundred feet in length. At one time it must have lain perfectly on its starboard side. Indeed, this fact is made evident by the massive intact bow structure, which rises more than twenty feet above the seabed. This bow section extends aft some fifty feet. Inside are three distinct deck levels. One can easily swim through these spacious decks and either squeeze through rust holes near the stem, or work through the plating to a "higher" or "lower" deck. In reality, though, it is easier

The picture above shows the displaced steering quadrant. The picture at right shows a displaced rudder assembly. Neither of these steering mechanisms are located at the stern, leading me to believe that they were cargo.

to reverse direction and exit the interior at the cut, then re-enter another deck.

A large, heavy-duty double towing bitt is secured to the very tip of the bow on the upper deck. The two bitts are positioned in fore-and-aft alignment. "Beneath" these bitts, the stem curves aft to become the keel. A deep washout has been scoured beneath the forefoot. At 74 feet, the bottom of this washout is eight to ten feet lower than the surrounding seabed. Crouching in the bottom is like sitting in the bottom of a semicircular pit. The washout cuts through the clay or marl, exposing the grayish substrate in three, steplike layers, above which the seabed consists of off-white sand and shell hash.

The double bottom hull construction is clearly in evidence where the intact bow section terminates sharply, abaft of which point the wreck is considerably broken down. The height of the double bottom measures about eighteen inches.

The broken-down section extends approximately one hundred fifty feet aft. The bottom is fairly evident. The hull in this area has collapsed in such a way that the wreckage consists largely of a jumble of beams and hull plates. Debris extends "upward" a considerable distance – perhaps fifty feet or so – implying that the vessel possessed some superstructure above the main deck.

Several small double bitts are scattered around the wreck in strategic locations. Another large, heavy-duty double towing bitt lies on the sand off the stern.

A huge rudder assembly is situated inconsistently in the middle of the wreck (or closer to the bow). This rudder assembly measures thirty-five feet in length. The plane surface measures some twenty feet in length and five feet in width. The curved upper portion measures five feet in length. The cylindrical rudderpost measures ten feet in length. At the very top of the rudderpost is the steering quadrant. The location of this rudder assembly makes it appear that it was being carried on the deck of the vessel at the time it sank.

Not in evidence were means of propulsion, machine parts, piping, valves, anchors, chain, or anything mechanical – not even winches or a windlass. I did not see hawse pipes in the bow. I am not even certain that the bow *was* the bow. The end that I took for the bow could conceivably have been the stern. The opposite end of the wreck is so

Virginia - Bone Wreck and Dragger 230

demolished that its configuration was not discernible.

The date on the recovered portholes is inconsistent with the metal hull construction. Double bottoms did not exist in 1867. I do not know how to reconcile this inconsistency, except to suggest that perhaps the portholes were recovered from another wreck, and that over the years, two distinct wrecks were given the same or similar names, and have become confused with each other.

The Bone Wreck appears to be the remains of a modern barge – not a square-ended shallow-draft work barge, but an ocean-going barge.

Whatever it may be, the Bone Wreck is definitely worth exploring. Visibility is generally good, even after stormy seas – this because of the large granular sand that surrounds the wreck. I saw some tautog and one conger eel, but I would favor calling the site the Sea Bass Wreck because of the incredibly large schools of black sea bass that live there.

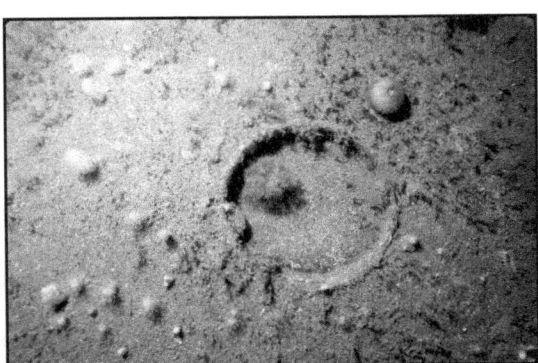

Dragger 230

Left and below: Two photos of an unidentified dragger that I named Dragger 230 because of the depth. The wreck was the first dive of a three-day offshore trip aboard the *Miss Lindsey*, from Lynnhaven Dive Center. I was not privy to the location. The second dive of the first day was on the *Ethel C*, which lay not far away. The dragger's hull was painted red; the wreck lay on its side so that the propeller was not buried in the sand.

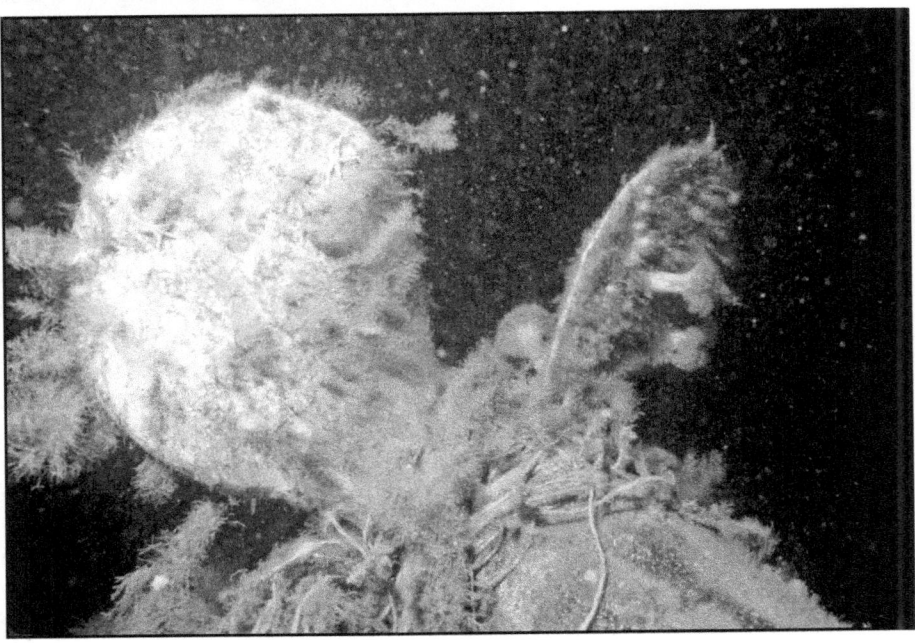

Screw Wreck
(alias Lightship, alias Winter Quarter Lightship)

The eponymous feature is the four-bladed iron propeller, each blade of which measures seven feet in length. Adding the two-foot diameter of the hub, the propeller measures fully sixteen feet from tip to tip. Ted Green remembers that when he dived on the wreck in the early 1980's, the stern section on which the propeller was mounted rose twenty feet or more off the bottom – a truly spectacular sight. He also remembers that the shaft was in line with the keel.

When I first dived on the wreck in 1991, the propeller hub stood ten feet above the bottom – still an impressive sight. However, the shaft lay at a right angle to the centerline, with the propeller pointing to port. Green speculates that one side of the hull crumpled, causing the stern to twist sideways as the wreck collapsed. It must have broken the shaft in the process. Today, the propeller has lost some of its former glamour because it stands only four feet or so above the bottom.

The rudder, rudderpost, and steering quadrant lie to starboard and forward of the propeller. How the assembly achieved such a position I refuse to speculate. The plane surface of the rudder measures ten feet in length. The rudderpost pierces the steering quadrant. Forward of the rudderpost assembly lies a twenty-foot-long ferrous metal cylinder that has all the appearances of a propeller shaft, complete with flanges at either end; perhaps it was a spare length of shaft.

The section with the propeller measures some thirty feet in length. Fifteen feet of empty space separates it from the main mass of wreckage. Apparently, this void was created when the connecting hull and bulkheads fell flat against the sand and were buried.

Proceeding forward, one can follow the propeller shaft to the place at which the engine used to stand. In some places, vestiges of the shaft alley housing are extant. The engine is broken down to its constituent parts, which are difficult to differentiate from the surrounding encrusted metal. The way to make sense of the wreckage is to hover eight to ten feet above the wreck, and look down. Let your eyes follow the shaft to its nether end. At that point you can see an eccentric or counterweight that is disarticulated from its connecting rod. Once you visualize the nearby connecting rod, you will be able to discern pistons and other connecting rods.

A propeller lies flat on the debris, abaft the engine on the port side of the propeller shaft, and close to the forward termination of the shaft. The blades of this propeller measure three to four feet in length: shorter than the length of the blades on the vessel's operational propeller. It is unlikely that this propeller could have been utilized as a spare. Indeed, the fact that this propeller lies *atop* the debris is difficult to explain. It is possible that the propeller was carried in the bottom hold as cargo, and that the upside down hull rusted away from it. But Green speculates that the propeller might have fallen or broken off the lightship when she drifted over top of the wreck when the wreck stood high; this could explain how it came to rest on top of the wreck's debris.

Forward of the engine pile is the wreck's dominating feature: a pair of boilers lying side by side. These boilers measure fourteen feet in diameter. The depth at the top of these boilers is 6 feet. An auxiliary boiler lies forward and to port, angled 45° off the centerline. This boiler measures eight feet in diameter. Green has informed me that this auxiliary boiler has been known to move. In fact, when I referred to my survey drawings

Virginia - Screw Wreck   131

– which I made nine years apart – I saw that I drew this boiler in different attitudes.

Much marine life is in evidence. Schools of three-foot-long striped bass congregate in and around the forward hatchway and skeletal boiler. Schools of triggerfish hover amidships. Sea robins and puffer fish clung to the bottom. Black sea bass swim everywhere. Shy tautog maintain station near openings and overhangs, ready to dart inside at a moment's notice or at the appearance of a spear gun.

Forward of the boilers the overlapping hull plates are evident. The port side disappears into the sand, while the starboard side stands a couple feet above the seabed. It appears that the hull collapsed in such a way that the port hull fell inboard (toward

I do not profess to be an artist or a draftsperson. The importance of my drawings is to recall and convey information about wreck sites. This drawing shows featured parts of the Screw Wreck in relation to each other.

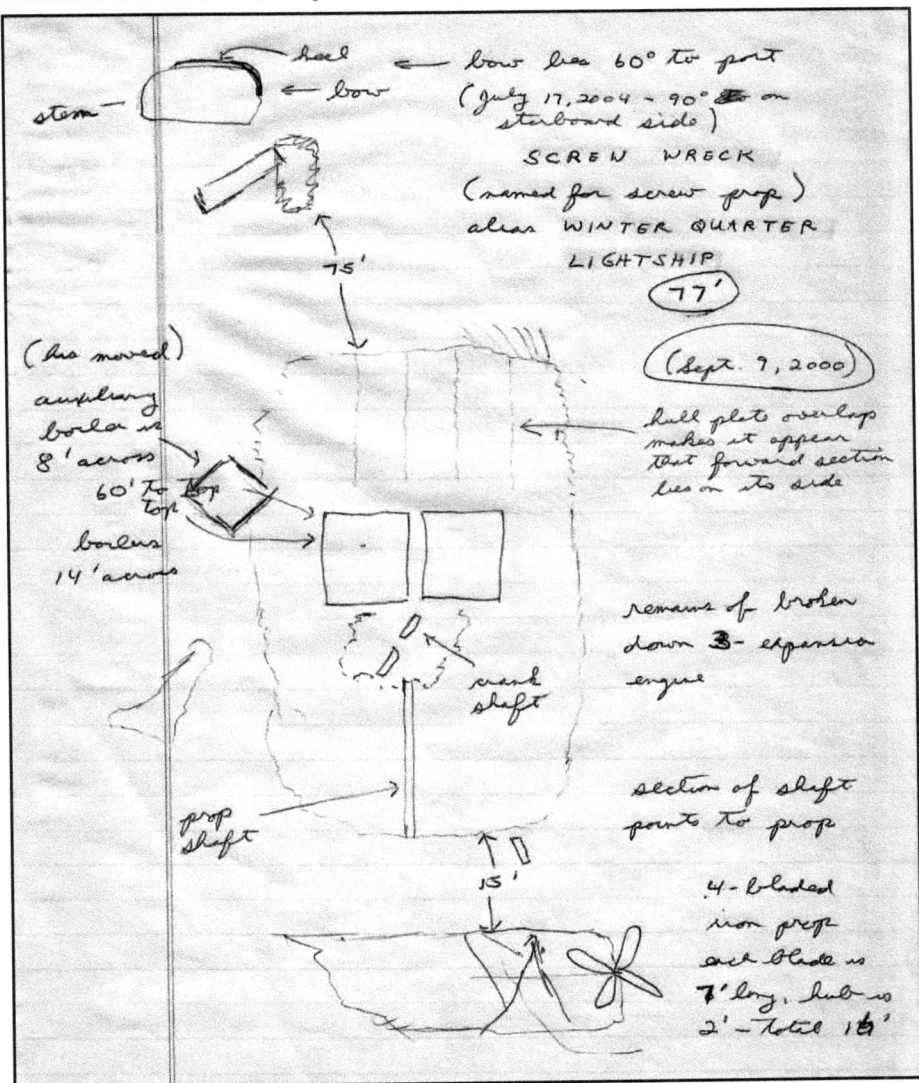

the keel), and that the exposed portion of plating that is visible is the port side of the hull. (Remember to mentally reverse port and starboard if the wreck lies upside down.)

The expanse of plating extends about fifty feet forward of the boilers. Then it terminates abruptly by diving under the white sandy bottom. The bow section lies out of sight across a void of barren sand.

To locate the bow section, divers are advised to tie a line to the leading edge of the hull. Proceed away from the wreck, and veer ever so slightly to the left – fifteen degrees should do the trick. At a distance of about seventy-five feet you will encounter a chunk of wreckage that lies at an angle to your line of progress. This rectangular chunk meas-

---

I found this photograph in the National Archives. It was titled "Mysterious Wreck of Winter Quarter Lightship." As the *Winter Quarter* lightship never sank, the title is an obvious misnomer. Under the title was typed, "When the steamship was first sighted, it was abandoned and partly submerged. It appears that she is an unreported submarine victim." The date of record (not the attack date or date of loss) was August 23, 1918. The citation read, "From *The New York Sun*." The photograph is indeed mysterious. Ted Green and I have pored over this picture and discussed it at great length, in order to decipher its origin and meaning, but without reaching any affirmative conclusion.

My hopeful interpretation is that the vessel in distress is the *Hermod* (which see), with the *Celtic* waiting in the background. The picture was not published with the article - perhaps because news of the tragedy travelled faster than the photo, and by the time the photo reached the wire services, the *Hermod* was old news (to use an accepted oxymoron). The picture was then kept as a file photo, possibly to be retrieved as an illustration for some other sinking for which no photographs were available.

Note the deck gun forward of the wheelhouse. Keep in mind that Norwegian vessels transited the North Sea where German U-boats proliferated, and sank numerous vessels. It is possible that the *Hermod* was therefore armed for self-defense. Although no gun has ever been seen in the wreckage, it may have been salvaged, especially as the Hermod sank in such shallow water and was exposed until it was battered to pieces.

Green finds favor with another option. He noted that the *Winter Quarter* lightship did not always stay on station, but periodicallly went into dry-dock for maintenance and repairs, during which time a relief vessel took her place. When the lightship returned to station, she might not always moor in the same exact spot. Thus she guarded the shoal from various but nearby locations off the shoal.

As he had identified the *Hermod* elsewhere, the vessel in the picture must be some other vessel: one which appears to be stranded on the shoal. He postulates that the picture was taken from the lightship, which was located a quarter mile from the *Hermod*. Furthermore, local lore has it that lightship crewmembers used to fish on the sunken wreck as the lightship swung on her mooring and drifted over top of the wreckage; this circumstance would explain how the small, displaced anchor came to rest on the wreck: the lightship's anchor struck the wreckage when it stood higher than it does today. Perhaps the wreck is one that hugged the shore as a way to avoid a chasing U-boat, and got too far out of course. In that case, it was not a U-boat casualty - all of which were annotated in both German and American records. Obviously, the *Hermod* and the Sub Wreck are two different wrecks, as they exist at two different locations. This begs the question: What is the name of the Sub Wreck?

Virginia - Screw Wreck and Steel Sailing Vessel

ures some thirty feet in length and four feet in width; it rises three feet from the bottom. The side that opens away from the main wreckage is open. The interior is generally swarming with sea bass, and the occasional lobster.

Ten feet farther past this isolated chunk is the main bow section. It lies perfectly on its starboard side, perpendicular to the centerline of the main wreckage. The stem is very evident. The stem curves around the bottom of the hull and becomes the keel. This bow section measures some thirty feet in length, and rises more than ten feet above the bottom. The side facing the main wreckage (and facing the angled chunk) is partly open and penetrable. Tautog hide inside the spacious interior, as do lobsters.

At left is the eponymous screw, or propeller, of the Screw Wreck.

Steel Sailing Vessel

GPS: 37-48.516 / 74-57.055 Loran: 26987.0 / 41974.9
Metal hull, medium relief Depth: 95 feet

On some charts this wreck is called the *Madrugada*. The site is close to the historic location given in official Navy documents. At first glance, the wreck is even similar to the *Madrugada* in size and general appearance. Yet it cannot possibly be the *Madrugada* for a number of reasons. The hull is ferrous metal whereas the hull of the *Madrugada* was wood, and there is no sign of propulsion machinery or associated piping or valves (the *Madrugada* was a diesel assisted schooner).

As a matter of precision, I favor calling this wreck the Ferrous Metal Sailing Vessel (or ex-Sailing Vessel). The rusted hull might be constructed of iron rather than steel, and only a laboratory analysis can determine the difference. Also, in sailing lingo, a "ship" was a precise description of a sailing vessel's rig. A ship had three or more masts that were rigged with square or quadrilateral sails (sails that spread from side to side). Thus a ship was clearly distinguished from a bark or brig or schooner. Ted Green thinks that my suggested name is pedantic and overly cumbersome, and I am forced to agree.

This wreck is absent any rigging, thus classifying the vessel as a barge. Most people picture a barge as a double square-ended vessel that is either pushed or towed. By strict definition, a barge is any unrigged vessel without means of propulsion. When the age of sail was waning, and steamships were taking the place of sailing vessels, many old sailing vessels were dismasted and converted to barges. Such a barge would still retain the hull configuration of a sailing vessel, and would then be classified technically as a schooner barge, a ship barge, and so on.

The Steel Sailing Ship appears to be a converted barge. From stem to stern the wreck measures some 225 feet. The highest point of relief is the extreme stern, where the gracefully flared hull supports the fantail and the post stubs of the taffrail. The rudderpost and steering arm reside on the remains of the after deck. Underneath, in a washout that goes as deep as 99 feet, the sternpost and rudder are clearly exposed. The rudder is canted at about 20 degrees, with the top in its proper position and the bottom disappearing into the sand several feet to starboard.

Moving forward, both port and starboard sides depict a clearly defined waist: like a bathtub buried to its upper lip. This waist is likely the turn of the bilge; the vertical sections of the hull appear to have collapsed outboard, and are not exposed. The height of the waist varies from two to four feet. The interior is filled with enough sand to cover the keelson. No cargo is in evidence.

Thick debris appears in the middle of the wreck about seventy-five feet forward of the stern. A metal ring along the centerline is likely the placement hole for a mast. Forward of the mast ring is the perfect outline of a hatch coaming. Wooden planks stretch fore and aft on the port side of this hatch. These planks appear to be remains of the upper deck. Forward of this area, the wreck (including the waist) terminates by descending gradually beneath the sand.

One might be inclined turn around at this point. However, by taking a nonintuitive leap of faith, one can traverse seventy-five feet of open granular sand that is the off-white color of eggshell, and reach the bow section. This section lists about 20 degrees to port, and rises to a height of eight feet or so. The length of the section is twenty feet or more. The stem is clearly distinguishable. The shiny metal of a hawsepipe can be seen underneath the port side. About ten feet abaft the stem, a massive windlass lies canted where it crashed through the deck and came to rest. A large anchor is resting against the windlass. The anchor stands vertically with the arms and flukes at the top, and the shank going down into the debris, appearing much like an artistic rendering of a capital "T".

I conducted this survey in the month of November. At that time, the wreck was inhabited by thousands of black sea bass. They schooled like a cloud of gnats, so thick that in places the visibility was reduced from thirty feet to less than ten. I could easily see a hundred at a single glance, even with the horse-blinder effect of a scuba mask. They hugged me so tight that I felt like a tuna fish in a can. The interior space of the bow section was choked solid with bass, so that there was hardly any room for them to swim. The hawsepipe was worn smooth, I suspect, by the constant rubbing of their bodies.

Amid this dense school of bass were the largest tautog I have ever seen. The monster of the pack was a yard long, with a girth that approached the size of my chest. No lobsters, though.

Virginia – Steel Sailing Vessel and Steel Vessel Barge

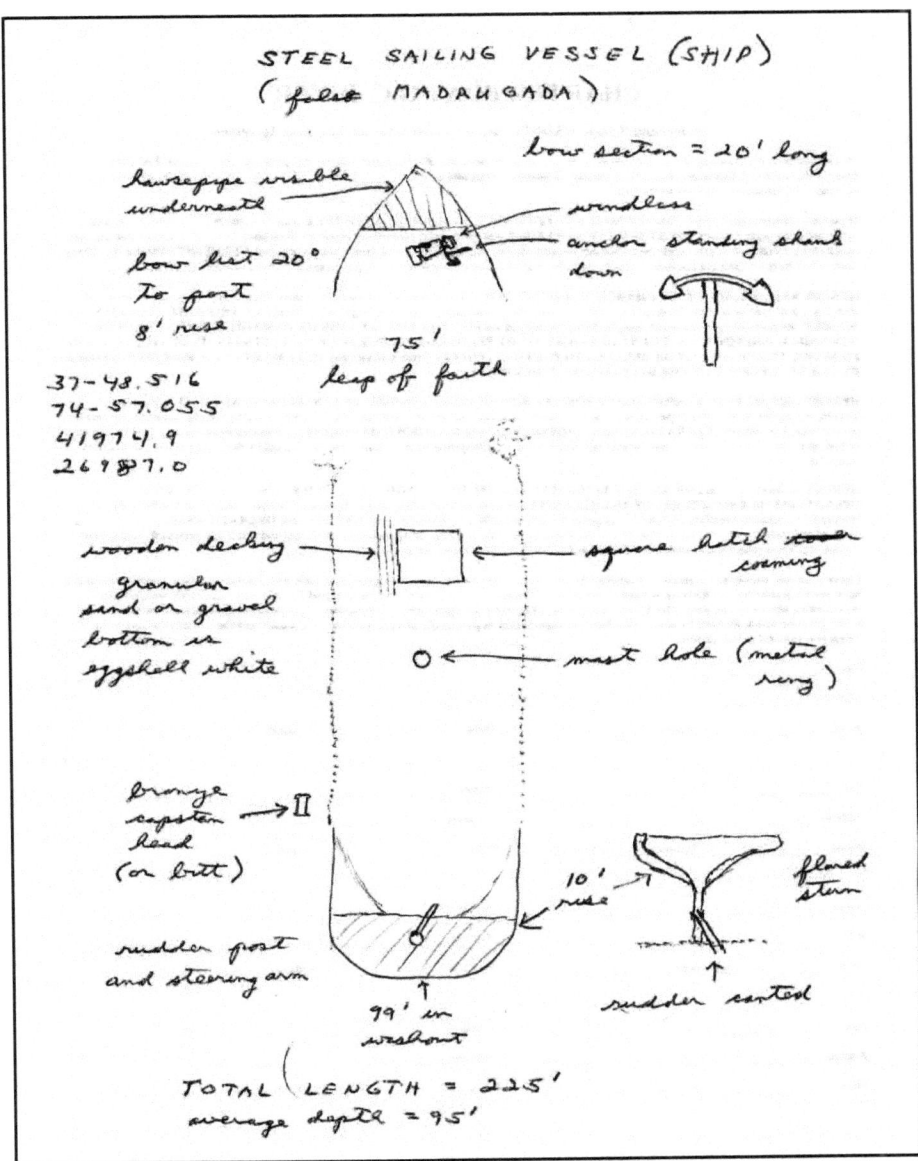

I called the Steel Sailing Vessel the false *Madrugada* because the real *Madrugada* had a wooden hull.

Steel Vessel Barge (alias False Powell)

GPS: 37-32.078 / 75-13.769 Loran: 27038.0 / 41766.4
Metal hull, high relief Depth: 95 feet

    The highest point of relief is the fantail, which rises 20 feet above the bottom. The list of the stern can be readily ascertained by the tilt of the rudderpost: about 45° to starboard. Forward of the rudderpost, near the bottom of the counter stern, the propeller

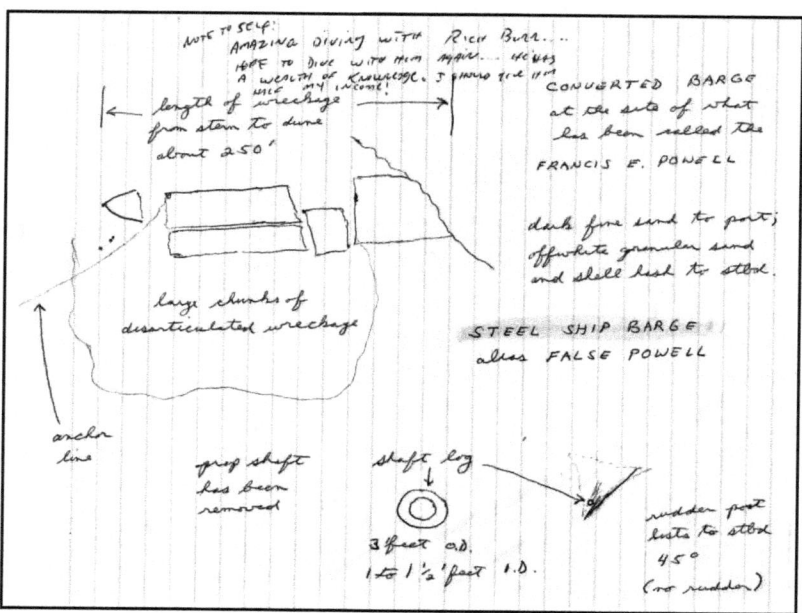

After I made this drawing, I changed my initial name from Steel Ship Barge to Steel Vessel Barge, in order to be generic instead of specific. Note that Richie Burr has been at it again, writing on the sheet, "Note to self: Amazing diving with Richie Burr. . . . Have to dive with him again. . . . He has a wealth of knowledge. I should give him half my income." This kind of camaraderie goes on all the time.

shaft gland implies steamship construction. Upon close inspection, however, one can see that the shaft gland does not contain the stub of a shaft – as it would if the propeller had been salvaged after the vessel sank. Instead, the gland is empty, implying that the propeller shaft must have been removed before the vessel sank.

Furthermore, no signs of propulsion machinery or associated steam pipe and fittings are visible anywhere on the wreck. The vessel was obviously constructed as a steamship, but removal of the engine and boilers converted the vessel to a barge. The outside diameter of the shaft log measures three feet; the inside diameter measures about one to one-and-a-half feet. One can see (and stick a hand or arm) a foot or two inside the gland. An interior bulkhead must have sealed the gland from the sea.

This stern section extends forward about thirty feet. A ten-foot space then separates the stern from the rest of the wreck, which extends forward and to starboard; the height of this wreckage ranges between four and six feet. Large sections of hull, with gaps in between sections, extend some 250 feet – before a sand dune marching from port covers the forwardmost section. No discernible bow or stem is exposed; rather, the wreck is gradually overburdened with sand until it is no longer exposed; the stem is buried under the dune.

Much disarticulated wreckage exists to starboard of the main hull sections. The sand on the port side of the wreck is dark and fine, while the sand on the wreck and to starboard is off-white and granular, and contains shell hash.

Large tautog and myriads of black sea bass inhabit the wreck; many large flounder were in evidence. Despite the presence of lobster pots on the wreck and along its perimeter, I saw few lobsters, and those that I saw were small.

Sub Wreck
(alias Bottle Wreck, alias Pipe Wreck, alias Norwegian Freighter)

GPS: 37-52.065 / 75-03.432 Loran: 27075.1 / 42519.0
Metal hull, low relief Depth: 85 feet

This wreck is most definitely not the *Hermod* (which see), as some people call it, for that Norwegian freighter ran aground on Winter Quarter Shoal.

The Sub Wreck (to call it by one of its aliases), is the wreck of a nineteenth-century steamship. The highest point of relief is the top of the compound engine, which stands nearly twenty feet tall. Forward of the engine lies a pair of boilers, side by side. Each boiler measures fourteen feet in diameter and twelve feet in length. A donkey boiler lies forward of the boilers, on the centerline. What appears to be a condenser lies on its end adjacent to the starboard side of the starboard boiler.

The rest of the wreck is considerably broken down. Most of the hull has fallen outboard so that the machinery area is surrounded by a large field of low-lying debris in the shape of a lozenge that exceeds two hundred feet in length. The only other major recognizable feature is a section of propeller shaft midway between the engine and the propeller. Two blades of the propeller are exposed, protruding upward like Mickey Mouse's ears.

Although this meager description makes the wreck sound less than exciting, the wreck holds a continuing fascination to divers because of the artifacts that have been recovered: clay pipes, Coke bottles dated 1909 (and still packed in cases, as discovered by Doug Buckley), and lead linotype in single column widths such as that which was printed on newspaper. Danny Fisher showed me some of the linotype that he recovered. The type was reversed, so I held one up to a mirror and read the heading: *The Admirable Crichton*. I let out a yelp when I deciphered the title because it has always been my favorite play; I read it in high school. James Barrie, the author of *Peter Pan*, wrote this classic piece of literature in 1902.

Scott Jenkins found a V nickel that was dated 1902. Part of the cargo that has withstood the ravages of time consisted of peanuts! Ted Green told me that the peanuts were tested, and found to be a Virginia hybrid. This implies that the vessel was outbound from the Chesapeake Bay when it sank.

Above right: An enlarged and reversed picture of the linotype so that the title is readable. Below: The full length of linotype. The lettering is not as legible as it should be due to corrosion from the chemical bath in which it was submerged for so many years.

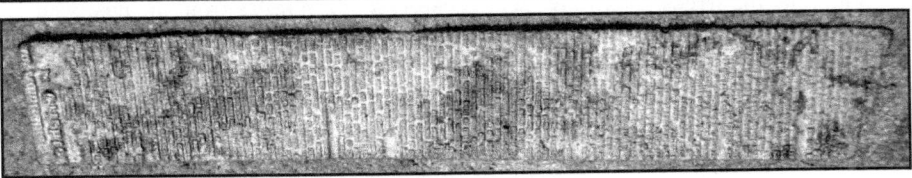

Agnes E. Fry (plus Virginius)

Have you ever wondered why the vast majority of shipwreck discoveries have been made by wreck-divers, and hardly any by marine archaeologists? There is a good reason for this disparity. The reason is dedication.

The average wreck-diver works a fulltime job during the week, and spends time, money, and effort to dive on the weekend. He (or she) buys his own equipment, pays for maintenance on that equipment, pays for air fills, pays his own transportation costs to the shore, and pays a charter fee upwards of $100 per day.

In my own case, I have done voluminous archival research on shipwrecks, purchased thousands of photographs, bought tens of thousands of pages of photocopied materials, and traveled to museums and archival facilities all over the country: and all at my own expense. This research led me to the approximate locations where unfound shipwrecks went down. In this manner, for example, I discovered all ten of the Billy Mitchell wrecks, among others. I also organized expeditions, chartered boats, and paid my own way in an endless search for lost shipwrecks, then discovered their locations and dived on them as a way of verification.

Some wreck-divers went a different and perhaps more expensive route. People like Rusty Cassway, Joe Mazraani, Harold Moyers, and Brian Simpson, spent tens or hundreds of thousands of dollars to build or purchase a dive boat for the express purpose of searching for elusive long-lost wrecks: and succeeded in achieving their ambitions.

On the other hand are marine archaeologists. They do research only when they are paid a salary to do it. They spend no money out of their own pockets. They do not devote their weekends or take time off work to conduct in-water search operations. What they do best is garner media attention when someone pays them to do their jobs.

Archs gripe about treasure hunters who take enormous financial risks to search for valuable shipwrecks which usually do not pay off. They claim that treasure hunters are money-grubbing thieves whose only purpose in the business is to make a profit. Yet the archs themselves are the real money-grubbers, for they spend their entire careers working for a salary. Archs are pots calling kettles black. The only time they search for shipwrecks is when they are given money to do so. Like this...

On February 27, 2016, such a shipwreck search project was funded by the National Park Service, and ultimately met with fortuitous success. North Carolina's Underwater Archaeology Branch (nee Unit) towed a side-scan sonar unit along the waterfronts off Caswell Beach and Oak Island, near the mouth of the Cape Fear River, where three Civil War blockade runners were known to have gone aground close to shore in about 10 feet of water: the *Agnes E. Fry*, the *Georgianna C. McCaw*, and the *Spunkie*.

It should have come as no surprise that they found a wreck, because historical sources placed three of them precisely at that spot. The reason why it (or they) had never been found before is simple: no one ever bothered to look for them. I should also mention that the wreck sites were located barely a dozen miles from the headquarters of the Underwater Archaeology Branch, at Fort Fisher.

At first there was some doubt about which wreck had been located. According to the side-scan sonar image, the length of the target measured 225 feet. This eliminated the *Georgianna C. McCaw* from being a contender because her hull measured only 179 feet from stem to stern. But this sidewheel steamer had to be nearby. She was

Agnes E. Fry. (From the author's collection.)

chased ashore on June 2, 1864, while attempting to make her first run through the Union blockade. Her hull and superstructure were so exposed that for the remainder of the war, Union blockaders used the wreckage as a waypoint when describing their locations in dispatches.

The USS *Victoria* shelled the helpless vessel and turned her to a demolished hulk. The shore battery added to the mayhem at daylight. Union forces boarded the vessel shortly after she grounded, and were the first salvors to recover valuables from the wheelhouse: "Two chronometers, one barometer, one sextant, one marine clock." Sixty tons of Confederate cargo was left to rot and rust. The boarding party set the wreck afire before they disembarked.

At 191 feet in length, the side-wheel steamer *Spunkie* was closer in size but too short for the cigar. She stranded on February 9, 1864 "a short distance west of Caswell." Union forces tried to pull her off the bar: "Two tugs have been daily employed since then in endeavors to extricate her from her position, but without avail, notwithstanding the very favorable weather we have had for several days past, but as the wind has veered to an opposite point S. W., with a lob barometer and threatening appearances, it is to be hoped she has made her last trip." This last sentiment came to pass. Heavy surf broke the wreck in two.

Furthermore, both vessels were constructed "of an earlier design." The *Georgiana C. McCaw* was built in Great Britain as the *Dundalk*, and had seen service under the British flag before she was purchased by the Confederacy. She was not purpose-built for speed and maneuverability as a blockade runner. The *Spunkie* was a riverboat that was built in 1857, and was not even designed for ocean service.

Ironically, in 1985, the Underwater Archaeology Unit (as the Branch was known at that time) mentioned both the *Spunky* (sic) and the *Georgiana C. McCall* (sic) in its massive tome entitled "National Register of Historic Places Inventory," but made no mention of the *Agnes E. Fry*. Nor had the Unit (or Branch) made any attempt to search for these wrecks over the span of 31 years – until the NPS paid NC archs to conduct a search.

In any case, an educated guess pointed to the *Agnes E. Fry* as being the submerged culprit because "it's the right shape." By that, it was meant that she was a purpose-built blockade runner, with a narrow beam and pointed stem so she could cut through the water with maximum speed while making radical turns to slip between Union blockaders and avoid enemy gunfire, much like the sleek rum runners of the Prohibition era.

NC archs told the press that the significance of the *Agnes E. Fry* was that it was the first Civil War blockade runner to be discovered in North Carolina waters "in decades," and "since the 1970's." What they neglected to mention was that the person who was the most responsible for researching, locating, and salvaging Civil War shipwrecks was not a State archaeologist, but a lone individual who single-handedly did everything on his own and at his own expense: E. Lee Spence.

Spence compiled two massive tomes whose titles are self-explanatory: *Shipwreck Encyclopedia of the Civil War: North Carolina, 1861 – 1865* (1991), and *Shipwreck Encyclopedia of the Civil War: South Carolina and Georgia, 1861 – 1865* (1991). Spence has done more research on Civil War vessel losses off the three named States than the entire staffs of the archaeology branches of all those States as long as they have existed. He has also discovered more Civil War shipwrecks, surveyed them, and salvaged them, than all three archaeological branches in the three named States.

'Nuff said.

The discovery of one more is a minor local detail, not a national media event. Nonetheless, the discovery of any previously undiscovered shipwreck has a value all its own. My point is that the *Agnes E. Fry* could have been discovered decades earlier if State archaeologists were more dedicated to their profession than simply viewing archaeology as merely a salary-paying job. They could have looked for it on weekends the way wreck-divers do, and paid for the cost of the search. But they didn't.

Again, 'nuff said.

Dives to the wreck revealed the absence of the machinery and paddle wheels, with only one boiler remaining. This evidence jived with the fact that the *Agnes E. Fry* was partially salvaged in the 1880's. I have often said (and written) that most shipwrecks are identified not by the recovery of an artifact with the name of the vessel given on it, but by a preponderance of evidence. This wreck fills the bill.

Best yet was a beautiful side-scan sonar image, courtesy of a high-tech and sophisticated 3-D state-of-the-art unit that was provided by the Charlotte Fire Department, plus a volunteer team of search and rescue divers who were experts at working under water in low- or no-visibility conditions. This resulted in a high-res sonar mosaic that is almost a photograph of the wreck.

North Carolina - Agnes E. Fry

Additionally, volunteer students from the ECU Maritime Studies Program helped in the project by diving and recording their findings. Divers recovered a knife handle, a deck light, and a lump of coal – but this is the kind of coal that an arch would like to find in his Christmas stocking.

The wreck lay a quarter mile from shore in 18 feet of water: deeper than when it initially sank due to continually shifting sand. Relief above the seabed was 6 to 8 feet.

So much for the wreck. How about the ship?

The *Agnes E. Fry* was built in 1864 by Caird & Company in Greenock, Scotland, under the name *Fox*. She was built for Crenshaw & Company specifically as a Confederate blockade runner.

During the Civil War, the Confederate States of America were desperate for supplies which their agrarian society could neither make nor manufacture. To prevent these much needed goods from reaching Confederate hands, the Union navy established a blockade of warships around each of the South's ports. The blockade threatened to force the Confederacy to its knees by figuratively starving the South into submission. This situation forced the Confederacy to have blockade runners built for them in British shipyards. Those blockade runners that passed the blockade found a ready market for everything they could provide, and a fantastically high prices.

The earnings were so extraordinary from successful deliveries that British entrepreneurs joined the business of blockade running. The profits that were generated by a single successful voyage almost paid for the construction of the vessel. Two successful voyages resulted in enormous profits for the owner.

From *Frank Leslie's Illustrated Newspaper.*

CAPTAIN JOSEPH FRY.—[FROM A PHOTOGRAPH BY T. LILIENTHAL, NEW ORLEANS.]

A blockade runner needed an audacious skipper. Enter Captain Fry.

Fry was born in Florida in 1826. At the age of eight he was sent to Albany, New York to live with his grandparents and to receive his formal education. When he reached his fifteenth year, he began his nautical career with the United States Navy. He attended the Naval Academy at Annapolis. After passing his examination and being promoted to midshipman, he earned his baptism of fire while serving aboard the *Vixen* during the Mexican-American War.

In 1849, Fry married his first cousin, Agnes Evelina Sands. He was then attached to the United States Coast Survey, where he served aboard the sidewheel steamer *Robert J. Walker*. (Parenthetically, the *Robert J. Walker* sank off the coast of New Jersey in

1860. Today it is a favorite fishing and diving spot. For complete details, see *The $25 Wreck of the Robert J. Walker*, by this author.) After that he commanded the coast and geodetic survey schooner *William A. Graham*.

After fathering a daughter, and still ranked as a midshipman, in 1851 he embarked on a round-the-world cruise that lasted for four years. The vessels on this expedition served under the command of Commodore Matthew Perry during his commerce negotiations with Japan, which at that time was an isolated sovereign nation that declined to trade with other countries. Perry's gunboat diplomacy included firing blanks at Yokosuka as a way to intimidate the Japanese into allowing him to land and to negotiate trade agreements. Instead, the Japanese wanted him to go to Nagasaki, the only port city that foreigners were permitted to visit. Perry declined. (The U.S. did not officially visit Nagasaki until August 9, 1945, when an atomic bomb was dropped on the city.) Eventually, the Japanese relented, and signed a very limited agreement.

From *Life of Capt. Joseph Fry the Cuban Martyr*, by Jeanie Mort Walker.

Fry returned to the States in 1855. The Navy assigned him to shore stations and short cruises that allowed him to spend more time at home, and enabled him to father six more children in his spare time. His second voyage to the South Pacific was far shorter than his first one.

Upon commencement of the Civil War, Fry resigned from the Union navy and joined the fledgling Confederate fleet. He was promoted to lieutenant. His first command was the *Ivy*, a small tender that steamed among the forts on the Mississippi River. Not content with courier service, and reporting movements of the blockading squadron, Fry took it upon himself to engage three Union warships that were protecting two Union blockaders that had run aground at the mouth of the river. Cannonading was hot and heavy.

Fry approached the stranded steamers. "Finding that it was useless to continue at long range, I ran down within easy range of the enemy, and firing so as to take perfect aim at him, my shell exploded alongside of his smokestack. It was then reported to me that the flag officer was calling us, and I reluctantly left at the moment when I was able, for the first time, to hull the *Richmond* every time."

Fry's one shell "struck her on the quarter," but the *Richmond* lived to fight another day.

Next, Fry took command of the *Maurepas*. His new duty was to defend Confederate forts along the river. On March 21, 1862, Fry wrote in a letter to his wife, "I have been leading a most active sort of life since I came here, and this is the first morning that I have not been up at daylight. I do not think I have averaged more than three hours' sleep in twenty-four for the last five days. . . . We have been struck eight or nine times by cannon balls, and probably by thirty or forty [minie] balls. The deck has been covered with splinters; my back, also; my stove-pipe cut in two in the cabin; my table, secretary [desk], sideboard, looking-glass, etc., all smashed and scratched; and yet nobody hurt, except one man, who had a twenty-four-pound cannon ball pass between his feet without touching him! – cutting his trousers, however, and knocking him, heels over head, about twenty feet."

The Confederates retreated upriver. Fry had the cannons removed from the *Maurepas* and transported overland to form a battery on high ground. On June 16, "A shot from one of Fry's heavy guns penetrated the steam-chest of the *Mound City*, by which she was immediately enveloped with scalding steam, her men leaping from the portholes into the water."

This short-term victory led to a long-term defeat. Fry was wounded by a minie ball that pierced his right shoulder, leaving his arm useless. He and a number of his men were captured by Union forces. He was later exchanged. While he was recovering from his wound, he spent several months with his growing family in Georgia.

When he returned to service, he was placed in command of the blockade runner *Eugenie*. Again he distinguished himself: "On one occasion the *Eugenie*, when coming in loaded with gunpowder, ran on the bar outside of Fort Fisher, within range of the guns of the blockading squadron. Fry was ordered from the fort to abandon his vessel in order to save his crew from what was considered an inevitable explosion. Determined to save his ship or perish with her, he sent off, in small boats, all of the men who would go; and then remained at his post, with shells falling in the water all around him; lightened her, and with the tide carried her safely in – a deed of cool gallantry not surpassed in the annals of war."

After a year of running the Union blockade, he worked in St. Thomas, Bermuda as a government agent for the Confederate navy.

On July 5, 1864, Fry received orders "to take command of a steamer purchased for Government by Crenshaw." He immediately embarked on a passage to Greenock, Scotland, where the *Fox* was under construction. Fry changed the name of the *Fox* to *Agnes E. Fry*, after his beloved wife. He oversaw her fitting out (the vessel, not his wife), then returned to Bermuda in order to boldly engage in running the brand new sidewheel steamer through the Union blockade.

Over the next several months, Fry made four successful trips up the Cape Fear River to Wilmington, North Carolina. After each inbound run, he then had to make an outbound run through the blockade to either Bermuda or Nassau, the Bahamas, in order to take on munitions and supplies for the following run.

This is not to say that he made every successful run on the first attempt. On more than one occasion the *Agnes E. Fry* was driven off by the blockading squadron and had to return to her port of origin (Bermuda or Nassau). Blockade running was a harrowing business. Audacity must be tempered. Knowing when to turn back was equally as important as sneaking between Union vessels in the dark of night.

According to the U.S. consul at Bermuda, "The *Stormy Petrel* is commanded by Captain Gordon, who has made twenty-seven voyages through the blockade." On the other hand, "The *Talisman* is commanded by Captain Gilpin, who has been captured three or four times."

Fry's successful runs – or his run of successes – ended on December 27, 1864. The *Agnes E. Fry* ran aground west of the Cape Fear River. Her crew rowed to shore in boats. The *Chickamauga* transported Fry and his crew to Wilmington.

At first, Confederate army forces thought that they might be able to salvage the *Agnes E. Fry*, or at least the cargo and machinery if not the hull. But after examining her position with respect to the reach of the cannons of the blockading squadron, the Confederates decided to abandon the wreck.

Meanwhile, Union forces thought that they might be able to salvage the wreck. According to U.S. Navy Lieutenant W.B. Cushing: "I respectfully represent that the Confederate steamer *Agnes C.* [sic] *Fry* is beached on the coast 2 miles to the southward of Fort Caswell. She is not bilged and is in first-rate order in every respect. She is built of five-eighths-inch iron, has splendid engines, is about 1,000 tons, and handsomely fitted out. The ship is about 20 yards from the low-water mark in a bed formed in the quicksand, and could easily be launched by proper means, that are not at our disposal here. She is worth, if launched, $150,000."

Such was not to be. A war was being waged, and the proper equipment was not forthcoming. So there she lay, her superstructure fully exposed.

As noted above, her machinery and one boiler were salvaged sometime in the 1880's.

Thus ended the short saga of the *Agnes E. Fry*. But this was not the end of Joseph Fry. The following spring found him in Mobile, Alabama in command of the *Red Gauntlet*. That command was short-lived. Soon Fry transferred his flag to the gunboat *Morgan*, guarding the river "to prevent the enemy from erecting batteries, and to shell their infantry."

From the thumbnail sketch of Fry's Confederate service that I have already provided, you will have an idea of his aggressive nature in attacking his assigned duties with gusto. Fry continued in this vein, "firing wherever there were indications of activity on the part of the enemy."

In April of 1865, Fry and his crew were down below eating dinner when the *Morgan* was struck by a shell. Fry immediately yelled, "All hands to quarters." The gallant men manned the cannons and returned fire on the Union battery, while shells whizzed through the air or struck the ship, inflicting severe damage. All too soon, the battery got the range and the *Morgan* ran out of ammunition. A plank was blasted out of the hull at the waterline. The hole was too large to plug.

Fry weighed anchor and steered the crippled ship toward shore. The *Morgan* steamed slowly up the Tombigbee River to Demopolis, where she sat for a week before the Union advance overtook the area, and Fry was forced to surrender the ship. Once again Fry became a prisoner of war.

The Civil War came to an uncivil end a few weeks later. Fry was released and returned to his family, who were then living in New Orleans, Louisiana.

For Fry came the doldrums. He was no longer a naval officer. He had spent his entire career in the navy, and knew no other kind of work. He had no job, nor any prospects of finding one. He spent the next eight years eating from hand to mouth, and often not eating at all. At times he was unable to feed his large family.

North Carolina - *Virginius*

Both woodcuts are from *Life of Capt. Joseph Fry the Cuban Martyr*, by Jeanie Mort Walker, which was published in 1875. The caption for the one above reads "*Tornado* in pursuit of the *Virginius*." The caption for the one below reads "Capture of the *Virginius*." On the following pages I will employ woodcuts to illustrate the executions of Joseph Fry and some of the passengers and crewmembers. The full story is told in *Shipwrecks of North Carolina: South*. Some of the following images are from *Frank Leslie's Illustrated Newspaper*. The weekly journal had neither a correspondent nor an artist on site, but used local stringers to piece together the awful events and to visualize how those events must have appeared.

SPANIARDS TRANSFERRING PRISONERS FROM THE "VIRGINIUS" TO THE "TORNADO."

GEORGE WASHINGTON RYAN.   JESUS DEL SOL.
BERNABE VARONA.   PEDRO CESPEDES.

He invented a process for processing ramie fiber by separating it from its bark, but was never able to obtain the funds to commercialize his invention. He joined the New Orleans Academy of Sciences. He worked on science projects. But he never found fulltime employment. . . .

. . . at which point we skip eight years and segue to his final command, the *Virginius*.

In *Shipwrecks of North Carolina: South*, I covered the *Virginius* Affair in exacting detail. There is no need for me to repeat the whole saga here. But after the earlier publication, I was able to obtain some additional information about Fry,

After the prisoners were transferred to the *Tornado*, they were landed and imprisoned until they were executed. (Above and opposite bottom are from *Life of Capt. Joseph Fry the Cuban Martyr*. Remainder are from *Frank Leslie's Illustrated Newspaper*.)

THE SPANISH OUTRAGE ON THE AMERICAN FLAG—CAPTURE OF THE "VIRGINIUS," AND KILLING OF RYAN, VARONA, DEL SOL, AND CESPEDES.

North Carolina - *Virginius* 147

CAPTAIN FRY OF THE "VIRGINIUS" TAKING LEAVE OF HIS COMPANIONS BEFORE THEIR EXECUTION.

and woodcuts that should have graced the original chapter, so I wish to publish them here. Furthermore, I wish to note connections between the *Agnes E. Fry* and the *Virginius*, especially as the two wrecks lay less than fifteen miles apart.

In July of 1873, broke and destitute, wearing nothing but rags, and without money

EXECUTION OF CAPTAIN FRY AND HIS COMRADES.

Spanish depredations began before the prisoners were dead. Above: Living prisoners were bayoneted. (From *Life of Capt. Joseph Fry the Cuban Martyr*.) Below: Spanish officers trampled prisoners who were still alive, by riding their mounts over them. (Source unknown.) Opposite top: Spanish soldiers drove horse-drawn carriages over the bodies. (from L'Illustration), Opposite bottom: The bodies of the dead were loaded onto carts. (Source unknown.)

The "Virginius" Butchery.
Spanish Horsemen Trampling the Dead and the Dying Victims into the Slaughter-house Trench at Santiago de Cuba.

LES EXECUTIONS DE SANTIAGO DE CUBA. — LES CADAVRES FOULÉS AUX PIEDS DES CHEVAUX, APRÈS L'EXÉCUTION.

to feed his family, Fry went to New York to try to find a vessel to command. He was lucky. He met General Manuel Quesada, an agent of the Cuban Republic that was trying to overthrow Spanish rule of that island in order to gain independence. Quesada owned a vessel in Jamaica which he planned to use to sneak arms and ammunition to the rebels.

The vessel was the Confederate blockade runner *Virgin*, which was built in Scot-

After the Shooting of the Crew of the "Virginius."
Negroes of the Chain-gang Tumbling the Dead Bodies of the Victims into Mule-carts.

THE LOST "VIRGINIUS"—TRANSFER OF THE CREW TO THE "OSSIPEE."

land in 1864, and specifically designed to run the Union blockade. She was now named *Virginius*, and was about to resume her original purpose. She was registered as an American vessel. This registration provided protection on the high seas from Spanish vessels that patrolled the island in search of Cuban junta vessels/

The *Virginius* needed a commander. Blockade running was a job that was right down Fry's alley. Quesada offered to pay him $150 per month, with payment for the first month's service to be paid in advance. Fry accepted the post. He immediately sent $100 to his wife. He kept $50 "to replenish his own dilapidated wardrobe and procure his outfit."

To make a long story short, the Spanish warship *Tornado* captured the *Virginius*, and imprisoned the passengers and crew. The four leaders of the expedition were executed at once. Joseph Fry and forty-eight others were executed later. Some of these men were British subjects.

The United States and Great Britain were on the brink of waging war against Spain. Without any sense of logic, Spain claimed that the *Virginius* was a pirate ship. A pirate is "one who robs at sea or plunders the land from the sea without commission from a sovereign nation." The definition fit the *Tornado* but not the *Virginius*, which was landing men and materiel.

Intense negotiations resulted in monetary reparations for the families of the deceased, and the return of the *Virginius* to the United States. The *Virginius* foundered before reaching safe haven.

In Fry's final letter to his wife – a letter that he wrote in a Cuban prison – he reminded her that when he resigned from the U.S. Navy in order to join the Confederacy, the Navy owed him money which he never claimed.

On June 11, 1878, a Congressional committee made the following report:

North Carolina - *Virginius* 151

The Committee on Naval Affairs, to whom was referred the bill (H.R. 272) for the relief of Mrs. Agnes E. Fry, widow of Joseph Fry, beg leave to report in favor of the passage thereof.

The claimant in this case is the widow of the late officer in the United States Navy who resigned in 1861, for the purpose of entering into the service of the Confederacy, and who did in fact enter into such service. At his time of resignation, there was due to this officer a small balance on account of salary, and the bill authorizes the Secretary of the Navy to adjust and pay this balance, amounting to less than $200.

The only reason for its non-payment heretofore, and that is the question in the case, is that, being "disloyal," under the prohibition of existing laws the claim cannot be paid.

In the opinion of the majority of the committee the non-payment of the amount due for services rendered to and accepted by the government prior to the alleged act of rebellion, would be "confiscation," illegal in form and man-

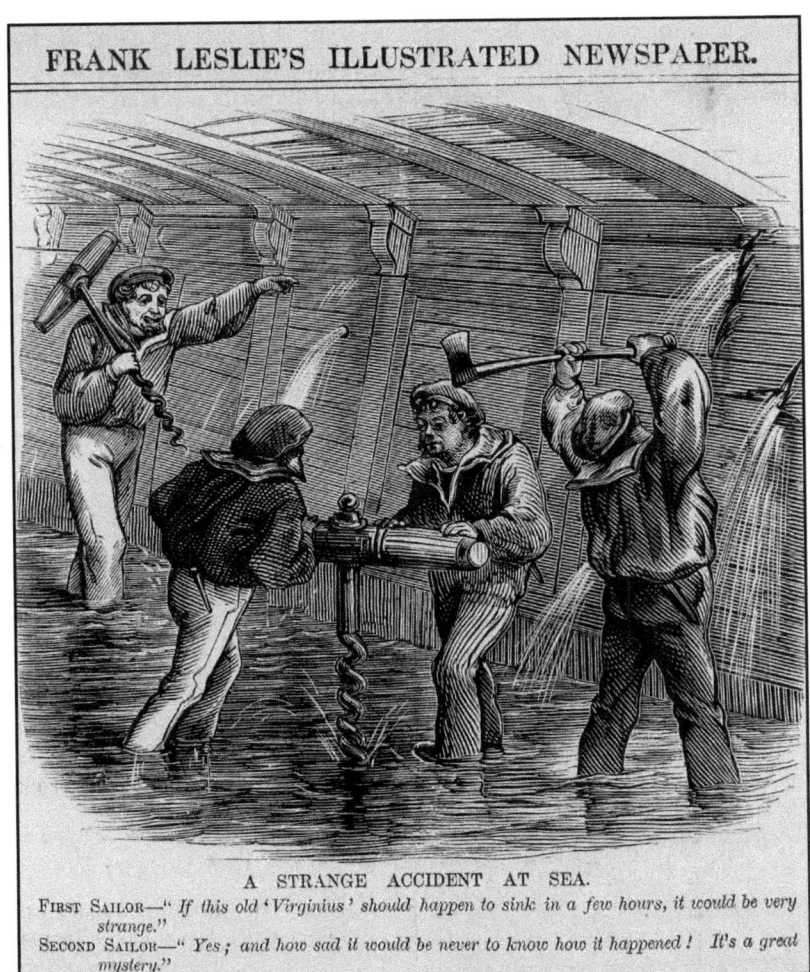

FRANK LESLIE'S ILLUSTRATED NEWSPAPER.

A STRANGE ACCIDENT AT SEA.
First Sailor—" If this old 'Virginius' should happen to sink in a few hours, it would be very strange."
Second Sailor—" Yes; and how sad it would be never to know how it happened! It's a great mystery."

ner, or repudiation of a just and legal liability. Wherefore they report in favor of the passage of the bill.

On March 19, 1885, Agnes Fry wrote a letter to Secretary of State Thomas Bayard. This letter explains some of the circumstances that followed the terrible tragedy that was brought about by the illegal capture of the *Virginius*. Note that her memory was remiss with respect to dates and numbers.

> Sir,
>
> I respectfully appeal too you in the matter of the *Virginius* Ind.[emnity] Fund.
>
> I am the widow of Joseph Fry, Captain of the Steamer *Virginius* when that steamer was captured off the coast of Cuba, in Nov. 1874 by a Spanish vessel – taken into port at Santiago de Cuba and with thirty six of his crew, executed on the 7th of Nov. 1874.
>
> Spain paid to the U. States Government a certain amount as indemnity for the execution of Capt. Fry and his crew. In 1875 those heirs of the men executed, who presented their claims, were paid by the Government a certain portion of this Ind. Fund – retaining the balance in case other claimants should present themselves.
>
> In this division I received, as the widow of Captain Fry, Six thousand dollars. It has been several years since the last claim was presented and from the fact of the small number of crew who were executed thirty seven in all for the benefit of whose heirs the "*Virginius* Ind. Fund" was paid, and that the heirs were well acquainted with the fact of Spain having paid the U. States this money for their benefit. If they have not to the present time submitted their claims there can be no possible or probable chance that any additional claimants will ever present themselves.
>
> I therefore respectfully appeal to you, that you will have this matter examined into, that Justice may be done me and my children who are sadly in need of the money justly due them, and which is now lying in the U.S. Treasury by ordering it distributed as the Government intended when Spain was required to pay it for their benefit.
>
> I have the honor to be your obedient servant
> Agnes E. Fry

Statistics (of *Agnes E. Fry*)

Built: 1864
Previous names: *Fox*
Gross tonnage: 559
Type of vessel: Iron-hulled, side-wheel, blockade runner
Builder: Caird & Company, Greenock, Scotland
Owner: Crenshaw & Company, Greenock, Scotland
Cause of sinking: Ran aground
Sunk: December 27, 1864
Depth: 18 feet
Dimensions: 236' x 25' x 13'
Power: Coal-fired steam
Location: Cape Fear River, 400 yards off the beach at Fort Caswell, North Carolina
GPS: coordinates withheld by the North Carolina Underwater Archaeology Branch

SINKING OF THE STEAMER "VIRGINIUS."

Alligator Creek Barges

This chapter is about a 2008 canoeing adventure and the recovery of a porthole without going underwater . . . or even getting wet. It came about partly by accident, but also partly because Cheryl Novak and I did a great deal of canoeing in the wilderness of the East Dismal Swamp, on streams that no one has paddled since Indians occupied the area.

One day we went canoeing on Alligator Creek, in Tyrrell County, North Carolina: about 20 miles west of Manteo, on Roanoke Island, which itself is east of the Outer Banks and towns like Kitty Hawk and Kill Devil Hills. Alligator Creek feeds the Alligator River near the Albemarle Sound. The river and sound are part of the Intracoastal Waterway. This particular exploratory trip carried us along the north shore region where no roads existed. We sought small inlets or animal trails that might lead us into the unknown interior.

Something caught my eye as I stared ahead and around: what appeared to be a long, low vessel against the opposite shore of the creek. The assignation of "creek" is somewhat of a misnomer that gives the wrong impression of the size of the waterway. Alligator Creek qualifies as a narrow body of water farther upstream, where we had begun our sojourn, but at our current location it measured a quarter mile in width; and farther downstream it measured nearly a mile across.

We paddled toward the vessel out of curiosity. As we approached closer, the vessel resolved itself into three overlapping steel barges that were sunken in the shallows. What I originally mistook as superstructure from a distance turned out to be a crane and a tugboat on top of one of the barges. We moored against the laden barge in order to investigate. The barges had been there for such a long length of time that trees had taken root in windblown dirt that had accumulated in crevices.

The decks were badly rusted. Where deck plates were missing I could look down into the water-filled holds. Miscellaneous equipment lay scattered about: a mushroom anchor, cracked bumpers, huge tractor tires, and so on. The crane was still fitted with its treads and derrick. The blunt-bow push-boat had been stripped of its engine and instruments in the wheelhouse, but – lo and behold – still had one of its iron portholes in place!

When we returned a few weeks later, the canoe was burdened with tools: the standard wreck-diver's assortment such as crowbar, sledge hammer, chisel, and drift-pin

North Carolina – Alligator Creek Barges

Opposite page: Barges as they appeared from the canoe. Note the huge tractor tires on the barge to the right.

Top: Trees growing on the steel deck.

Above: Mushroom anchor and bumpers.

Left: Steering quadrant.

Alligator Creek Barges - North Carolina

Above: Crane and push tug.

Left: Engine room of the tug with a view of the wheelhouse.

Opposite bottom: Starboard side of the engine room. Note the porthole on the right.

Opposite above: The porthole after it was removed.

North Carolina - Alligator Creek Barges

punch; plus box wrenches, open-end wrenches, socket wrenches, and a pipe wrench. The porthole was bolted to the hull. I tried finessing off the nuts with wrenches, and succeeded with some of the nuts. But the rest were rusted in place. As it turned out, brute strength was easier: I easily sheared off the heads with a chisel. And I didn't have to come up for air! To add to the day's haul, I removed an inclinometer from the crane.

I asked Charlie Ogletree about these barges. He had lived in the area for thirty years or so, and was somewhat of a historian on local events and happenings. He told me that the barges had been used to support construction of the bridge across Croatan Sound in the early 1950's. The bridge connected Roanoke Island with the mainland.

The barges had been laid up ever since, rusting away because the bridge builder did not want to pay to have them removed. And there they rested (and rusted) for more than fifty years.

The eyesore barges have finally been hauled to the scrap yard, thus beautifying the creek shore.

Curlew

The *Curlew* is one of those shipwrecks that is known by only a few people who delve into archives in order to conduct primary research. Yet the history of the wreck is fascinating and should be popularized.

The *Curlew* was an iron-hulled side-wheel steamer that was propelled at 10 knots by a pair of paddle wheels that measured eighteen feet in diameter. A coal-fired boiler provided steam to turn a walking beam engine whose iron shaft was geared to the two paddle wheels.

The *Curlew* was built to the order of Thomas Warren: a wealthy farmer and part-time doctor. He was the president and principle investor in the Albemarle Steamboat Company. The *Curlew* commenced commercial service in 1856. Her five-foot draft enabled her to navigate shallow waters. For the next five years she served as an excursion boat to the outer banks, and transported freight along the rivers and sounds in the vicinity of Edenton, North Carolina.

At the approach of the Civil War, North Carolina seceded from the Union. To protect the State from Union aggression, North Carolina embarked upon a program to acquire arms, ammunition, an organized militia, and vessels to patrol the waterways of the State. The *Curlew* was one of those vessels that was purchased during this military build-up. Under this new guise, she operated as a troop transport.

North Carolina joined the Confederacy at the outbreak of war. Thus the *Curlew* became part of the Confederate Navy. Her skipper was Captain Thomas Triplett Hunter. Some of the after structure was removed in order to make space for a gun. Another gun was emplaced on the bow. The *Curlew* was now officially designated as a gunboat.

The *Curlew*'s first engagement occurred on September 29, 1861, when she found the Union transport *Fanny* anchored off Roanoke Island (the present site of Manteo). The *Curlew* blocked the inlet while the *Fanny*'s crew transferred supplies to a lighter. Backup soon arrived in the form of two more Confederate gunboats: *Junaluska* and *Raleigh*. For half an hour the three Confederate gunboats traded shots with the *Fanny*. Neither vessel was seriously harmed in the engagement. Nonetheless, because the *Fanny* was outgunned, the skipper decided to run his boat aground so that he and his men could avoid capture. The Union sailors got away, but the Confederates obtained a valuable cargo.

In early October the *Curlew* accompanied five other gunboats in an attempt to kick the Union soldiers off Hatteras Island. Constant shelling of the fort forced the Union army to retreat – but only long enough until reinforcements arrived. The Union quickly reoccupied the fort while the Confederate soldiers beat their way back to the boats, which then departed.

For the next three weeks the *Curlew* was engaged in reconnaissance patrol. On October 24, she made contact with two Union vessels: *Cor>*

win and *Stars and Stripes*. Both sides opened fire from a distance of three miles, with guns from a Union-held fort lending assistance, but none of the vessels sustained any damage.

This kind of waterborne guerilla warfare and cannonading sniper fire continued throughout November with very little fanfare and hardly any consequence except to keep the Union soldiers and sailors at bay. The year ended ignominiously with neither side taking nor yielding ground.

Then the Burnside Expedition arrived. General Ambrose Burnside was an indefatigable Union officer whose massive mutton chops gave birth to the whiskery name "sideburns." In February of 1862, Burnside arrived at Hatteras with some 17,000 Union soldiers, to combat less than 2,000 Confederate defenders. In addition, Admiral Goldsborough commanded twenty gunboats against the slap-dash Confederate fleet of eight.

General Ambrose Burnside. (Courtesy of the National Archives.)

Thus the Confederate ragtag army was both outmanned and outgunned in what came to be called the Battle of Roanoke Island. Fighting commenced on February 7, 1862. Troop strength approximated eight and a half to one on the side of Union forces; naval guns measured four and a half to one against the Confederacy. The outcome was a forgone conclusion. The only statistics that held any meaning were how many men would die, and how many vessels would sink.

The naval battle took place in Croatan Sound: between Roanoke Island and the mainland to the west. The *Curlew* was struck twice by Union gun fire. The first shell badly wounded the pilot, Eli Williamson. The second shell smashed a hull plate and opened the hull to the sea. With the *Curlew* fast taking on water, Captain Hunter took his vessel out of action and steered toward shoal water in case the *Curlew* sank.

Captain Parker, skipper of the Confederate gunboat *Beaufort*, noted: "Her captain, finding she was sinking, started for the shore, and as he passed me, hailed; but I could not make out what he said, and he being a very excitable fellow (the North Carolinians called him Tornado Hunter) I said to Johnston that I thought there was nothing the matter with him. 'Oh, yes there is,' said J., 'look at his guards.' And sure enough he was fast going down. I put after him in the *Beaufort*, but he got her ashore in time."

Parker added this likely apocryphal tale, "To show what an excitable fellow Hunter was: he told me afterward that during the fight this day he found to his surprise that he had no trousers on. He said he could never understand it, as he had certainly put on a pair in the morning. I told him I had heard of a fellow being frightened out of his boots, but never out of his trousers."

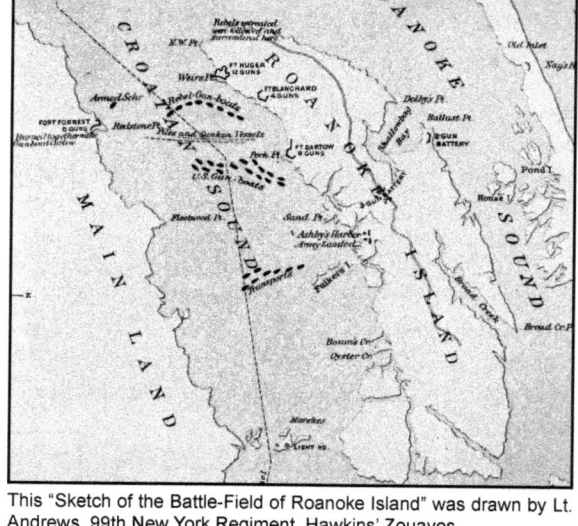

This "Sketch of the Battle-Field of Roanoke Island" was drawn by Lt. Andrews, 99th New York Regiment, Hawkins' Zouaves.

Parker's latter sentiment sounds improbable. His first observation was definitely inaccurate: the *Curlew* ran aground on a midstream shoal half a mile from land, not on shore.

Although the *Curlew* was *hors de combat* (French for "out of action"), she still could serve a useful purpose as her magazines contained cannon powder and shot that could be employed on fellow gunboats. Thus the *Fanny* drew alongside the stranded *Curlew* so that ammunition could be transferred from one gunboat to the other.

By the end of the day, the Confederates has expended all their ammunition and were forced to retreat to Elizabeth City via the Pasquotank River and the Dismal Swamp Canal. That night, under cover of darkness, three Confederate vessels were dispatched to recover from the *Curlew* the remaining ammunition, the cannons, and everything that was worthwhile taking.

Hostilities resumed the following day. Ironically, the presence of the grounded *Curlew* proved to be a threat to her Union counterparts, because Union forces did not know that she was unable to move; they believed that she was anchored there to protect the Confederate Fort Forrest, which stood nearby on the western mainland.

Soon, however, Union soldiers were on the verge of capturing the fort. Colonel Henry Shaw, the highest ranking officer and in charge of the Confederate troops, ordered the cannons to be spiked, the ammunition to be detonated, and the fort to be set afire before the trapped soldiers were forced to surrender to superior forces.

The torch was also put to the *Curlew* so that she could not be salvaged by the Union fleet. And so the *Curlew* was destroyed where she sat on a sandbar. Captain Hunter and the crew of the *Curlew* were rescued by the Confederates, and continued to fight the battle in other ca-

North Carolina - *Curlew*

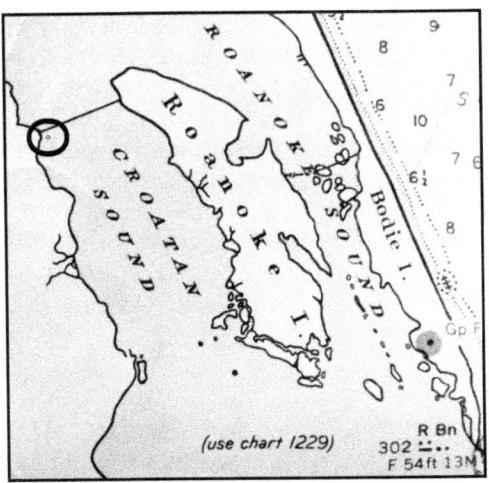

I drew a circle on a modern nautical chart where I think the *Curlew* likely lies, but the wreck could lie either east, south, or southeast of this approximate position.

pacities . . . all for naught.

Union forces overwhelmed the Confederate army and navy by sheer might of numbers and fire superiority. Within two days after the Battle of Roanoke, the Confederate soldiers either surrendered or scattered out of harm's way, and the remainder of the Confederate fleet either fled or was captured or scuttled.

Resting in only 10 feet of water, with her walking-beam engine rising high above the surface, the *Curlew* stood as a tragic monument to the fierce battle that had raged in Croatan Sound and on Roanoke Island. This tall marker lasted until 1863, when a salvage outfit removed the engine and associated machinery. That left little if anything exposed except at extreme low tides. Eventually the hull collapsed altogether so that nothing of the wreck protruded above the waves.

And there she lay, forlorn and forgotten . . . until 1988, when a youth group of international students located the wreck after a five-day search with a magnetometer. These recreational divers recovered a host of artifacts that included portholes, pottery shards, cannonballs, and ultimately the builder's plaque, the latter of which confirmed the wreck's identity.

Disarticulated wreckage lay scattered across the bottom in a geometric oval that measured approximately one hundred feet in length. Low relief prevented the wreck from being a hazard to navigation. While the existing wreckage may not be much to see, the sunken *Curlew* serves as a link to the past, when Civil War raged, when soldiers and sailors fought and died, and when the country was divided by opposing cultural standards.

There is an unusual follow-up to the loss of the *Curlew*. When the Confederates removed the guns, ammunition, and other supplies from the stranded steamer, they also took the two flags that the gunboat carried in the face of battle: an English Union Jack and a nine-star flag of the Confederate States of America.

The Union Jack was flown in order to disguise the true nationality of the vessel when running a Union blockade or passing a Union fleet, stalling or avoiding altogether an enemy attack.

The particular Confederate flag in question was a rarity. According to Paul DeHaan, one-time owner of the flags, the nine-star flag was "authorized only after the admittance of Arkansas to the Confederacy on May 18, 1861, and before the admittance of the tenth state, North Carolina, on May 21, 1861. Confederate naval records reveal that the CSS *Curlew* was commissioned on that very day – May 21, 1861."

According to the provenance, the *Curlew's* flags were captured from the CSS *Ellis* – one of the three vessels that stripped the *Curlew* before demolishing her – when Union forces overran the Confederate troops and captured the gunboat afloat. The flags passed through a litany of owners until they were purchased by Civil War collector DeHaan.

It is supposed that there are less than five nine-star Confederate flag still extant.

Statistics

Built: 1856
Previous names: None
Gross tonnage: 236
Type of vessel: Iron-hulled side-wheel steamer
Builder: Harlan & Hollingsworth, Wilmington, Delaware
Owner: Confederate Navy
Cause of sinking: Shelled, stranded, then set afire
Location: About 300 yards, nearly equidistant from the bridge to the north and the shore to the west

Sunk: February 7, 1862
Depth: 10 feet
Dimensions: 135' x 23' x 8'
Power: Coal-fired steam

Estelle Randall

She was beautiful in her heyday and essential for providing the transportation of goods and people who lived along the shores of the Potomac River and around the Chesapeake Bay: her primary operational area for most of her career, from 1897 to 1909.

In those nascent colonial times, in case you have forgotten your high school history, Washington threw a silver dollar across the Potomac River. He could not perform such a feat if he were alive today, because a dollar does not go as far.

The country was rough and rugged in the days before paved roads, tractor-trailers, and sleek automobiles. The three modes of conveyance available to fin de siecle Americans were horse-drawn wagons, railroad trains, and vessels that were driven by either sails or coal-powered steam engines that turned paddle wheels or propellers. The *Estelle Randall* was one of the latter.

Life was hazardous and travel was more hazardous. For those who lived near inland waterways, carriage by boat was the fastest, safest, and most luxurious way to go.

The *Estelle Randall* possessed a fully paned salon that extended nearly half of her registered length of 111 feet and all the way across her beam. Fore and aft of her center salon, plus a full-length upper deck that was open to the air, afforded accommodation to as many as 600 excursionists. The *Estelle Randall* could very well have been named the Esteemed Randall without any attempt at exaggeration.

This extravagance earned for the *Estelle Randall* the praise of "one of the largest and most magnificent passenger and freight steamers in North Carolina."

Which is not to say that there were no complications . . .

In 1899, "The steamer *Estelle Randall* collided with the steamer *Kent* in Port Tobacco Creek. The case was investigated November 22, 1899, and the license of Harry S. Randall, master of the steamer *Estelle Randall*, was suspended for a period of fifteen days."

This may be difficult to imagine today, but in 1905, the Potomac River was frozen solid. According to a DC newspaper account on February 4, "In the lower course of the river, where the channel is more pronounced and the ice generally thinner, the ice offers great difficulties to navigation. Three powerful naval tugs, the *Triton*, *Tecumseh*, and the *Choctaw*, attempted to take a barge laden with material to the power factory at Indian Head, Md., yesterday. Battling with cakes frozen together to the thickness of three or four feet, they broke several big hawsers in pulling the barge between here and Alexandria, where they arrived after being in the river nearly all forenoon. The *Estelle Randall* left yesterday morning with the mail for Glymont. At noon she was about Fort Foote. A steamer arrived from Norfolk about midnight Friday morning, and the report was that from off Ragged Point to the city the river was frozen over with a solid sheet of ice."

Explosives were used to break up the ice. Those were what folks refer to as "the good old days."

But wait! There's more! Two weeks later, the river ice had grown thicker. "The past few days of biting cold weather have had the effect of solidifying the coating of ice on the river so that in many places it is now three and four feet thick. Harbormaster Sutton is making plans for opening a channel.

This antique image of the *Estelle Randall* is from the author's collection. Note the name in reverse on the after flag.

NEW POTOMAC RIVER PASSENGER PROPELLER ESTELLE RANDALL, BUILT BY WILLIAM E. WOODALL & CO., AT BALTIMORE.

"Tugs will be sent down the river to open up a passage through which the ice can go when broken up. The larger tugs of the fleet under command of Mr. Sutton will break the ice above the bridges and the smaller boats will be detailed in the work of preventing it from jamming at the piers. The following tugs will be called into service. . . .

"The harbor boat *Vigilant* and the Randall Line steamer *Estelle Randall* will also aid. The latter is armed with a plow and is able to break through the heaviest ice."

On March 4, 1905, in anticipation of a parade to celebrate the inauguration of Teddy Roosevelt as President of the United States, "The steamboat *Estelle Randall* arrived last night and reported having followed in the wake of the transport *Arcadia*, containing the Porto Rican troops, all the way up the river from Mathias Point, where the latter had been aground for two days. The *Arcadia* is now anchored at Alexandria and the troops will come from there by rail this morning."

It was not until April of 1905 that "Four companies of artillery, which will participate in the maneuvers on the Potomac this summer, were taken to Fort Washington by the steamer *Wakefield* yesterday. The eleventh Company of Coast Artillery, consisting of seventy-three men, under the command of Capt. R. R. Ward, arrived yesterday morning by rail from Key West, Fla. and preceded the other companies on the regular trip of the *Estelle Randall* to the fort."

I should mention at this point that the so-called Randall Line was owned by licensed captain Ephraim Randall. The *Estelle Randall* was named after his daughter. Harry Randall was the elder master's son.

In July of 1905, it was noted, "The United States army quartermaster's department tug *Gibbon* has taken her place on the route between this city and fort Washington and Fort Hunt, in place of the steamer *Estelle Randall*, which has returned to mercantile service on the river."

North Carolina - Estelle Randall

No sooner had she returned to mercantile service than on July 14, "William Crowley, a member of the crew of steamer *Estelle Randall*, was drowned in the harbor of Washington. Case investigated October 12, and found that no licensed officer was responsible for said drowning while acting under the authority of his license."

The *Estelle Randall* continued to operate on her usual rounds. In 1907, it was reported that "Henry Wilber, thirty years old, of Pisgah, Charles County, Md, was taken in an ambulance to the Casualty Hospital yesterday afternoon [July 28] from the steamer *Estelle Randall*, at the Eighth street wharf, suffering from a severe gash in the leg. The wound was inflicted with an ax during a fight at Glymont, Md. The man was suffering greatly when he was admitted to the hospital. It is said that the fight was the result of differences over the ownership of a number of tools."

Later in 1907: "The excursion of the Audubon Society to Fort Washington this morning on the Steamer *Estelle Randall* from the Eighth street wharf, will start at 8 o'clock instead of 9 o'clock, as previously announced."

And still later in 1907: "William Dentz, colored, a deckhand on the steamer *Estelle Randall*, narrowly escaped drowning yesterday. He was washing the upper deck of the steamer when he lost his balance and fell into the river. Deckhands rescued him. The steamer was anchored at the Seventh street wharf."

Somewhere along the way, Ephraim Randall changed the name of his solely-owned company, as is shown in the following article.

In 1909, "The steamer *Capitol City*, of the Potomac and Chesapeake Line, while en route from Norfolk to Washington, ran aground a short distance below James Point Light, Alexandria, during a sense fog early yesterday morning. When the fog lifted the *Estelle Randall*, of the same line, and the naval tug *Tecumseh* went to her assistance, but it was found that she was firmly imbedded in a mud bank, and her passengers were transferred to the *Tecumseh* and carried to Washington. During the day several efforts to dislodge the *Capital City* were made, but it was not until high tide, about 7 o'clock last night, that she was floated and it required the united efforts of the *Estelle Randall* and the *Wakefield*. The *Capital City* it is stated, was not injured."

In case you missed the point, the *Estelle Randall* stayed to render assistance because both she and the *Capital City* were owned by Ephraim Randall's company.

The following notice appeared within weeks of the incident above: "The steamer *Estelle Randall*, which for the last eleven years has been running on a route between this city [Washington] and Glymont, Md. [on the Potomac River], has been sold by the Potomac and Chesapeake Steamship Company to parties in Norfolk. The steamer was turned over to them at Norfolk Friday [December 3, 1909]. She is to be used on a route between Norfolk and Elizabeth City, N. C., through the Dismal Swamp."

This area of North Carolina was practically inaccessible by land because of its location in the aforementioned Dismal Swamp. The place was called the Dismal Swamp because it was, well, dismal, and because, well, it was a swamp. Still is (or still are).

I know a great deal about the area because I have owned a rental property there since the year 2000, and because I spent a great deal of time and effort on exploring its highways and byways – mostly its byways: the swamp land and streams that are seldom hiked or paddled.

The *Estelle Randall* also collected from and delivered mail to towns to which the word "rural" was a gross exaggeration: towns that bordered the sounds inside the Outer

Banks; sounds such as the Albemarle and Pamlico, and population centers such as Elizabeth City, Edenton, Columbia, and other whistle stops. My house is located in Columbia, in Tyrrell County.

Consider this modern comparison. I was born and raised in Philadelphia (which is a city that fills the entire county). Two million people reside in Philly. The current population of Columbia is around 600.

Tyrrell County is twice the size of Philadelphia, yet the population is only 4,000. There's a lot of empty space for growing corn, cotton, and soybean. And a lot of swamp that is practically impenetrable except along the waterways.

Now imagine how remote and isolated this area must have been when the *Estelle Randall* was in service. Her route from Norfolk led to Virginia Beach, thence onto the Dismal Swamp Canal (today part of the Intracoastal Waterway), thence to Elizabeth City and into the Albemarle Sound, and thence to all points on the compass.

The new owner ("parties in Norfolk") was the Farmers & Merchants North Carolina Line. The *Estelle Randall* proved not to be a worthwhile investment for this company, for barely a month and a half later she was destroyed by fire on the Scuppernong River at the downtown wharf in Columbia. Fourteen people were on board at the time of the catastrophe. All but one managed to escape with their lives.

A year later, "The American Security and Trust Company, acting as trustee of the Potomac and Chesapeake Steamboat Company, yesterday [January 13, 1911] instituted suit for $10,000 against the Hartford Fire Insurance Company in the District Supreme Court, through Attorneys C A. Douglas, Paul Dulaney, and Hugh H. Obear. The action grows out of the alleged refusal of the insurance company to live up to the terms of a fire insurance policy which, it is claimed, entitled the trustee to considerable money when the steamer *Estelle Randall* was burned."

I figure that the American Security and Trust Company must have been holding the mortgage on the boat. They should have known that avaricious insurance companies make money by collecting premiums, not by paying claims.

According to the North Carolina Office of State Archaeology, "The North Carolina Underwater Unit has been spearheading an effort to record and recover significant portions of the wreck's machinery and artifactual content prior to a waterfront clearing project. The work is a cooperative effort between the Underwater Archaeology Unit and Columbia and Tyrrell counties to conduct research and restoration on the remains of the *Estelle Randall*.

"The majority of excavation, which was necessary for the recovery of the machinery, has been conducted by volunteer divers Eddie Congleton, Mitch Moore and Kenneth Bland. During this work they recovered a large variety of shipboard implements, personal effects, and machinery accessories such as steam gauges and grease lubricators. With the help of heavy equipment and operators donated by Waff Contracting, Inc. of Edenton, the machinery from the Estelle Randall was recovered in November 1992. The major items retrieved were a vertical, direct-acting, vertical air pump; a duplex feed-water pump; an early Westinghouse generator housing and the ship's rudder.

"The unit is in the process of inventorying and stabilizing the many small artifacts. Within the next year restoration will begin on the machinery. A collection of small artifacts is now on display in Columbia and it is hoped that the interest generated will lead to a local museum that deals with the area's maritime history and features the *Es-

telle Randall."

As noted above, I had a rental property built in Columbia in the year 2000. As a result, I spent an inordinate amount of time in Columbia. Yet in all those years, I was unaware of the display of any artifacts from the *Estelle Randall*. Perhaps, in the eight years since the recovery operation and the time I built my house, the artifacts had been placed in storage or returned to the Unit.

While I am on the topic, I must assert that the above three paragraphs that were devoted to the recovery operation are grossly understated. Those who worked on the project received short shrift for doing a job of such monumental proportions. Granted that the water is shallow, but visibility in the Scuppernong River varies from 0 to 1 foot; it rarely in the plural.

I made my first dive on the *Estelle Randall* in 1995. My dive buddy was Jon Hulburt. By dive buddy I mean that we both went into the water at the same time; but we never saw each other on the bottom. When my head ducked under the surface, I could see for at least several inches in the ambient light of a sunny sky. But a foot under water the visibility dropped to zero, as in none, nothing, nada, zip, zilch, and diddly squat. I could not see my dive light in front of my face. I could not see the wreck at all but it *felt* good and solid.

I groped my way around the wreck with my dive light switched off. What was the point of wasting battery life when the only time I could see the tortured beam was when I pressed it against the face place of my dive mask? The iron hull was thinly encrusted with what felt like rust. Touch was my only working sense. The metal surfaces were rough and jagged. When I reached the river bottom at the edge of the hull, there was no need to be careful of stirring loose mud in order to prevent a silt out. This was already the ultimate braille dive.

I occasionally popped to the surface and waited for Jon to do the same. We conversed about our feelings; that is, our shipwreck feelings. After exploring the perimeter and crisscrossing the wreckage, I perceived a strong mental image of the wreck's appearance: much like a side-scan sonar image after processing and refining. We discussed distinctive features that each of us had "observed."

Jon gave me directions to specific features by telling me to feel my way along an obvious structure that each of us had explored, then turning at notable waypoints which he described in detail. I did the same in return. In this manner I returned to certain places and followed his conceptual map in order to feel features that I had missed; and vice versa.

I also explored off the wreck in the hope of finding ancient discarded bottles. After all, the wreck lay within a few feet of a no-long-existent wharf from which people were likely to toss glassware into the water. Searching for bottles proved fruitless because the riverbed was overburdened with trees and branches that had drifted downstream from the swamps to the north. This wildwood litter prevented me from reaching the bottom anywhere except in the immediate vicinity of the wreck site.

Nonetheless, I made one startling discovery. I felt a curved object which possessed a bumpy outer surface and a smooth inner surface that was marked by metal interruptions. I worked my hands around the object which proved to be circular. This round whatsit was connected by two bars to frame of some kind. The doohickey frame led me to another protrusion that was shaped like a flumadiddle T, which enabled me to move the circular thingamabob.

A bicycle! I had found a bicycle!

I pulled it out of the muck and tangled tree limbs, then dragged it to shore. Except for a few rust spots, the bike appeared to be in excellent condition. After the dive, I gave the bike to my friend and attorney Charlie Ogletree. He and his wife Midge lived right on the waterway, where the *Estelle Randall* lay in front of their yard. Charlie turned over the bike to the police. Their investigation established the ownership of the bike, and solved a three-month-old case of theft. They returned to stolen bike to the rightful owner: a local high school student. Case closed!

After a two-hour bottom time with no decompression penalty, Jon and I finally surfaced above the *Estelle Randall,* and swam thirty feet to shore, where our other halves waited patiently. I can't say that the dive was fun, but it certainly was instructive. And both of us now possessed a comprehensive perceptual likeness of the parts of the wreck that the archaeologists left behind.

Several years later, I did a solo dive on the *Estelle Randall*. Charlie Ogletree asked me to inspect his boat mooring in front of his house. I made the inspection, found the mooring sound and in good condition, then moved a few feet away to the wreck site. I did this because I had an unbelievable 1 foot of visibility – on the bottom!

This time I could see features that I had previously only felt. With this newfound ability of ocular observation, I circumnavigated the wreck and examined every speck of the innards. Only a true wreck-diver can comprehend the satisfaction that I gained from this fortuitous and unusually great visibility.

Divers should know that the best time to dive on the wreck is in calm weather and especially during a drought, when the swamps that feed the Scuppernong River are less likely to push dirty water downstream.

As a point of interest, I found it disturbing that North Carolina archaeologists were responsible for conducting a salvage operation when the standard archaeological doctrine is preservation in situ. "In situ" is Latin for "in place," and with regard to archaeology it means to leave a wreck alone and let it rust, rot, and otherwise deteriorate without human interference or disturbance of the site. In other words, let nature take its course and let the wreck collapse and disintegrate.

The salvage of the *Estelle Randall* is a prime example of a double standard. Many, perhaps most, wreck-divers recover relics and artifacts from abandoned shipwrecks in order to display them in their homes or to donate them to museums for public exhibition. The Graveyard of the Atlantic Museum in Hatteras is holding hundreds of artifacts that were donated by wreck-divers. Yet those artifacts are not on display. They are stored in a huge back room because the archaeological community refuses to grant permission for the museum to display artifacts that were rescued by wreck-divers. Because NOAA partially funded the construction of the museum, it holds the reins on the way the museum operations. Because of NOAA, the museum is allowed to display only those artifacts that were recovered by NOAA salvors or by professional archaeologists.

. . .

. . . with two exceptions: the bell from the *Diamond Shoals* lightship, which was rescued and conserved by Uwe Lovas, Rom Lovas, and Stephen Lang; and the enigma machine from the *U-85*, which was rescued and restored by Jim Bunch, Richard Hunting, and Roger Hunting. All these people are dedicated wreck-divers. Apparently, the

North Carolina - Estelle Randall

importance of these artifacts outweighed NOAA's objections to their display. It's a good, thing, two, because without them the museum's display area would be totally devoid of artifacts that were rescued from local wrecks.

Meanwhile, enough artifacts to fill a warehouse are languishing out of public view because NOAA's bigoted hatred against wreck-divers, and archaeologists' egotistical vanity and outlook of holy supremacy, allow only these two relics to serve as exemptions from their very own rule.

It seems as if the archaeologists who were responsible for organizing the salvage of the *Estelle Randall* said, "Do what I say, not what I do." Or perhaps they believe that they have the God-given right to recover artifacts, but that wreck-divers do not.

Which makes me wonder whatever happened to the *Estelle Randall's* machinery and other artifacts. A very few small items are on display in the Columbia Theater Cultural Resources Center (a fancy name for "museum"). The majority are tucked away out of sight and sound. The public won't even hear about them, much less see them.

Statistics

Built: 1897
Previous names: None
Gross tonnage: 212
Type of vessel: Iron-hulled passenger/freight steamer
Builder: William E. Woodall & Company, Baltimore, Maryland
Owner: Farmers & Merchants North Carolina Line, Norfolk, Virginia
Port of registry: Washington, DC
Location: Scuppernong River, Columbia

Sunk: January 17, 1910
Depth: 8 feet
Dimensions: 111' x 24' x 7'
Power: Coal-fired steam
Cause of sinking: Burned
GPS: 35-55.07.26 / 76-15.18.17

Charlie Ogletree had this painting of the *Estelle Randall* especially commissioned. The wreck is located in the Scuppernong River almost directly in front of his house. The painting hangs on a wall in his living room.

Home

When I wrote the chapter on the *Home*, the wreck had not been located. Now it has!

Well, part of it, anyway. According to survivors' accounts, the *Home* gradually broke apart into a number of pieces as it drifted along the coast while passengers and crewmembers fell into the water one by one, and drowned. One piece drifted to shore and grounded on the beach, eventually to be covered with sand. That piece contained the machinery.

Years after I published the account of the *Home* in *Shipwrecks of North Carolina: South*, George Purifoy called me to tell me that on the way from the *Shurz* to the *Cassimir* he found a piece of wreckage that could be part of the *Home*. Afterward, George's son Bobby dived on either the same piece or another piece of wreckage which he identified as the *Home* by recovering a shipwreck's most prized artifact: the bell.

The bell weighs on the neighborhood of 200 pounds, stands 23 inches high, and measures 23 inches across at the base. No name was stamped on the bell, but raised letters read:

JAMES P. ALLAIRE
1837
NEW YORK

The *Home* was built in 1837 for the Southern Steam Packet Company, which was owned by James P. Allaire. The port of registry was New York. This is what I call proof positive.

Location withheld by both Purifoys. But George did tell me that the wreck lay in 115 feet of water some 30 miles offshore. The piece of wreckage was small - one might say tiny - perhaps little more than the slab of wood on which the bell was mounted.

I guess it's true: there's no place like home.

From *Early American Steamers*, by Erik Heyl.

Pulaski

Rob Penn spent a great deal of time in searching for the wreck – or parts of the wreck – of the *Pulaski*. After seven years, a fisherman friend handed over a set of co-ordinates which he thought might be the answer to his prayers. It was.

The location of the wreck not a secret. Many anglers fished on the Onslow Bay site without knowing its identity. To them, it was just another fishing spot. But when Penn descended to the wreck, and observed an old-fashioned engine with a paddle wheel shaft and an old-style boiler, he knew he had found and identified the *Pulaski* at last.

Recently I learned that he was no longer allowed to dive on the wreck because a treasure salvage outfit had arrested it: a legal process which establishes salvage rights in the name of the arrester, and which prevents interference in ongoing salvage operations; and, by doing so, denies further access to any and all.

The salvors in possession trade under the name Deep Blue Exploration: one of several subsidiaries of a Florida-based company called Swordfish Partners. The wreck was "discovered" by another subsidiary called Endurance Exploration. As the substitute custodian, Deep Blue Exploration has contracted Blue Water Ventures International to conduct the underwater operations.

According to a BWVI press release, dated November 2, 2017, they "have deployed to a shipwreck site thought to be the wreck site of the *Pulaski*, a paddle wheel steamship that sank in the waters off North Carolina in 1838. . . .

"Expedition personnel on board the BVWI Recovery Vessel Blue Water Rose are now conducting operations to undertake a systematic excavation of the wreck. Dive teams are making the necessary preparations on specific areas of the wreck, so members of the marine archaeological team can focus on positively identifying the wreck. Other members of the expedition are engaged in additional surveying and mapping of the overall site."

Another press release – dated January 3, 2018 – announced that the salvage divers "have begun recovery of coins and other artifacts from a shipwreck site believed to be the *Pulaski*, a paddle wheel steamship that sank off North Carolina June 18, 1838.

"The coins being found by the operations dive team are dated no later than 1836 and consist of early United States silver issues AND Spanish silver coins from the late 1700's. These recoveries provide further evidence that will lead to the identity of this shipwreck."

For updates, stay tuned to the expedition website: http://www.bwvint.com/.

After the wreck was identified, Pete Manchee apprised me of what he calls "kismet." The dictionary definition of kismet is fate or fortune, but in this regard it refers to irony or to an incredibly unlikely coincidence. The *Pulaski* is located only four miles from the *Cassimir*. Polish-born Casimir Pulaski was a well-known freedom fighter who fought against Russia in the Polish revolution, then fought against the British in the American Revolution. Very few people would have made the connection between the two shipwrecks. I know of only one.

Location of the *Pulaski* withheld by everyone.

Pirates of the
Queen Anne's Revenge

According to the age-old cliché, there's good news and there's bad news. In this case there is only bad news.

In a gross usurpation of personal and intellectual property rights, the State of North Carolina has signed into law a two-pronged Act which specifies that all State-owned, -funded, or -affiliated museums and similar historical repositories will automatically assume ownership of all cultural resources (specifically shipwreck artifacts) that are on temporary loan for public display, and will automatically strip copyrights from photographers who have let State agencies display their pictures and show their video recordings.

With regard to the latter part, the new law provides that, "All photographs, video recordings, or other documentary materials of a derelict vessel or shipwreck or its contents, relics, artifacts, or historic materials in the custody of any agency of North Carolina government or its subdivisions shall be a public record pursuant to G.S. 132-1. There shall be no limitation on the use of or no requirement to alter any such photograph, video recordings, or other documentary material, and any such provision in any agreement, permit, or license shall be void and unenforceable as a matter of public policy."

By placing photographs and video recordings in the public record, anyone in the world may use the images and recordings in any manner whatsoever (including advertising) without payment to the copyright holder.

In one fell swoop, North Carolina has authorized gross infringement of copyrighted materials by bureaucratic fiat.

This drastic measure was motivated by a recent lawsuit that was initiated by the discoverer of the *Queen Anne's Revenge*: a vessel that was under the control of Blackbeard the pirate when she ran aground in 1718 and was subsequently abandoned. A company called Intersal located the wreck in 1996. Intersal designated Nautilus Productions as a partner that was tasked with conducting underwater photography and videography of the wreck site.

Whenever North Carolina published photographs or showed video footage that belonged to Intersal, Intersal was supposed to be paid usage fees in accordance with its contract. However, the State reneged on payment, so Intersal filed a lawsuit for more than $8 million.

The State legislature's kneejerk reaction was to enact pre-emptive legislation against future usage and dissemination of copyrighted materials. The House bill to control media rights has been called Blackbeard's Law: a clear case of modern day political piracy.

I discussed this issue with a North Carolina attorney. After stating that the current Assembly was out of control with respect to this and other absurd bills, he noted that the Act is unconstitutional because its seeks to supersede federal law with regard to copyright infringement. This means that the State will get away with infringing on the copyrights of image makers until someone takes the issue to court.

As a result of this unethical law, Rick Allen (of Nautilus Productions) canceled

North Carolina - Queen Anne's Revenge

his participation in the 2016 shipwreck symposium that has been and will be sponsored by the Graveyard of the Atlantic Museum in Hatteras, North Carolina. I followed his lead and canceled my participation as well.

This is only a brief account of current events. Initially, I intended to include a long chapter in *Shipwreck Potpourri* in order to provide some history of Blackbeard's career, the events that led to the loss of the *Queen Anne's Revenge*, the discovery of the wreck, the subsequent archaeological work, the recovery of cannons and other artifacts, and an in-depth report on Blackbeard's Law and the resulting lawsuit. As the suit is still ongoing, I could use that as an excuse for not making this chapter longer than it is, but that would be dishonest. In truth, after doing some initial research, I soon realized that the whole story is so long and complex that nothing less than a book could do justice to the subject. Perhaps I will write such a book someday.

Although I cannot tell the entire story, I must at the very least emphasize the most important part of it: that the blatantly unconstitutional law was enacted purely as a measure to punish the hard-working people who discovered the wreck and captured images of it on film, by refusing to pay them their due.

Blackbeard was perhaps the most notorious pirate in the history of the world. Now his reputation has been superseded. Today the most notorious pirate in the world is the State of North Carolina. Here is hoping that the political pirates who framed Blackbeard's Law shall be hung not only in disgrace, but on gallows in public view.

In the 1951 Disney movie *Alice in Wonderland*, the Queen of Hearts shouted "Off with their heads." This is an appropriate quote and an acceptable action for the political pirates who legalized the theft of property: a sneaky, unethical, and unlawful way to avoid paying its debts. But in Lewis Carroll's original book *Alices Adventures in Wonderland*, the queen shouted "Off with his head." She said it only once, and she was referring to the Cheshire Cat. Come to think of it, North Carolina's politicians resemble the conniving cat: in action if not in appearance.

X Marks the Spot - or Does it?
Mixed-up Merchant Vessels (Continued)

In *Shipwreck Sagas* (2008) I wrote a chapter titled "Shuffled Shipwrecks of North Carolina," in which I furnished evidence that supported the notion that the identities of some of the vessels that were sunk by German U-boats in World War Two had been misidentified. I corrected the identities as best I could.

There was little doubt that my deductions – as well as those of other researchers – were correct. Yet the evidence was not conclusive; some of it was inferred.

To recapitulate: the first indication that all was not as it seemed occurred in 1987, when I recovered the bell from the wreck that was shown on the nautical chart as the *Malchace*. The name that was stamped on the bell was *Manuela*:

The *Manuela* bell had only part of the lip exposed.

After excavating the bell by hand I exposed the entire lip and the clapper.

a wreck that lay barely a mile away. Subsequently, observations of the layout of the not-*Manuela* established that it was instead the *Malchace*.

Another pair of freighters whose positions shared an inshore/offshore relationship were the *Buarque* and the *Equipoise*.

In 1992, I dived on the offshore freighter whose name on the chart was given as *Equipoise*. However, I recovered a pair of steam gauges whose place of manufacture suggested that the wreck was in fact the *Buarque*. By inference, if the *Equipoise* was then *Buarque*, then the *Buarque* should be the *Equipoise*: names that were interchanged a la *Malchace* and *Manuela*.

North Carolina - Mixed-up Merchant Vessels

Buarque gauges.

This assumption proved to be wrong. The so-called *Buarque* turned out to be the *Mexicano*. The *Equipoise* has so far not been located or identified.

Then in 1996, Robert Smith became the first person to announce the theory that a handful of tankers did not deserve the names that were given to them. After ten years of study – both historical research and dives on the wrecks – the fallout resulting from The Lost Tanker Project proclaimed the following: the so-called *Papoose* is the *W.E. Hutton*; the so-called *W.E. Hutton* is the *Ario*; the so-called *San Delfino* is the *Papoose*; and the so-called *Ciltvaira* is the *San Delfino*. The *Ciltvaira* has yet to be located or identified.

Smith has continued his researches throughout the years. He also formed a group of dedicated wreck-divers who go under the cognomen of the Surface Interval Diving Company, or SIDCO. The purpose of the group is to provide more evidence to prove that the newly given identities are accurate beyond a shadow of a doubt, or found guilty as charged, in order to convince recalcitrants of the absolute truth of the situation.

Some people – I call them Santa Claus huggers – are slow or reluctant or downright repudiative to adopt new ideas despite the overall validity of the facts before their eyes. These people prefer to maintain their dogged, self-delusional beliefs rather than to accept verified reality.

Notwithstanding the above, SIDCO found indisputable evidence that the wreck that was originally thought to be the *W.E. Hutton* is indeed the *Ario*, because they found a third mast on the wreck site. Topside photos of the vessels show that the *W.E. Hutton* was fitted with only two masts, whereas the *Ario* was fitted with three. As Smith noted in his project work report, the third mast was not exposed until recent storms and deep ground swells washed away sand and sediment.

The report also noted that the *Papoose* drifted for five days before finally sinking. When last seen, the *Papoose* was far offshore in the vicinity of the wreck that has always been called the *San Delfino*.

Best guess now is that the wreck that is alternately called the Green Buoy Wreck and the *Mirlo* is the *San Delfino*. For the future, SIDCO plans to concentrate its efforts on exploring the Green Buoy Wreck in order to confirm its identity; and to "try to locate and ground truth the *Mirlo* using the updated information we now have on her and the circumstances of her sinking."

I wish them great success in their underwater endeavors.

H. C. Brooks

I do not believe in omens, but in retrospect an incident that occurred aboard the *H. C. Brooks* certainly seemed like a portent of bad things to come. Consider this narrative:

The brig *H. C. Brooks* arrived at the anchorage on the 5th of August, (1870), seven days from Havana on the morning of July 28, and the Captain [Jefferson Briggs] sickened a few hours after he got to sea. Upon his arrival here [Charleston, South Carolina], he was quite weak from the attack, but fresh beef and champague [sic] in a few days restored him to ride out a quarantine of thirty-two days, making thirty-nine (39) days from his leaving Havana. No other cases occurred on board the *Brooks*. Her cargo was sugar and molasses.

The pestilential disease that concerned authorities the most was yellow fever. There had been outbreaks on other vessels in which scores of crewmembers died. Thus the reason for quarantine. With Captain Briggs out of action, a replacement captain was in command a month later when the ultimate disaster occurred:

The brig *H. C. Brooks*, Captain Shea, sailed from this port [Charleston, South Carolina] on Tuesday, the 18th instant, with a cargo of lumber, for Providence, (R. I.) On Monday afternoon, the 19th instant, in latitude 32 degrees, longitude 78 degrees, experienced a heavy Northeast gale, in which she sprung a leak. Keeping all hands at the pumps, the leak kept steadily gaining, and the vessel settled down. On Tuesday made a sail to leeward which proved to be the schooner *Zela Psi*, from Charleston for Philadelphia. The *Brooks* having become water-logged and unmanageable, the crew were compelled to abandon her, and were kindly received on board the schooner *Zela Psi*, which vessel brought all hands safely to Charleston, late Tuesday night. During the blow three seamen attached to the brig were washed overboard, but were fortunately rescued. There was nothing saved from her.

Pete Manchee thinks that a site known as the Ledge Wreck is the remains of the *H. C. Brooks*. He found very little wreckage and no cargo. As the cargo consisted of lumber, it would have been eaten away by rot, bacteria, and wood-boring mollusks (known as ship worms) over the last century and a half. The dominating wreckage and main relief is a pile of anchor chain and two large anchors. Manchee also found two mast steps, which would make the wreck a brig.

Manchee noted in correspondence to me, "Noting that absolutely identified this wreck as the HC Brooks......but, if it looks like a duck, quacks like a duck, swims like a duck......good chance it's a duck!"

The corollary to Manchee's principle of shipwreck identification is Occam's Razor, which states: "All things being equal, the simplest explanation is usually the best."

I have always said that most shipwrecks are identified not by the recovery of an item with the name stamped on it, but by a preponderance of evidence. Granted that a

South Carolina - H. C. Brooks

pair of mast steps and the absence of cargo hardly constitute a preponderance, the fact that the location somewhat approximates the very general latitude and longitude that were given in the newspaper article supplements the appearance of the wreck. The name will have to stand until the discovery of another brig is found in the area.

As information, the construction description states thus: "One deck, two masts, square stern, no galleries, a billethead." Undoubtedly, all these wooden accessories have long since rotted into nothingness along with the cargo.

The nickname Ledge Wreck was applied because the wreckage, such as it is, rests alongside a ledge that stands two feet in height.

Statistics

Built: 1854
Previous names: None
Gross tonnage: 162
Type of vessel: Wooden-hulled brig
Builder: Columbia, Maine
Owner: William Lindsey and Nathaniel Lindsey, Fall River, Massachusetts
Port of registry: Fall River, Massachusetts
Cause of sinking: Foundered

Sunk: September 19, 1870
Depth: 134 feet
Dimensions: 96' x 16' x 9'
Power: Sail

Loran: 45217.9 / 59802.2

Pete Manchee took this photograph of the chain pile and one of the large anchors. Very little else is exposed.

Leif Eriksson

In *Shipwrecks of South Carolina and Georgia* (2003), I wrote, "It has been suggested to this author that a wreck known locally as the Anchor Wreck might be the remains of the *F.J. Luckenbach*, but I think otherwise. The *F.J. Luckenbach* was propelled by a compound engine . . . [I observed] that the engine was a triple expansion engine and not a compound engine." This difference in the number of cylinders meant that the Anchor Wreck was some wreck other than the *F.J. Luckenbach*; some wreck that was propelled by a triple expansion engine.

Mike Barnette found such a wreck in a *New York Times* piece, and communicated his finding to South Carolina's offshore shipwreck expert Pete Manchee. According to the 1905 article:

> The Standard Oil whaleback steamship *City of Everett* arrived here [New York City] yesterday with twenty seamen which she had rescued from the Norwegian steamship *Leif Eriksson*, which the *Everett* struck and sank off Cape Romaine, on the east Florida coast, last Saturday in a heavy gale and thick fog. The second engineer, Oster Ostersen, and Johann Johanssen, one of the Norwegian seamen, were drowned.
>
> The *Leif Eriksson* sank in less than ten minutes. The whaleback was badly hurt in the crash. After the collision, although she was bound for Sabine Pass, Texas, she turned around and headed back to New York.
>
> The *Leif Eriksson* was on her way to Philadelphia from Matanzas, Cuba, with a cargo of sugar. Suddenly the whaleback darted out of the mist and fog ahead. A minute later the steel prow of the *City of Everett* cut into the hull of the *Eriksson*, ripping her to pieces as if she were just so much cardboard. Great seas were running at the time, and the wind was howling with a fierceness that made it almost impossible for even a siren or a fog bell to be heard. Capt. Bunting of the *Everett* had his sirens bellowing and bells clanging furiously.
>
> The collision was followed by a wild scramble on the part of the crew of the Norwegian craft, and two lifeboats were immediately launched, into which nineteen of the men jumped. The chief engineer stuck to his post until the last minute, and then jumped overboard and was picked up by a lifeboat from the *City of Everett*.
>
> That any of the crew were able to live in the tumultuous waters that separated the two vessels was considered by the men on both steamers little less than a miracle.
>
> Yesterday afternoon Capt. Savard of the *Leif Eriksson* said that he had been a sailor for twenty-two years, and that the accident was the first that had ever befallen a craft with which he was connected.

To this account I must add a more succinct version (from the *New York Maritime Register*) which nonetheless contains additional information that is of particular historical interest, and which corrects a gross error in the account given above:

> *City of Everett* (ss), from New York Jan 29 for Sabine Pass, returned to

South Carolina - Leif Eriksson 179

Courtesy of Pete Manchee.

New York Feb 9 with her bow stove and with twenty of the shipwrecked crew of the Norwegian str *Leif Eriksson*, from Matanzas and Cardenas for Philadelphia. The *City of Everett* was in collision with the *Leif Eriksson* on Feb 4 off Cape Romain, SC, in a dense fog. The second engineer and one seaman of the *Leif Eriksson* were drowned. The barge *No 95*, which left New York in tow of the *City of Everett*, was afterwards turned over to the str *Capt A F Lucas*, which passed Sand Ket Feb 5 from Wilmington, NC, for Port Arthur, Tex.

The astute reader will have noticed that in the first article, misspelled Cape Romaine was located off the Florida coast; whereas in the second article, spelled correctly, it was located off South Carolina. This might not seem to make much difference as Florida and South Carolina lie adjacent to each other. But to a shipwreck researcher this error makes a great deal of difference. In this case it might explain why a dedicated shipwreck researcher of South Carolina wrecks (Pete Manchee) found no mention of such a wreck in South Carolina waters, and why a similarly dedicated shipwreck researcher of Florida wrecks (Mike Barnette, who has written two books about shipwrecks off Florida) *did* find such a mention . . . and was willing to share his information.

Barnette suspected that the Anchor Wreck might be the remains of the *Leif Eriksson*, so he contacted Manchee and, based on the information in his possession, alerted Manchee of his suspicions. Manchee then procured a photograph of the *Leif Eriksson*. By enlarging the photo, he was able to discern that portholes on the vessel were fitted with a built-in shade or spray guard, which prevented water from pouring into the porthole when it was opened. Manchee had recovered such a porthole from the Anchor Wreck. He also recovered a piece of machiner with a brass flange on which was stamped "Goteborg," which is in Sweden, thus attesting to Scandinavian construction. This pretty much confirmed Barnette's hypothesis.

Not content with that, Barnette continued researching the *Leif Eriksson*, and found, in his words, "another article regarding the disposition and pending salvage of the wreck, which was documented to rest upright and intact in 14 fathoms of water 30 miles off Cape Romain." According to that article:

> The legal disposition of a wreck, which may possibly also include its mechanical disposition, is told in a dispatch from Charleston of the sale of a steel steamship with a cargo of sugar.
>
> The *Leif Eriksson* is her name, and she lies in 14 fathoms, about 30 miles south of Charleston light, off Bulls bay.
>
> With her topmasts above the surface and her funnel, derricks, gear and decks visible in clear water, the steamer has furnished to craft sailing over her an interesting and weird study for the better part of three months.
>
> The *Leif Eriksson*, a Norwegian streamer of 2128 tons register, Capt. H. Savard, bound from Cardenas for Philadelphia, was sunk off Bulls bay, with the loss of her second engineer and one seaman, on Feb. 14, by the whaleback streamer *City of Everett*. The remaining 20 men of the steamer were saved by the whaleback.
>
> The *Leif Eriksson* cost $240,000. She sold for $5. Wrecking her in 14 fathoms will be easy, and the prospects of her speculative purchaser are rosy."

Barnette hypothesized that the cluster of three anchors which gave the wreck its name might have been left by salvors.

When Manchee made me aware of this new turn of events, it made me wonder how *I* missed finding the *New York Times* piece. In the 1970's, when I first started to research shipwrecks, I visited my local library where I found the complete multi-volume indexes of the *New York Times*, plus the NYT on microfilm. This quickly became my first place to look whenever I found a wreck that I wanted to research. The NYT did not cover every shipwreck in the world, or even off the eastern seaboard, but it covered many of those that pertained to local interest, or that were somehow significant, such as those that suffered great loss of life. I used the NYT so often that I was forced to make numerous trips to the library just to ascertain if the NYT ever covered a wreck in which I was interested. This became such a burden that I soon decided that it would be more convenient to have the index handy next to my desk.

I could not afford to spend thousands of dollars for the hardbound books, some of which were hefty tomes the contained more than a thousand pages. But I could afford discrete photocopies. So I photocopied the index pages that listed Marine Intelligence, Shipping Casualties, and Naval Action. Thus I created a personal research guide some two inches thick. When I started to write my Popular Dive Guide Series, I studied every shipwreck that was listed in the index from the comfort of my own home, with a cup of coffee in one hand and a colored marker in the other. I looked not only for names that were already familiar to me, but for locations where unfamiliar wrecks had sunk.

The reason I missed the *Leif Eriksson* article is because, by some quirk of fate, the NYT Index failed to list it – even though the newspaper had published an article about her loss. Welcome to shipwreck research . . .

I found the notice that was published in the *New York Maritime Register*, but that was after the fact. Knowing the name and date makes research so much easier. Here is an excerpt from another article that supplements the facts:

The *Leif Eriksson* was first seen crossing the bow of the *City of Everett*. The latter is a whaleback and has an overhanging, cigar-shaped bow, which cut into the *Eriksson's* hull deeply and ripped her open far below the water line. Several of the bow plates of the *City of Everett* were stove in.

Captain Bunting stated that after the collision the crew of the *Erickson* [sic] became panic stricken and that the two men were lost during a wild rush for the boats, in which the lifeboat on the port side was capsized. He added that Chief Engineer Lars Steffens was the last man to quit the sinking ship. He jumped over the side and clung to the log line until rescued by a boat from the *City of Everett*.

The value of the sugar aboard the Erickson [sic] is placed at $260,000. The vessel and cargo were covered by insurance.

The *City of Everett* had the upper part of her bow crushed and she will be sent to dry dock.

One item that none of the above articles failed to mention was the temperature. According to the *Charleston News and Courier*, at the time of the collision:

All day the temperature was below freezing, and the ice that formed on the pavements Friday night melted but little during the day, though the biting northern winds eased up a bit towards nightfall, and the cold was not so disagreeable.

Cold weather prevailed in general over the State and South as well, temperatures of 20 degrees being reported from Columbia and Knoxville. The ice rendered walking somewhat dangerous and more than one pedestrian went down the street, there being two ways of going down – horizontal and vertical. Horses and mules slipped about, and messenger boys had no little difficulty in riding their wheels to points about the city. The cold along the wharves was especially penetrating the wind having a clean sweep down the rivers."

This meant that *Leif Eriksson* crewmembers who went into the water must have suffered badly from exposure. And even those who rowed lifeboats in the open air must have agonized from the cold. Further in this regard, because the ice storm tore down the telegraph lines, local newspapers did not learn about the catastrophe until long after the news was old.

Statistics

Built: 1889
Previous names: None
Gross tonnage: 2,128
Type of vessel: Steel- and iron-hulled freighter
Builder: Laxevaags Msk. & Jnrskb, Bergen, Norway
Owner: S. M. Kuhnle & Son, Norway
Cause of sinking: Collision with *City of Everett*
GPS: 32-41.269 / 79-09.280
Note: Frames and plating are steel; remainder is iron

Sunk: February 4, 1905
Depth: 100 feet
Dimensions: 274' x 38' x 18'
Power: Coal-fired steam

Port of registry: Bergen, Norway

Loran: 45314.6 / 60179.0

Ozama

The *Ozama* had a varied, interesting, and not always law-abiding career that lasted a baker's-dozen years near the end of the nineteenth century. She was named *Craigallion* when she slid down Scottish ways in 1881.

Although the *Craigallion* was designed as a freighter and not as a tugboat, on two occasions she was used to tow vessels long distances: in 1884 she towed a dredge from Philadelphia, Pennsylvania to Colon, Panama, during the French attempt to dig a canal across the Panamanian Isthmus; in 1885 she towed a damaged steamer from Colon to a shipyard in Baltimore, Maryland.

Shortly after the towing job, the *Craigallion* anchored in the Bahamas in order to wait out a storm. The wind blew so hard that her hawsers snapped like rotten string. The freighter was blown onto a reef near Watling's Island. At first blush the stranded steamer was described as "a total wreck." But further investigation found that her hull was still sound.

The wrecking tug *Resolute* was dispatched to her aid, and soon pulled the *Craigallion* off the bar. The *Resolute* then towed the damaged freighter to Norfolk, Virginia for repairs. Upon completion, in 1886, the *Craigallion* was purchased by the Clyde Steamship Company, which then had her registered in the United States under the name *Ozama*.

The *Ozama* plied Atlantic waters unnoticed until the end of December 1888, when she came into prominence by transporting munitions and materiel from New York to Haiti: "nine Gatling guns, fifty cases of rifles, several hundred thousand cartridges, and soldiers' uniforms." She was given the pejorative of "gun-runner," although that term is generally used when military arms and ammunition were smuggled without knowledge of authorities. On the contrary, the military cargo was duly listed on the *Ozama's* manifest, which made their transport perfectly legal.

Port authorities noted the cargo on the *Ozama's* manifest but found nothing suspicious about its means of transportation or its ultimate destination. The fact that the military freight was undoubtedly intended for Haitian insurgents known as Hippolytes had no bearing on the matter. The *Ozama* was permitted to depart and to deliver her cargo because in doing so she violated no American or international laws.

Fanning the fire was the continuance of the *Ozama's* practice of bearing arms and non-military supplies to the Haitian port of Gonaives, which was under control of the Hippolytes and not the official government of the island nation. A rather undignified contretemps occurred in 1889, when the *Ozama* once again planned to make a delivery to Gonaives. Perhaps "contretemps" is too much of an understated word to use under the circumstances that eventuated. According to a contemporary account:

> New York, July 1 – Captain Rockwell, the commander of the steamer *Ozama*, was interviewed this evening concerning the seizure of his ship by the Haytian authorities. His story is as follows:
>
> The *Ozama* left this city on June 2, bound for Gonaives, Hayti. She carried a cargo of provisions, but no arms or ammunition of any kind. On the morning of June 9, when the *Ozama* was about 32 miles from Gonaives, three Haytian gunboats were discovered rapidly approaching. Captain Rockwell,

not wishing to be delayed by any of the whims to which the Haytian war vessels are constantly subjecting American vessels, piled on steam and forged ahead as fast as he could. The gunboats he soon made out to be some of the Legitime's ships. They were the *Defense*, the *Marseilles* and the *Toussaini l'Ouverture*.

The *Ozama* had not gone far when suddenly from the long gun on the bow of the *Defense* came a flash, and a cannon ball whizzed across the bow of the *Ozama*. That settled matters, and Captain Rockwell hove to. The *Defense* was now alongside and a boat was lowered. It was pulled alongside of the *Ozama* and the first officer clambered up the side and said, "The Captain of the *Defense* wants you to come aboard his vessel."

ROCKWELL'S TART ANSWER

"Tell your Captain," answered Captain Rockwell, "That if he wants to see me he can find me on board my ship." The officer saluted, returned to the *Defense* with Captain Rockwell's answer, and soon returned with an official known as the Secretary of the *Defense*. This individual asked to see the *Ozama's* papers. They were shown him.

"Gonaives is blockaded," he told Captain Rockwell, "and you cannot go there. You will have to go with us either to Port-au-Prince, Jacmel, Jeremie or Aux Cayes. You can go nowhere else"

In vain, Captain Rockwell protested against his being detained, but he finally had to give in and said he would go to Port-au-Prince. He knew he would be more likely to meet an American man-of-war there than anywhere else. Under the escort of three gunboats, the *Ozama* arrived in the outer harbor of Port-au-Prince at midnight that night.

Early next morning the *Ozama* was taken into the inner harbor and anchored under the guns of the fort. Captain Rockwell immediately went ashore and sought out Minister Thompson, who represents this country in Hayti. The American Minister asked the Haytian Government why the *Ozama* was detained, and demanded her release. Not the slightest attention was paid to the letter, and no answer was received that day.

A CHANGE IN AFFAIRS

Next morning the American man-of-war *Ossipee* steamed into the harbor with Captain Kellogg on board. As soon as she anchored Captain Rockwell pulled out to her and met Captain Kellogg coming in. Both gigs stopped and Captain Rockwell told how he had been captured, and that the Haytian Government would not let him go out. Captain Kellogg said he could take her out.

Both commanders then went ashore and proceeded to the American Minister's house. The entrance of the *Ossipee* into the harbor had evidently stirred up the Haytian dignitaries, for they were at the American Minister's house in full force. There were three or four officials, Captain Rockwell says, but he didn't remember who they were. After being introduced the Haytians were ready to argue the matter.

"We are very sorry that this happened," they said, all smiles and very polite, "but, of course, it couldn't be prevented. The port of Gonaives is blockaded and the vessel cannot proceed in."

"There is no use of this palavering," said the Captain of the United States man-of-war. The ship has got to be released at once. You have no right to detain her, and I want you to distinctly understand that as long as I am here you cannot interfere with American ships."

There was more arguing on the part of the Haytians, but their smiles had disappeared. Captain Kellogg then said, "I will give you until 3 o'clock, and if the ship is not released by that time I will come and take her by force."

It was then 10 o'clock A. M. The doughty Captain by this time had his dander up, and his anger was increased when one of the officials said:

"Well, we will release her, but she cannot go to Gonaives."

By —— she will go to Gonaives, and she will go tonight, and I am going to take her, too."

This settled matters and the Haytians withdrew. Captains Kellogg and Rockwell went to their respective vessels.

About noon a formal release was sent by Legitime to Minister Thompson and the latter sent it to Captain Rockwell. The latter immediately weighed anchor, hoisted the American flag, and with his whistle screaming defiance, sailed out from under the guns of the port and anchored alongside of the *Ossipee*. Three hearty American cheers were given by the crew of the warship, and they were returned with a vengeance. At sunset on the same day the *Ossipee* and the *Ozama* proceeded to Gonaives with no further molestation. Captain Rockwell went on board of the *Ossipee* after they arrived and thanked Captain Kellogg.

It is important for the reader to understand that there was political unrest in Haiti, with opposing political factions residing in Port-au-Prince and Gonaives. There was also antipathy against the United States. These factors combined to create the situation above. The reader should also compare the similarities between the Haitian blockade of 1894 with the Union blockade of the South during the American Civil War. Only then can you begin to understand the hostilities involved.

Four months later, the year that started with a bang for the *Ozama* ended with a whimper. According to a local account:

On November 23, 1894, the tug *W.B. Congdon* picked up off the Georgetown Bar Captain Bennington and twelve men of the steamer *Ozama*, bound from Philadelphia to Charleston in ballast. Captain Bennington reported that at 7:30 p.m. on November 15th the *Ozama* struck on Cape Romain shoals and stove a hole in the engine room compartment. The water quickly filled the fire rooms, rendering the engines useless. The steamer floated off the shoals soon after striking, and at 3 a.m. sank in six and one half fathoms of water. The crew took to the boats, saving only part of their clothing. The engineer with ten men went to board the steamer *Planter* from Charleston but missed her and it was thought they landed "on Romaine beach."

The wreck was gone and practically forgotten after this ignominious end. The site was not discovered until 1979, but not identified until 34 years later. How those events

South Carolina – Ozama

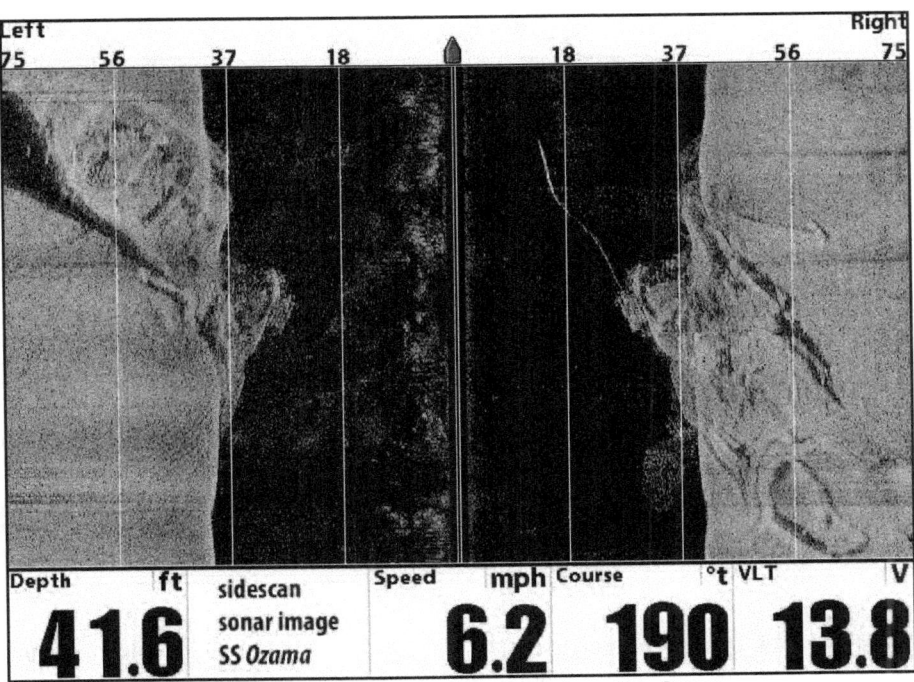

Side-scan sonar image of the *Ozama* is courtesy of Lee Spence.

came about can best be told in the words of South Carolina's best known underwater archaeologist Lee Spence, who has discovered more shipwrecks off the State of South Carolina than any other person, and more than all the archaeologists in all the years of the existence of the South Carolina Institute of Archaeology and Anthropology.

This is the wreck of an iron-hulled steamer. The site is in approximately 40' of water about ten miles from the mouth of the Santee River and six nautical miles off the lighthouse at Cape Romain, South Carolina.

I first located the site in 1979 while searching with a proton magnetometer for a much earlier shipwreck with treasure on it. I can write about it now only because the United States Federal District Court has already ruled that I am the "true and exclusive owner" to all of the wreckage (not just the *Ozama*) that I have found on and around the outer shoal of Cape Romain. I have a five mile radius exclusive area.

Because of the wreck's general type and condition, I suspected it dated from the late 19th or early 20th century. It was definitely not my original target, so I simply made a note of it as something to investigate later and moved on finding more and more shipwrecks in its general vicinity. They were all cataloged for future work.

In January of 2012, I included the site in an admiralty case that I filed with the United States court, claiming rights, as both salvor in possession and as the discoverer of lost and abandoned property, to all of the unidentified and abandoned wrecks that I had found within the area specified in my pleadings.

In August of 2012, the court officially recognized me as the "true and exclusive owner" of the wreckage.

In February of 2013, while doing research, I came across an 1894 newspaper account that gave me my first real clue as to this wreck's identity. The paper told about the loss of the *Ozama*, an iron propeller steamer, which sank in six and a half fathoms (39') of water, about six miles off the lighthouse. That fit with my wreck perfectly. Even the compass heading given in the article matched.

A sonar survey, on site inspection and measurements made of the wreck and compared with those recorded for the *Ozama* in *Lloyd's Register of British and Foreign Shipping*, have further confirmed the wreck's identity. She is definitely the *Ozama*.

So far Spence has recovered portholes, china, and miscellaneous brass objects from the wreck, but there is much more work to be done before the wreck is fully explored.

Statistics

Built: 1881
Previous names: *Craigallion*
Gross tonnage: 1,028
Type of vessel: Iron-hulled freighter
Builder: Ramage & Ferguson's Shipbuilding Yard, Leith, Scotland
Owner: Clyde Steamship Company, New York, New York
Port of registry: New York, New York
Cause of sinking: Stranded then foundered
GPS: Withheld by Lee Spence

Sunk: November 15, 1894
Depth: 40 feet
Dimensions: 216' x 76' x 30'
Power: Coal-fired steam

Below: Pete Manchee took this picture of me swimming above cannons on the *Philadelphia*.

Philadelphia

The *Philadelphia* was one of those wrecks whose discovery was kept a closely guarded secret. The reason at first was that it was teeming with fish. Later it was discovered that it was loaded with cannons. Unloaded cannons, fortunately, so no one had to worry about them exploding. They were harmless. But very valuable.

Rick Skimmyhorn was a commercial angler who was trolling twenty miles off Cape Romain when he hit a spot that was swarming with fish. He started catching them left and right and down the middle. He marked the location. Every time he returned to the spot, he caught great batches of fish. The site was an angler's delight: a sure thing when every other fishing hole failed to produce. He fished the spot for six years, during which time it never failed to yield large quantities fish.

In 1997, he told local scuba diver Rufus Perdue about the site. Skimmyhorn was not a diver, so he asked Perdue if he would go out on one of his trips in order to dive on whatever object attracted so much sea life. Perdue said he would. That was when Perdue descended the anchor line and saw right away that the attracting object on the bottom was a shipwreck.

Perdue also saw that in addition to the schools of fish that inhabited the site, the wreck was littered with cannons, railroad rails, and heavy train wheels. There were more cannons than Purdue could count, but he estimated that he saw at least fifteen, and speculated that others might lie underneath them and beneath nearby wreckage.

Neither Skimmyhorn nor Perdue knew the name of the wreck, but that did not matter at the time. Skimmyhorn and Perdue took another tack.

In 2006, the South's oldest daily newspaper – *The Post and Courier* – published an article about Skimmyhorn's find and Perdue's observations, in which it stated, "They brought in fellow Murrell's Island resident Rodney Thomaston, owner of Long Bay Salvage, to help them figure out how to recover 7-ton cast-iron cannons from 80 feet of water.

"Still, they did not know exactly what they had found. They hired Wes Hall, an archaeologist from the Clive Cussler team that found the *Hunley*, to map the site and give his professional opinion. Gary Gentile, a historian they knew, found *The News and Courier* article that put a name to the ship that matched the description Hall came up with. It seemed there was little doubt they had found the *Philadelphia*."

I don't know who researched and wrote the previous paragraph, but he or she did not get the information from me. I was never interviewed for the article. Furthermore, I had nothing to do with identifying the wreck. Pete Manchee identified it. He combed through thousands of microfilmed pages of old newspapers before he came upon one that fit the wreck site. Afterward, he gave me the name of the vessel and the date of her demise. All I did was locate corroborating data when I went on my next research trip. I found the *Philadelphia's* listing in the *Record* of the American Bureau of Ships (which confirmed the tonnage), and in the *New York Maritime Register* (which confirmed the date of loss and subsequent salvage operations).

According to an 1877 issue of *The News & Courier*:

Total Loss of a Schooner. – The schooner *Philadelphia*, Capt Boeman, sailed from this port [Charleston, South Carolina] on Wednesday, February

28, having on board a cargo of heavy cannon and some old railroad iron. She was towed to sea, and, on getting outside the port, had the wind from the southeast moderate, with some sea rolling in. The vessel was kept on her course on Wednesday night and during Thursday, the wind in the meantime increasing in force, with a large volume of sea. On Thursday night, about 12 o'clock, the captain found that the schooner was leaking badly, and, on going below, discovered the water coming in the seams in large quantities. It was evident that the schooner was settling fast and that she would sink in a short time. The boat was immediately placed overboard, and the schooner was abandoned about 1 A. M. on Friday, and she sunk ten minutes afterwards. She lies in about thirteen fathoms [78 feet] of water, Cape Romain bearing W. N. W. twenty miles off. The boat was headed for the beach, which was struck near Cape Romain. The boat and crew afterwards proceeded to McClelianville, where all were capably taken care of by Mr. DuPre, and they then proceeded inward to Charleston and landed at Dewees' Island, where they were kindly received by Mr. McElroy.

The captain and crew reached this city yesterday in their boat, having stood by the inland passage. The *Philadelphia* was a good schooner of 254 tons, was about three years old, and was mostly owned in Philadelphia, where she is probably moored. The wreck of the schooner was right in the track of Northern bound vessels, and something should be done to remove her spars so as to prevent accident.

Note that Boeman was spelled Bowman in the *Record*. In addition the the above article, Manchee also found three follow-up pieces. The first was dated March 9:

The Sunken Schooner *Philadelphia*. – The steamer *Resolute* returned here yesterday from making a trip to the sunken schooner *Philadelphia*, which was found in thirteen fathoms of water, about twenty miles east southeast from Cape Romain. There were taken from the wreck several sails, some rigging and a sextant. They were secured by a diver descending some twelve fathoms deep. The topmast of the *Philadelphia* stands above water, but it is quite likely that the first spell of heavy weather will break up the vessel.

And, on March 13:

The Schooner *Philadelphia*. – The wrecking steamer *Resolute* arrived here yesterday forenoon from the above vessel. By working under water at an unusual depth, the *Resolute* has succeeded in securing the foresail, jib and a considerable quantity of rigging, a portion of one mast was obtained and brought up, and another was loosened from the hull, but got away afterwards. A search was made for the captain's pantaloons, said to contain in one of the pockets $125, and which were accidentally left behind when the vessel was sinking, but nothing was seen of them. The masts have now all been removed to a sufficient extent to permit the deepest vessel to pass over the wreck in safety.

South Carolina ~ *Philadelphia*

Finally, on March 14:

> Sale of Wrecked Property. – The hull of the Norwegian bark *Lief*, as she lies on the breakers off the Hunting Islands near Fripp's Inlet, was sold at auction yesterday by Mr. J. A. Enslow for the sum of one dollar. The wrecked materials saved from the same vessel brought eight hundred dollars. The sails, rigging, &c., from the schooner *Philadelphia*, sold for eight hundred and fifty dollars.

News & Courier, 2006: "Using air bags and a lift bar, Thomason and Perdue have so far raised five of the cannons (Skimmyhorn sold his share of the wreck a few years ago.) Raising the guns is a massive undertaking, requiring 35 hours of sailing just to get one of them to shore – not to mention the time to raise it."

But raise it they did. Or rather, them. Yesteryear's trash is today's treasure. Treated properly, iron that would have been sold for scrap was a valuable antiquity in today's market. The modern salvors did not simply plop the cannons on the grass to serve as lawn ornaments. They were not interested in kitsch. They wanted to preserve the cannons for future generations to enjoy and appreciate.

Perdue built a large caisson, filled it with fresh water, built an electrolytic reduction system, and connected a cannon to electrodes that were powered household electricity. After a while the encrustation started to flake off the iron, revealing the slightly pocked surface of the barrel of a cannon that was from the era of the Civil War . . . pardon me, the War of Secession, alias the War of Southern Independence, alias the War of Northern Aggression. This was yet another reason to keep the wreck site a secret. In fact, very

Pete Manchee (in the camoflage crush hat) and Rufus Perdue peer into the caisson at a cannon that is in the process of being cleaned of encrustation by means of electrolytic reduction. Note the lid that usually covers the bath in order to keep foreign objects (including small children) from getting into the liquid solution.

few people even knew about the cannons that were recovered from the wreck until a decade after the fact.

What is not made clear in the modern article is that only one cannon was raised at a time. The next one was not raised until the previous one was fully preserved and removed from the chemical bath. That way the newly recovered cannon could be placed immediately into the caisson.

After the salvors went public, they produced a video of the entire operation, including underwater footage and the history of the wreck. This all goes to show what non-professional divers, historians, and archaeologists can do to enlighten the world about incidents of the maritime past.

Statistics

Built: 1873
Previous names: None
Gross tonnage: 254
Type of vessel: Three-masted schooner
Builder: Smyrna, Delaware
Owner: Philip Fitzpatrick & O.
Cause of sinking: Foundered

Sunk: March 2, 1877
Depth: 80 feet
Dimensions: 119' x 32' x 6.9'
Power: Sail

Port of registry: Philadelphia, Pennsylvania
Location withheld by all three participants

The trunnions of this restored cannon are set in balks of wood that are stacked in order to simulate a carriage, which in this case is a car trailer, which can be towed for exhibition purposes.

Ringborg (and Runa)

You won't find the *Ringborg* in *Shipwrecks of South Carolina and Georgia* (2003). So I need to tell you about it.

For one thing, at the time I wrote the book I had never heard of the *Ringborg*. Worse yet, local shipwreck historian and research expert Pete Manchee had never heard of it. But don't let me hog the show. Let Manchee tell the story, in a letter that he wrote to me on April 24, 2007.

Hi Gary,

Thought you might find this interesting. As you know, I've been trying to identify the ORE FREIGHTER for roughly 18 years without success. Last year I teamed up with Rob Penn, of Carolina Beach, NC and Danny Campbell of Inman, SC. Both of them had the same desire to know what the wreck is. We made quite a few dives on her last year and began an extensive search of the engine for builders' plaque. In the process, we collected various pieces of the engine and noticed that most brass pieces had the number 673 stamped on them. We figured that it must be the particular engine number, but without knowing the builder, the information was useless. Danny made a research trip to the Mariner's Museum to research various wrecks and one of the resources he returned with was a book by Joan Charles entitled, *North Carolina Shipwreck Accounts – 1790 to 1950*. Danny and I both, though independently, also began combing through *Disasters at Sea From 1824 to 1962*. Danny found a reference in both to the SS RINGBORG. There were differences in cargo between the two entries, but the dimensions and position were in agreement. We now had a date to track. I went to the *Charleston News and Courier* and there it was on 10/01/1924. The position had been listed in both of the before mentioned sources as 34 N., 75 W, some 150 miles from the ORE FREIGHTER. However, the newspaper article puts the position at "20 miles west, southwest of Frying Pan" ......right were the 18 FATHOM wreck is!

Now, with a name and date, we found a reference on the Internet to the builder Wm. Gray and Co. That lead to copies of the company's ledger books from the various yards. Imagine my surprise and delight at finding that the LEONIS (RINGBORG's previous name) was built at yard number 673. You've seen the brass helm stand from the wreck at my place and I think I told you years ago that I had gone over the wheel with a magnifying glass because bored sailors scratch and carve all sorts of stuff in brass objects while on watch. I got out my notes and drawings of the inscriptions I had found on the wheel, to see if anything looked like LEONIS or BENGALEN or RINGBORG......nothing. But, I did notice that there was a reoccurrence of the initial W in several places on the wheel. I had originally thought that it was the product of some egotistical maniac trying to leave his "mark" in as many places as possible. I went back through the material that I had collected on the builder and the original owner and bingo, there was the house flag for H.M. Wrangell, W, the original owner. The W is made in a very distinctive way. It took me a week to get the smile off my face!! After 18 years, it sure

feels good.
Pete.

House flag courtesy of Pete Manchee.

That's the kind of dedication that is required for successful shipwreck research!

To allay any confusion, the wreck site has been known as both the Ore Freighter and the 18 Fathom Wreck: the first because of the visible cargo, the second because of the depth.

Now note the inconsistencies in the Lloyd's reports. The *Lloyd's Register – Wreck Returns* states: "*Ringborg*, 2641 tons, Norwegian, steel screw steamer, from Santa Lucia to New York, carrying iron ore, foundered in Lat. 34 N., Long. 75 W."

According to *Dictionary of Disaster at Sea During the Age of Steam Including sailing ships and ships of war lost in action 1824-1962*, which was published by Lloyd's Register of Shipping: "Norwegian ship *Ringborg* sprang a leak and sank on October 1st, 1924, in 34°N., 75° W, while she was carrying sugar from Santa Lucia, Cuba, to New York."

Such contradictory information is only one facet of what makes shipwreck research so difficult. To make matters worse, now read a local newspaper article about the incident:

> Norfolk, Va., Sept. 30. – The Norwegian steamer *Ringborg* was in a sinking condition twenty miles west, southwest of Frying Pan Shoals and had been abandoned by her crew, according to a radio message received here tonight, from the American steamer *Comanche*. The steamer *Enare*, also Norwegian, according to the message, was standing by the stranded steamer and had taken her crew aboard.

In the first sentence, the article stated that the *Ringborg* was sinking. In the second sentence, it stated that she was stranded. "Stranded" means "ran aground." A vessel cannot sink if she has run aground.

Another article stated: "The Norwegian steamer *Ringborg* sank off the Frying Pan Shoals. The tug *Keen* witnessed the stern of the ship sink below the waters."

A longer report was published the following day. The headline read "*Ringborg's* Crew Arrive in Port." The sub-headline read "Ship Sank Yesterday." The sub-sub-headline read "Twenty-seven Survivors of Ill-Fated Vessel Rescued by the *Enare*." In somewhat illiterate and ungrammatical form, with vessel name italics added by me, the article read:

> The crew of the ill-fated Norwegian steamship *Ringborg*, which sank at 6 o'clock Wednesday morning about twenty-one miles south by east of the *Frying Pan Shoals* lightship, was brought into port here yesterday by the Norwegian steamship *Enare*, which vessel stood by the *Ringborg* until it sank.
> According to the story told by Capt. Thornvald Monsen, of the *Ringborg*, the vessel left Santa Lucia, Cuba, Friday and ran into heavy seas Sunday, which began to break over its decks, by Monday morning the full force of the

South Carolina - Ringborg

Courtesy of Pete Manchee.

storm which had been sweeping up the coast struck the *Ringborg* tearing the tarpallins [sic] from the hatchways allowing the water to reach the cargo and this with the constant rolling of the ship caused it to list heavily. Capt. Monsen, at this time, made an effort to reach the port of Wilmington, but without success.

Tuesday afternoon the *Enare* came in sight and upon request of the *Ringborg* stood by the disabled vessel. The *Enare* took the officers and crew of the *Ringborg* aboard for the night and Wednesday morning while preparing to return the officers and crew to their vessel the *Ringborg* suddenly sank. The *Enare* than [sic] proceeded to Charleston with the rescued men.

The crew of the *Ringborg* consisted of twenty-seven officers and men and upon arrival here were taken in charge by Mr. Christian J. Larsen, Norwegian consul. They were provided with clothes and will be paid off probably today, some will then leave for New York.

During the storm the crew worked energetically at the pumps in an effort to save their ship and only abandoned it Tuesday night as a matter of precaution. The storm at that time had practically subsided.

Captain Monsen has been at sea twenty-five years, having begun service when fifteen years of age, and has been a captain for the past nine years and this, he stated, is the first time that a vessel has gone down under him. He also stated that he has never been shipwrecked although he had sailed the seas all during the World War.

From here Capt. Monsen will go to New York before sailing for Norway.

So there you have it. Or do you? There is still the cargo inconsistency. Was the *Ringborg* transporting sugar or ore? And from which Santa Lucia? There is a port city named Santa Lucia in Cuba, which has long been known for its production of sugar.

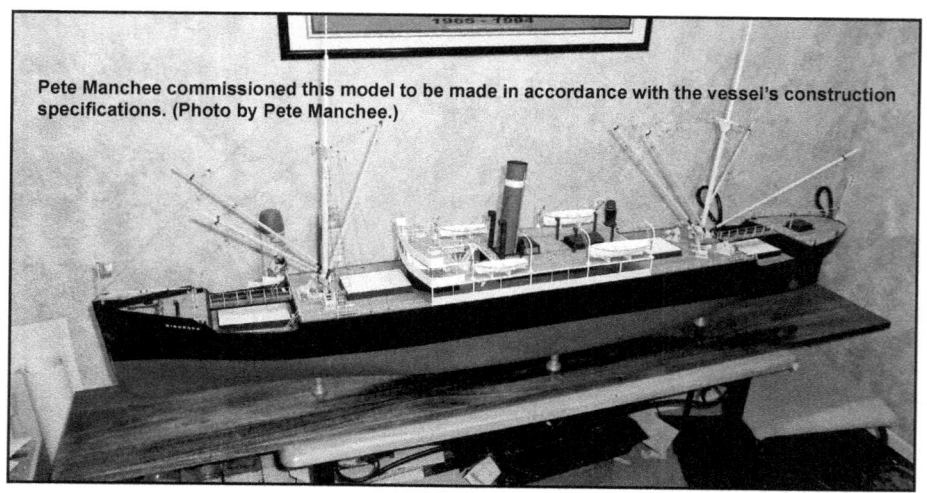

Pete Manchee commissioned this model to be made in accordance with the vessel's construction specifications. (Photo by Pete Manchee.)

But there is also a port city named Santa Lucia in Italy, where silver mines abound.

I found ore in the forward holds, but obviously I did not find sugar; it had been stowed in the aft hold and had long since melted.

As information, on a night dive I saw numerous moray eels swimming through the darkness; their skin was greenish with speckles. I caught a number of shovel-nose lobsters. And I spotted (but couldn't catch) an unidentified species of spiny lobster; it measured six inches in length, and was fire-engine red with a swirled pattern of similar hues.

But there's another facet to this story. Actually two. In 1985, treasure salvor Denny Breese recovered ore samples from the wreck. According to the assay, the ore contained approximately 24 % copper. The ore also contained about .012 ounces of gold per ton. Breese estimated that the quantity of ore onboard was around 6,000 metric tons, and at the then-current price of copper, the total value of the ore was nearly four million dollars (disregarding minute quantities of gold and silver).

Breese arrested the wreck in 1988. In Admiralty lingo, the arrest granted him salvage rights and relief from interference by competitors against "the unidentified, wrecked and abandoned shipwreck, under the navigable waters off the coast of North Carolina, her tackle, apparel and cargo, located within twenty-five hundred (2500') yards of a point located at coordinates 33° 12.16' N Latitude and 77° 47.60' W Longitude." (Note the error: the symbol ' means feet, not yards. Note, too, that this "complaint in rem" was made before the wreck was identified.)

Breese was unable to obtain financing for his planned recovery operation; nor was he successful in interesting investors or venture capitalists to fund the project. A requirement of a salvage arrest is that salvage be ongoing. You can't simply arrest a wreck to keep it out of the hands of other salvors; you must actively and continuously work the wreck. Thus Breese's salvage arrest soon lapsed due to inactivity.

Breese renewed his interest in (if not the arrest of) the wreck in 1995. But again, nothing came of it.

But Breese was nothing if not persistent. Over the period of 2008 and 2009, he contracted with a commercial diving outfit called Aqua Quest International, based in

South Carolina - *Ringborg* and *Runa*

Tampa, Florida, to recover the ore. Aqua Quest anchored its salvage vessel in the wreck, then commenced diving operations. The plan was to raise chunks of ore with an airlift. When the divers descended to the bottom, they encountered a large school of sand tiger sharks that were roaming over the wreck.

This was not an unusual situation. Sand tiger sharks often hung around shipwrecks. I have seen numerous sand tiger sharks on the *Ringborg*. Despite their fierce facial expression – with rows of jagged teeth hanging out of their mouth – they are fairly harmless, and quite skittish. A yank of the tail or a punch to the body will send them zooming away like a rocket sled. Wreck-divers ignore them and go about their business.

Rumor has it that the Aqua Quest packed up their gear and skedaddled back to Tampa with their beaver tails between their legs. Like most rumors, this was more of an urban legend than actual fact. Aqua Quest divers videotaped the sharks, and wrote about the "absolutely incredible place to be working" while surrounded by curious and non-lethal sharks.

However, they did eventually pack up and head back to Tampa, but for a different reason than the one which urban legend speculated. To recover chunks of ore, Aqua Quest used an airlift which they named Orasaurus. The nozzle and pipe of the Orasaurus measured a foot or so in diameter. They expected to simply vacuum the ore chunks off the bottom the way industrial vacuum equipment sucks up small stones and pebbles. It didn't work that way.

The ore on the wreck is concreted into a solid mass. Divers had to break this concretion apart with chisels and prybars – to release a chunk at a time. Video footage shows single-tank divers at work at this laborious task, sucking up one or two chunks as divers broke them free from the concretion, and placed the chunks in front of the nozzle to be sucked up to the deck of the surface vessel. They recovered some ore, but at such a slow rate that the job would never prove to be economically feasible. Rather than being scared off by sharks, it is more reasonable to presume that Aqua Quest quit the job because it cost more to recover the ore – in terms of time and operating expenses – than the ore was worth.

If they had had a giant claw like the CIA used to recover a Russian submarine . . .

Runa

At the time I wrote *Shipwrecks of South Carolina and Georgia,* Manchee considered the possibility that the Ore Freighter alias 18 Fathom Wreck was the *Runa*. I wrote a chapter under that name and described the dual-named site in detail. Now that it has been established that the wreck in question is the *Ringborg*, one must wonder where the *Runa* is located. Manchee has found the answer.

In a letter dated August 23, 2006, he wrote:

> We haven't talked about the *Runa* for a while, but I am leaning more and more towards the Rosin wreck being the *Runa* also. [Remember that this letter precedes the one above, about the *Ringborg*.] I have found nothing on the wreck that positively shows that she is the *Runa*. However, last fall I did come across some of the railing that I had not seen before that pretty closely matches the *Runa's* railing. Also, the Rosin wreck lies almost exactly 35 mi[les] from the Lifesaving Station at Southport......this is the same distance that was de-

scribed at the time. Her cargo [rosin] would indicate a Southern port of departure (Savannah) so that fits. The two ships are very close in dimensions so that plans of the *Runa* could fit either ship.

The piece de resistance came a few months later, when Manchee received an email from Bob Birmingham. The email was dated January 8, 2007:

> Hi Pete,
>   The *Runa* was built as the *Maria De Georgio* (sp?) in 1911. George [Purifoy] recovered some silverware with the name that can barely be made out. The hull length is exactly correct, a number of artifacts recovered were built in Norway and Sweden (gauges, valves…..), and she perfectly matches a picture, comparing the fo'csle and the forward hull with port spacing and anchor.

The correct spelling of the *Runa's* previous name was *Marie di Giorgio*. I wrote a detailed description of the Rosin Wreck in *Shipwrecks of South Carolina and Georgia*.

So again, there you have it. As long as wreck-divers keep diving and doing research, unidentified wrecks will continue to be identified, and unknown wrecks will be discovered – not by chance but by the hard work and effort of underwater and archive volunteers.

Statistics (*Ringborg*)

Built: 1903
Previous names: *Leonis, Bengalen*
Gross tonnage: 2,660
Type of vessel: Steel-hulled freighter
Builder: William Gray & Company, West Hartlepool, England
Owner: H. M. Wrangell & Company, Haugesund, Norway
Port of registry: ?
Cause of sinking: Foundered
GPS: 33-12.120 / 77-47.545

Sunk: October 1, 1924
Depth: 120 feet
Dimensions: 317' x 45' x 20'
Power: Coal-fired steam

Loran: 45138.6 / 59398.2

Runa

GPS: 33-35.391 / 77-27.205

Loran: 45170.2 / 59156.7

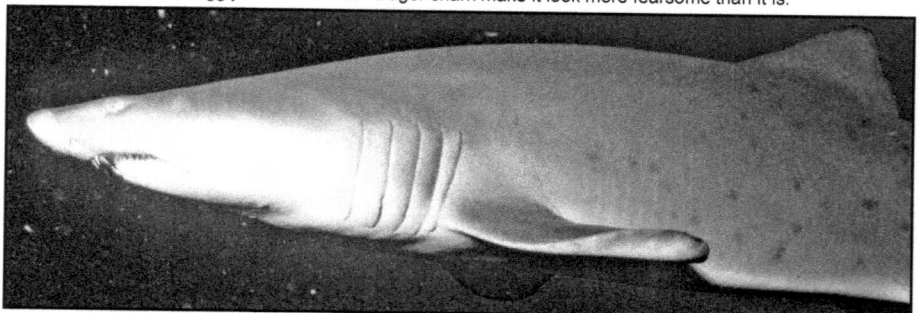

The scraggly teeth of the sand tiger shark make it look more fearsome than it is.

Sailing Yacht

The saga of this sailboat is long, involved, and as yet unsolved. Nonetheless, I am including the story in this volume in the hope that one of my readers will be able to shed some light on the mystery. As with so many of South Carolina's shipwreck discoveries, this one started with Pete Manchee.

On August 17, 1985, Manchee chartered the *Boss Hog* to locate a 37-foot Hunter that had sunk six weeks earlier. The insurance company, which paid the claim for loss in the amount of $64,000, provided loran numbers 14580 / 45182: an approximation that was derived by means unknown to Manchee. At that location, the water depth was 120 feet. A thorough search of the area by means of depth sounder failed to reveal a wreck or obstruction of any kind. Further search was waived, and the sailboat was all but forgotten: a write-off for the insurance company, and nothing but a footnote in shipwreck history.

Fourteen years later, in 1999, Manchee invited me on a trip to dive on some known wrecks and to investigate a set of "numbers" in the offshore waters of South Carolina. On September 29, the dive boat *Safari III* took us to a site that showed a tiny "spike" on the depth recorder. The sky was bright and sunny, the seas were flat, the ocean was a clear cerulean blue, and the water temperature was 75 degrees. The downside was the current: it was not quite ripping but it was strong to say the least.

The target on the bottom was so small that the grapnel couldn't catch it. Undoubtedly the current pulled the grapnel off the bottom so that it sailed over the wreck without touching it, much less hooking it. After several failed attempts to snag the wreck, we decided to deploy a weighted marker buoy, use the line to descend to the bottom, and hope that the wreck lay within sight of the weight.

We donned our gear and jumped overboard upcurrent of the float. We drifted to the marker with incredible celerity, then commenced our descent to the bottom.

The technique for descending a buoy line is different from that of descending an anchor line. Because an anchor line is secured to the wreck, a diver can pull his way down to the bottom with less energy than it takes to kick fins against the current. But pulling on an unsecured marker buoy lifts the weight and causes it to drag. Furthermore, if the current is strong enough, the current alone against the buoy line can drag the weight along the bottom.

We used the downline as a guide but had to be careful not to hold onto it. I found this almost impossible to do. The current was so strong that I quickly got out of breath. And if I stopped kicking in order to rest, I was either propelled backward away from the line, or – if I held onto the line – I dragged the weight away from the site.

The descent was such a severe struggle that at times I could not help but hang onto the line in order to make headway. Worse yet, due to the extreme depth of the wreck, the scope of the line was incredibly long: 400 feet or more.

As we approached the bottom, the curve of the line straightened almost asymptotically so that eventually it stretched nearly parallel to the seabed. When I finally settled on the bright white sand, I dug my knees and hands into the white crystalline granules so I could catch my breath without being shoved farther away from the weight. Then I crawled along the bottom for 50 feet or more, until I reached the weight.

At that point I took time to read my gauges. I had breathed an unusually large volume of air during the descent, but I still had enough to continue the dive. When I looked at my depth gauge, the digital readout displayed 290 feet!

The boat's depth recorder had showed 270 feet, and we had hoped to hover 20 to 30 feet above the wreck and look down at it from a shallower depth. Manchee settled down next to me and made a gesture of disgust because the wreck was nowhere in sight – and the ambient visibility was 75 feet.

I felt committed to our objective. As long as we had come this far, I thought that we should go a little farther and try to locate the wreck. A drag mark in the sand pointed the way.

I did not have the strength to carry the heavy weight forward. The current against the long length of line created too much pressure. I unclipped my wreck reel from its D-ring, hooked it onto the downline, and proceeded to crawl along the drag mark. Manchee was right with me. If we did not locate the wreck, we could easily find our way back to the downline and ascend to our first decompression stop.

Crawling was tough going because the current on the bottom was just as strong as it was in mid-water. The saving grace was that we didn't have to kick fins – the least effective way of making progress against a current – but could push with our knees and pull with our hands. I could use only one hand for pulling because I had to play out the line from the reel with my other hand.

A fuzzy dark silhouette appeared in the gloom ahead. This is a common phenomenon under water. No matter where you look, and no matter what the visibility, the far distance always appears darker than the near surroundings. The phenomenon is an optical illusion: a function of the eye's inability to see clearly in gradually diminishing light at the limit of visibility. I can't count the number of times I have been fooled into thinking that I was approaching a wreck or reef, only to never find it because it was always out of reach – like either end of a rainbow. A phantom wreck is just as imperceptible in every direction.

Only this time the silhouette assumed a darker form. A hazy shape extended left and right. It looked much like the hull of a boat as if seen through a thick layer of gel. As I bent back my head and looked upward, I could nebulously perceive what appeared to be a mast pointing toward the surface. But nothing would come into focus. The boat appeared like a photograph that had been taken while the subject was in motion.

It will come as no surprise that I was suffering from nitrogen narcosis. Yet I felt mentally alert. After all, I had unclipped my wreck reel and secured the clip to the downline without a glimmer of doubt about what I was doing; nor had I fumbled with my equipment, or lost dexterity. When we reached the wreck, I secured the reel to the gunwale so that later we could follow the guideline back to the weight; and so the weight could no longer move as the current put pressure on 400 feet of downline.

But now, after several minutes on the bottom, the delayed onset of narcosis was catching up with me. Although I was functioning fairly well mentally, I found it increasingly difficult to concentrate. Worse, despite the superior visibility, I was unable to obtain a clear picture of the boat and its contents.

The problem was not only with my eyes. It was with my memory. I could make observations, but I promptly forgot what I was seeing. It was like being in a daze, then crossing my eyes so that I saw objects in double. About the only thing I truly remembered after the dive was a red plastic cooler that sat in the cockpit. I thought it was odd

Brochure picture of a 27-foot Hunter. (Courtesy of Pete Manchee.)

that the cooler had not floated away. I vaguely remember that the doorway to the cabin was open. But the interior was nothing more than a dark void. In short, my perception of the sailboat was unclear and imprecise.

I checked my air gauge meticulously. At first I found myself lifting the gauge panel to my face, glancing at it, and letting it go – without ascertaining where the pressure gauge needle was pointing. In other words, I was acting perfunctorily as I always did, and regarded the face plate for a moment, but did not comprehend any meaning. I had to grab the gauge panel again, keep in front of my face for several seconds, and force myself to stare at the needle until I read and comprehended the number to which it pointed. My mental acuity was dull to say the least.

Finally, Manchee and I exchanged okay signs and agreed to terminate the dive. I unclipped the wreck reel from the gunwale, then commenced to reel in the line the way an angler reels in a fish; except that instead of pulling a fish toward me, I was pulling myself toward the weight. The current propelled me ahead like a tailwind on a sailboat.

I unclipped the line from the weight, clipped the wreck reel to the appropriate D-ring on my tank harness, and started up the downline. Bottom time was 13 minutes. We did 40 minutes of decompression: first breathing air, then breathing Nitrox-40, then breathing pure oxygen.

Back on the boat, Manchee laughed as he asked me, "Do you remember anything about that dive?"

The truth was, "Not much."

We compared notes about what we saw (or thought we saw). I swore I saw the cooler, but could offer no explanation about why it hadn't floated away. Additionally, the cooler's rectangular lid was resting inside the cooler with the lid positioned perpendicular to the longest length of the cooler. Manchee made other observations about parts of the wreck that I had not visited or noticed.

A week later, after my return home, I composed a request for information from Robert Browning, the Coast Guard historian and head of the CG's historian's office. I knew Browning personally because I had done research in Coast Guard archives numerous times throughout the years. Here is my letter in full:

Dear Bob,

I have a poser for you. Last week some buddies and I were checking out hang numbers off South Carolina – obstructions that we believed had never been dived before. One wreck turned out to be that of a sailing yacht. I have no knowledge of such a boat having been lost in the vicinity. This suggests two possibilities: that we found a boat that disappeared with all hands and may have solved a mystery, or that a rescue was effected and that the Coast Guard has a record of the casualty.

The loran coordinates are 45146.4 and 59685.4. This is about northeast of Charleston and approximately east of Georgetown, and some thirty or forty miles offshore. Our survey of the wreck was short and superficial, but here are our observations.

The yacht is approximately 50 to 60 feet in length. We definitely observed one mast forward of the cockpit, suggesting that it was a sloop, but there may have been a broken mast aft, making it a ketch.

The amount of encrustation suggests that the boat has been down no more than five years, although it may have been down for as long as ten or fifteen years. The wreck is covered with a thin layer of brownish encrustation. Bright white barnacles were smaller than dimes. Where the hull was visible – in small unencrusted patches – it appeared to be painted green, although color aberration due to depth tends to filter natural light and alter its visible characteristics. We saw partially obscured letters on the starboard bow but were unable to decipher the name due to the encrustation, and did not have enough time to clean off or scrape off the encrustation.

The hull and top appeared to be intact and we did not observe any massive overt damage. One window in the cockpit windscreen was broken, but the glass in the others, as well as in the side windows, appeared unbroken. Nor did we observe any reason for the vessel to have foundered. A cooler with a lid sat in the cockpit on the port side. The door to the interior was located on the starboard side of the cockpit; it was either open or missing, as we could look forward and inside.

Trapped on the sand under the bow was what appeared to be a deployed but deflated life raft about eight feet in length. It may be too that this was part of a bunched up sail – we did not study it too closely but noticed it only in passing.

Please acknowledge receipt of this message so I will know that it was transmitted successfully via e-mail. Otherwise I will post a paper copy.

Browning replied within hours: "I received the message. I can not confirm the name of this vessel without a name or a date. You might check with the local Coast Guard command. The wreck sounds fairly recent and with the information you now know, the vessel should be identifiable.

An hour and a half later, he added the addresses and phone numbers of the commands in Charleston and Georgetown. I fired off letters to both.

The rest of this research story was a three-year saga of additional appeals for information that led to filing several requests pursuant to the Freedom of Information Act. Readers of my books about NOAA (*NOAA's Ark: the Rise of the Fourth Reich*) and the Navy (*The Great Navy Wreck Scam*) might jump to the conclusion that the Coast Guard intentionally blocked my applications for evidence about the identity of the Sailing Yacht (as I now referred to the sailboat), but in this case they would be wrong.

South Carolina - Sailing Yacht

Whereas NOAA has habitually denied my FOIA requests, and the Navy has either refused to divulge requested information or lied about having it, the Coast Guard appeared to be trying to help but was unable to find any pertinent records.

Within a couple of months, they sent a complete set of records about the loss of the fishing vessel *Sherry Ann*. According to the Incident Brief, "32' F/V *Sherry Ann* sank in 100' of water 30NM SE of Charleston. The 3 people onboard abandoned vsl into a liferaft. Coast Guard Airsta Savannah helo CG6508 recovered all 3 POB safely by hoist and transported them to MUSC for evaluation. There were no serious injuries to the crew and the cause of sinking could not be determined due to the rapid ingress of water and the urgency to abandon the vessel."

Obviously, the Sailing Yacht was not a motorized fishing vessel. Either the Coast Guard FOIA officer did not know the difference, or did not bother to correlate the description that I provided about the sailboat with that of the fishing vessel. I had to start the FOIA process all over again by requesting a broader search of Coast Guard records.

On February 13, 2000, I indicated the differences between the two vessels, then wrote: "I hereby request the USCG to conduct an additional search of its records for a marine casualty which more closely fits the description of the vessel to which I originally referred. I am certain that older records must be searched – records in the range of 5 to 10 years past, prior to 1995.

"Alternatively, it is possible that the vessel to which I referred was logged as overdue or missing with all hands, and that no search and rescue operation occurred. Consideration should be given to researching sailing yachts that went missing."

I received a prompt reply two days later:

> The Coast Guard maintains an electronic database on search and rescue case information called SARMIS (Search and Rescue Management Information System). We conducted a query of SARMiS searching for cases of capsized, flooding or sunken 40 – 65 foot sailing vessels in a 25 nautical mile radius around the position you provided. This query was conducted for fiscal years 1990 through 1999. SARMIS did not identify any cases that corresponded to these parameters.
>
> You suggest that there are two possibilities with respect to your discovery: either this was a vessel that disappeared with all hands, or that a rescue was effected and the Coast Guard has a record of the casualty. It is impossible for us to give you a conclusive answer as to which scenario is true because of the limited information available. If the later scenario is true, it is quite possible that the vessel drifted for hours, days, or even weeks after a rescue was effected, before sinking in an unknown location.
>
> As such, without the ability to limit the number of potential cases via SARMIS, it is not feasible for us to conduct a physical records search to determine which search and rescue case, if any, correlates to the vessel in question. If further information becomes available, such as the vessel's name or registration number, we would encourage you to submit a request for another SARMIS query to be made. Regrettably, the Coast Guard responds to many incidents where the vessel or aircraft in question is simply lost without a trace.
>
> We regret that this reply cannot be more favorable to your request.

I couldn't argue with such well-thought reasoning. The explanation was not an excuse or justification, but a clarification of the limitations of the SARMIS database. So the ball was back in my court.

Manchee and I were not able to schedule a return trip to the Sailing Yacht until October 2, 2001, this time aboard the *Safari IV*. Furthermore, this time we were equipped with a breathing gas that would prevent nitrogen narcosis and keep us clear-headed. Our bottom mix was trimix-17/44 (17% oxygen, 44% helium, the balance nitrogen). For decompression gases we had nitrox-32 (which we started breathing at 130 feet), and nitrox-80 (to which we switched at 30 feet).

With these gases, we dived to 290 feet for 14 minutes, and did 62 minutes of decompression. Manchee took a scraper; I took my camera. The idea was to scrape off barnacles that covered the name board, and to photograph features of the wreck that might help to identify the type. Lateral visibility in natural light was 100 feet. Water temperature was 77 degrees from top to bottom. And most important of all, the current was slight if there was any at all. Because we were able to hook the wreck, most of our bottom time was spent on the wreck instead of traveling between the downline and the wreck.

Being clear-headed, I confirmed that there was indeed a cooler in the cockpit, and that the lid was tucked inside it. The mast had fallen by the wayside. Part of the hatchway was missing: probably it had broken off.

Encrustation was worse than it had been before. Barnacles were attached so thickly to the fiberglass hull that Manchee was unable to scrape them off the counter stern where we had hoped to read the name board. My photographs did not portray any conclusive evidence of any kind.

After all this, in a flash of insight Manchee suddenly recalled the 37-foot Hunter for which he had searched in 1985. He considered the possibility that the Sailing Yacht that we found could be that very same vessel. The problem was that his buddy Sam, who had been the contact with the insurance company, was now deceased. Manchee did not know the name of the insurance company, so there was no way to backtrack and obtain the name of the vessel.

The distance between the site of the Sailing Yacht and the coordinates that were furnished by the insurance company measured 27 nautical miles, or 30 statute miles. After Manchee informed me of the possible connection, I started a new round of research. One last hurrah occurred between me and the Coast Guard when I submitted an updated FOIA request in which I suggested the possibility of the wreck being that of the 37-foot hunter, along with information about the 37-foot Hunter, including its location. I also spoke on the phone with Coast Guard personnel, in order to fine-tune my request and suggest alternative ways of accessing their database. This resulted in the Coast Guard sending case files known as Marine Casualty Investigation Reports on vessels that tangentially met the new search criteria.

Once again the Coast Guard complied with my request by supplying incident reports from their database. According to Coast Guard FOIA agent Bruce Schmidt:

> I conducted a thorough search of the Boating Accident Report Database (BARD) system and found no records that are responsive to your request. The BARD system contains records of recreational boating accidents based on accident reports required by federal regulations (33 CFR 173 – 4) that are filed by the owners / operators of the vessels involved in the accidents. Boating accident (BAR) forms are filed with the State Boating Law Administrator (BLA) in the State where the accident occurred. The search of the BARD system looked for any recreational boating accidents that occurred in South Carolina over the June – July 1985 time period.

Relative incidents were (chronologically):

The flooding and eventual loss of the *Miss Mt. Hope* en route to Puerto Rico, in which all three occupants were saved, on January 30, 1987.

The sinking of the pleasure craft *Amo*, in which one person drowned, and which was dated April 20, 1989.

The fishing vessel *Capt Ronald Wayne*, which foundered in the Intracoastal Waterway on November 24, 1989.

The capsizing of the fishing vessel *Skipper*, which sank at sea on September 4, 1998, and in which two of the three occupants were missing and presumed dead, in tropical storm Earl.

The sinking of the 68-foot wooden fishing vessel *Griffin Elizabeth* off Shallotte, North Carolina, in which all three occupants abandoned ship and were subsequently rescued, on October 14, 1998.

Only the first two casualties occurred prior to our first dive on the Sailing Yacht, but these were the reports that the Coast Guard database generated in accordance with our parameters (except for date).

And that's all she wrote, as the expression goes.

By implication, the Coast Guard did not conduct either a search or a rescue operation in this area at that time. Perhaps the 37-foot Hunter was a totally different incident than that of the Sailing Yacht. The Sailing Yacht might be the remains of a vessel that was lost with all hands, and had departed from one port hundreds of miles away, never to arrive at its destination hundreds of miles in the other direction.

At the present time, no one knows.

Valour

For the most part, large vessel losses are a thing of the past. Shipboard radar, and skilled merchant mariners who are adept at interpreting the images on the screen, prevent most collisions and running ashore. Up-to-date charts warn seafarers of shoals and approaching shallows. Onboard fires occasionally occur. Foul weather sometimes overwhelms ships at sea. But by and by, most vessel casualties happen to commercial fishing vessels and other small craft.

The *Valour* was a rare exception to the rule. A tugboat is often described as a giant engine surrounded by a hull. This is because a tug does not carry cargo or passengers, but is designed to push or tow those vessels that are not equipped with propulsion machinery, or that a suffer mechanical breakdown and need help in reaching safe harbor.

Tugs are built to withstand exceptional sea conditions. But even a tug can meet wind and wave conditions which it is not able to withstand. That is what happened to the tug *Valour*.

The Coast Guard investigative report provided a succinct account of the *Valour's* final hours afloat:

> On January 17, 2006, the uninspected towing vessel, *Valour*, on a course of 220 degrees true at a speed made good of 3 knots was towing astern the fully loaded cargo barge *M 192* in transit 40 miles off the coast of Wilmington, NC. The wind was blowing approximately 40 to 50 knots gusting up to 70 knots from 180 degrees true. The seas were 15 to 20 feet and the water temperature was 64 degrees Fahrenheit. At approximately 2320, the Master sounded the general alarm as a result of a significant port list brought on by the filling of the #18 port ballast tank and subsequent unanticipated hydrostatic balancing of the #4 and #5 fuel tanks and the washwater tanks. At approximately 2330, the Chief Mate, enroute to the engine room, fell down the ladder leading from the pilot house to the 01 deck (referred to as the Stack Deck) passageway. It is believed that both of his legs were broken. He later went into cardiac arrest, died, and presumably, went down with the vessel. At approximately 2338, while trying to assist the Chief Mate out on deck for medical evacuation, one of the Able-Bodied Seaman fell overboard. After calling the Coast Guard and during man overboard rescue operations, the Master turned the *Valour* toward the east which brought the wind and seas off the starboard beam. This aggravated the situation by increasing the vessel's roll. On January 18, 2006, at approximately 0009, barge *M 192* was released as a result of its overtaking of the *Valour* on the port side, presenting a hazardous tripping situation. Coast Guard Helicopter *6553* arrived on scene at 0050, located the man overboard, and hoisted him onboard the helicopter at 0106. Shortly after 0100, the tug *Justine Foss* arrived on scene to provide assistance and positioned itself approximately 50 yards away from the *Valour*. The helicopter dropped a 20 person liferaft in the vicinity of the *Valour* and departed at 0140. At approximately 0145, after the Master determined that they could not save the *Valour* from sinking, he mustered all the crew on the bow. During this time the port list increased in severity and fuel had escaped from the port

fuel tank vents. At approximately 0225, the stern submerged and the bow of the *Valour* went straight up in the air. The Chief Engineer and an Able-Bodied Seaman fell from the bow landing on the superstructure and then went into the sea. The Able-Bodied Seaman was located by the *Justine Foss*, but could not be rescued and was lost at sea. The Chief Engineer was the last crewmember to be rescued by the *Justine Foss*. He died onboard the *Justine Foss* from shock brought on by hypothermia. Three more of the crewmembers were individually washed into the sea and later rescued by the *Justine Foss*. The Master, Assistant Engineer, and the Cook were the only crew still left on the *Valour*. They all went into the water together and were rescued together. While in transit to Wilmington, NC, the Assistant Engineer was medically evacuated by Coast Guard helicopter due to diabetic issues. The crew of the *Valour* was transferred to another vessel and brought into Wilmington. The *Justine Foss* recovered barge *M 192* and safely towed it back to Wilmington.

This uninspiring summary of tragic and dramatic events possesses none of the trauma that the sailors must have felt as they fought for their lives, never knowing if they would live or die in the water. Keep in mind that this drawn-out incident occurred under the cloak of night. Imagine what it must have been like to float in the water in complete darkness. Had it not been for the heroic efforts of the crew of the *Justine Foss*, all would have perished alone on the wide, wide sea.

Furthermore, the Coast Guard report redacted the names of those who perished and those who survived:

Sister ship of the *Valour*.
(Courtesy of Pete Manchee.)

Deceased: Chief Mate Fred Brenner, Chief Engineer Richard Smoot, and Able-Bodied Seaman and Tankerman Ron Emory.

Survivors: Captain Michael Lynch, Second Mate Jim Garnett, Assistant Engineer Lou Gatto, Able-Bodied Seamen and Tankermen James Hamilton and Earl Sheppard, and Cook Jay Templett.

As soon as the survivors landed, "Each was handed a cell phone and $750 cash to replace clothes and belongings lost on the *Valour*. Maritrans dispatched grief counselors not only for families and survivors but to crews of its 16 vessels and workers at offices in Tampa and Philadelphia. The company flew executives, survivors and their spouses to all three funerals."

It was also reported that "the accident marked the company's first deaths since 1988 and the only loss of a tug in its 78-year history."

The Coast Guard investigates vessel losses not necessarily as a way to ascribe blame (except in collision cases), but to determine the cause(s) of the loss, ascertain how such a loss could be averted in the future, and decide what kind of regulatory changes might be made in order to help prevent similar losses from recurring. Regulatory changes may apply to both vessel construction and operation. The Coast Guard takes into account such factors as vessel maintenance, hull stability, crew training, and so on.

In the present case, the Coast Guard found that the probable causes of the *Valour's* initial list and subsequent sinking was due to inherent instability which produced a natural starboard list, and a lack of understanding on the part of the operators of the importance of maintaining proper ballast tank levels, especially in extreme foul weather in a crosswind.

Motorists may find it difficult to believe that ballast weight can cause instability. Consider this: the *Valour* was equipped with six ballast tanks: four along the centerline for trim (two forward and two aft), and one on each side. The capacity of these tanks totaled 72,033 pounds, or 36 tons. Assuming that the average family vehicle weighs about two tons, the ballast water on the *Valour* weighed as much as 18 vehicles.

In addition, the *Valour* was fitted with six fuel tanks (three on each side), whose combined capacity totaled 123,984 pounds, or 61,992 tons, or 31 vehicles.

Sloshing was reduced by baffles, but nonetheless, all this liquid leaned to one side whenever the hull listed. Consequently, maintaining proper ballast was an important, even crucial issue.

Interrogation of survivors revealed the press of ongoing events during the *Valour's* final hours. Pandemonium reigned from the din of the storm. Despite chaotic conditions, the skipper and crew kept a firm grip on their actions. Yet there seemed to be a lack of communication as orders were passed from the skipper to his crewmembers, or between certain crewmembers.

The number one priority was dealing with the ever-increasing list. *Valour* started the voyage by emptying all ballast. According to the Coast Guard report, "The *Valour* had no tank level indicators (TLI) and had no way of knowing how full their ballast tanks were." The ballast pump operated at the rate of 250 gallons per minute.

On January 17, Chief Mate Fred Brenner, the officer on the afternoon watch, corrected a slight list by ordering Second Engineer Lou Gatto to pump water into the star-

South Carolina - *Valour*

board ballast tank. Fifteen minutes of pumping let 3,750 gallons of water into the tank. This corrected the list.

Captain Lynch was the evening watch officer, and Chief Engineer Richard Smoot was his engine room engineer. At 7:30 p.m, Lynch ordered Smoot to empty the starboard tank. This returned the tug to its normal slight list. He also ordered a reduction in speed from 7 knots to 5 knots.

At 9:30 p.m., Second Mate Jim Garnett relieved Captain Lynch as watch officer in the wheelhouse. By this time the wind speed had increased to 60 knots with gusts up to 70 knots. Seas were 10 feet. Under such conditions, Garnett prudently asked the skipper to remain with him in the wheelhouse, whereupon Lynch rested on a nearby settee while Garnett stayed alert to enduring conditions.

A slight starboard list became noticeable around 10 o'clock. Lynch called Smoot to confirm that he had emptied the starboard ballast tank. Smoot confirmed that he did. Lynch then ordered Smoot to put 15 minutes of ballast into the port ballast tank in order to correct the slight list.

For reasons that are unclear, Smoot took it upon himself to put 45 minutes of ballast into the port ballast tank. By 11:15, the *Valour* had not only leveled out, but then started listing to port. Lynch ordered Smoot to empty the port ballast tank.

"Shortly afterward Capt Lynch called C/E Smoot and asked him what he was doing and told him he was getting scared. Capt. Lynch then ordered C/E Smoot to pump out all of the ballast. At this point Capt Lynch lost his trust with C/E Smoot. Capt Lynch took the helm and ordered 2/M Garnett to go to the engine room and see what was going on. . . .

"At 2320, Capt Lynch sounded the general alarm, slowed their speed to 3 knots, and shifted the helm from autopilot to hand steering. He told the crew over the public announcement system that there was an emergency in the engine room and to assist the C/E as needed but not to overcrowd the engine room. Additionally, he told the crew to get their lifejackets and survival suits. Several of the crew either didn't hear him or didn't follow his direction. The *Valour* was listing approximately 15 degrees to port in rough seas at this point."

Again, Lynch dispatched a crewmember to the engine room for a report, but still he was unable to obtain accurate information. Due to the noise in the engine room, Smoot used sign language to indicate water in the bilge. Lynch was "increasingly nervous," and "was not confident with the information he was receiving from Smoot."

"At 2330, Capt Lynch radioed the tug *Independence*, another tugboat operated by Maritrans approximately 30 miles away, that they have 'a little too much water in the boat.'" The Coast Guard intercepted the transmission, "who immediately initiated contact with the *Valour*." Lynch told the Coast Guard "that they appeared to have the situation under control."

Yet four minutes later, Lynch "issued a Mayday transmission to the Coast Guard."

Events escalated with amazing celerity. As the tug wallowed broadside, Chief Mate Fred Brenner fell "from the wheelhouse to the stack deck passageway." Brenner's situation was critical. Both legs appeared to be broken and he was having trouble breathing. He soon went into cardiac arrest.

Lynch called the Coast Guard and requested a helicopter evacuation.

A refrigerator was breaking loose so two men worked to secure it.

The list increased to 25 degrees.

At 2338, seaman Earl Sheppard fell overboard.

Wave heights increased to 15 feet.

The digital display of the gyrocompass ceased to function.

Despite the man overboard, Lynch kept the tug headed into the wind and seas – else the boat might be blown over and capsized.

The list increased to 35 degrees.

The barge was passing the *Valour* on her port quarter, and was in position to trip the tug by dragging her sideways into the waves.

"The entire port gunwale and the stern of the tug were underwater with a couple feet of water on deck."

Brenner stopped breathing. Cardiopulmonary resuscitation was performed on him, but he was nonresponsive.

Lynch ordered the barge to be released. James Hamilton and Jim Garnett struggled to release "both the winch hand brake and the air brake" that secured the cable to the barge. "All of the towline payed out but the end of the wire hung up on a connecting U-bolt and failed to release."

Captain Lynch activated the EPIRB (Emergency Position Indicating Radio Beacon) so the helicopter could home in on the transmitted frequency.

In addition to CPR, Garnett gave oxygen to Brenner and used an automated external defibrillator on him. He remained nonresponsive.

Lynch tried to right the tug by pumping water into the starboard ballast tanks.

Lou Gatto "jiggled" the towing cable and managed to break the bitter end free from the winch. The sideways pull on the tug was released as the barge floated free.

Despite these emergency actions, "the *Valour* would lay almost all the way over to port when she rolled."

Once liberated of the barge, Lynch was able to maneuver the tug. He backed in order to close the distance to Sheppard. The crew gathered ring buoys "in the event that they got close enough to him." With incredible seamanship, Lynch managed to bring the badly listing tug within range of Sheppard. The crew tossed the ring buoys, Sheppard "was able to retrieve one. The crew tried several tactics to bring him onboard the *Valour*; however all attempts to recover him failed."

While everyone's attention was occupied with these lifesaving attempts, the *Valour's* life raft floated away "still in its case, undeployed."

The *Justine Foss* arrived on the scene at 0100.

The Coast Guard helicopter rescued Sheppard from the water. By this time, the helicopter no longer had enough fuel to linger in the area. The helicopter's crew dropped a 20-person life raft, then headed for port through the storm. Lynch maneuvered the tug "in such a way that it was stationed at and touching their port side for approximately 30 seconds. Capt Lynch gave the crew the option of making for the liferaft or staying on the tug. The crew opted to stay."

By this time, "CG video footage showed that the *Valour* was heeled over, rolling hard to port and squatting. The aft main deck was completely awash."

Lynch order to crew to muster on the bow. He was afraid of being trapped in the wheelhouse if the tug rolled over, so he joined them.

"At 0223, when the *Valour* was severely trimmed by the stern, the bow shot straight up into the air. AB Hamilton immediately fell into the water and C/M Smoot and AB Emory fell from the bow, landed on the superstructure, and then fell into the water."

In the heaving swells, the crew of the *Justine Foss* attempted to rescue Emory. After several failed attempts, Emory "went face down in the water. The decision was made by the master of the *Justine Foss* to leave AB Emory and retrieve crewmembers that they knew were alive."

Lynch, Gatto, and Garnett were on the bow of the *Valour* until large waves washed them off the fender. They stayed together, and "at 0246 were all rescued together by the crew of the *Justine Foss* approximately 15-20 minutes after going into the water.

Another Coast Guard helicopter arrived on site and located Hamilton. The aircraft remained overhead until the *Justine Foss* rescued him.

Coast Guard screen capture.

"The *Justine Foss* located C/E Smoot who appeared to be alive and had him aboard at 0325. He appeared to have a broken leg and arm. Shortly after getting onboard he stopped breathing and went into cardiac arrest." Crewmembers conducted CPR and used a defibrillator on him, but he soon died of – according to the medical examiner – "hypothermia/exposure."

The *Justine Foss* spent several hours searching for the missing AB, but were unable to locate him.

"At 1354, a Marine Corps Helicopter lowered three Coast Guard personnel on to barge *M 192* to rig an emergency tow line. At 1235, 2/E Gatto was medically evacuated by Coast Guard Helicopter. At 1354, the *Justine Foss* took barge *M 192* in tow bound for Wilmington, North Carolina."

The barge measured nearly 500 feet in length; her holds were filled with 5.5 million gallons of heavy fuel oil.

Thus concluded a long and tragic episode that resulted in three fatalities and the loss of the tug *Valour*.

In the aftermath, the Coast Guard conducted an exhaustive examination not only of surviving personnel, but of the wreck, using divers to ascertain the position of the cross-connect valve between fuel tanks.

The primary cause of the catastrophe was obviously the state of the sea. But contributing to the tug's ultimate loss of balance were other factors, none of which was solely responsible but all of which together combined first to initiate and then to exacerbate a deteriorating situation.

> The skipper did not know about the tug's natural port list.
> The skipper was not familiar with the tug's stability characteristics.
> The chief engineer conducted ballast operations on his own recognizance, without direction from the wheelhouse.
> The chief engineer shifted three times the ballast that the skipper ordered.
> Communications between the wheelhouse and engine room were inef-

fective during ballasting operations.

Neither the fuel nor the ballast tanks was equipped with level indicators; thus "there was no way to tell how much liquid was in any of the tanks without going out on deck to use a dipstick.

The cross-connect valves between port and starboard fuel tanks were left open, thus allowing fuel to pour from one tank to the other whenever one of the tanks was higher than the other, such as when the vessel was listing.

There were no valve position indicators on the fuel tanks, so that "each valve would need to be manually manipulated in order to determine if it were opened or closed. Additionally, if the valve's packing was tight causing the valve to be 'stiff,' meaning that it was particularly difficult to manipulate, it may have confused the valve operator into thinking it was open or closed."

"The tank capacity plans for the *Valour* were grossly inaccurate and there were no sounding tables for the #18 port and starboard ballast tanks."

"The engine room has two supply and two exhaust vents. They each have manual closures which are stored between the stacks bolted to the bulkhead. They are not installed while the engine room is in operation. In this case, this is the source of downflooding that eventually led to the sinking of the *Valour*."

"The decision to release the tow did not occur until barge *M192* began to overtake the *Valour* and threatened to trip the tug. The time to release the tow was when AB Sheppard fell overboard. Releasing the tow would have provided instant maneuverability."

The Coast Guard castigated Captain Lynch for not recognizing when his vessel was in extremis, and for not ordering abandon ship on two occasions: first when the helicopter deployed a life raft which came close to the tug; second when the men were grouped on the bow.

To quote the Coast Guard's view: "Giving the crew the option to abandon ship effectively relinquished his responsibility and duty as the *Valour's* master."

I strongly disagree. The Coast Guard viewed these situations in retrospect, with full knowledge of the eventual outcome. At the time these events occurred, no one could have predicted which recourse was the best one to take. Had Lynch ordered the two men to leap for the raft against their will – and against their strong pronouncement that they did not think that they could make it – and they died in the process, then the Coast Guard might have castigated him for ordering them to their deaths. Damned if you do and damned if you don't, as the old saying goes.

With respect to the raft, crewmembers voiced their doubt as to their ability to reach or land on the raft, and opted to stay on the tug. An *order* to abandon ship might have condemned them to death. The same argument applies to the second situation; no one could foresee that the tug would actually sink. She could have stayed afloat for hours.

Coast Guard investigations result in recommendations whose intention is to prevent or mitigate similar situations from recurring. The number one recommendation in the case of the *Valour* was to "issue a safety advisory to the towing industry emphasizing the importance of strict adherence to stability requirements."

Eleven additional recommendations related to ballast, stability, and tank level knowledge and retrofitting.

The Coast Guard also recommended that the skipper, second mate, and assistant engineer have their licenses suspended and revoked.

On the bright side, "It is recommended that the master and crew of the *Justine Foss* be put in for Silver Lifesaving Awards."

The wreck lay at a depth of 107 feet. The top of the smokestack extended some 80 feet above the keel. Thus the clearance depth of the wreck was 25 to 30 feet, depending on the depth of troughs in a rough sea. The Coast Guard marked the site as a hazard to navigation. The Coast Guard also conducted diving operations as part of its investigation, in order to establish the positions of certain valves.

Maritrans initially contemplated salvaging the tug and refurbishing it. Later in 2006, Maritrans was purchased by the Overseas Shipholding Group. Neither Maritrans nor the tug's new owner did much toward salvaging the vessel. After a year of inactivity with regard to total hull salvage, a company representative stated, "the weather has not been cooperative."

Salvage never eventuated, and the vessel was abandoned to the underwriters. As a final recourse, the wreck was razed down to the upper bridge. It no longer poses a menace to navigation.

Despite the shallow depth, the *Valour* is not a popular dive site, perhaps due to its distance from inlets and harbors.

Statistics

Built: 1975
Previous names: None
Gross tonnage: 193
Type of vessel: Twin screw tug
Builder: Main Iron Works, Houma, Louisiana
Owner: Maritrans Valour Company, Tampa, Florida
Port of registry: Wilmington, Delaware
Cause of sinking: Foundered

Sunk: January 18, 2006
Depth: 107 feet
Dimensions: 125' x 36' x 19'
Power: Diesel

Loran: 59335.0 / 456137.0

Courtesy of Pete Manchee.

The United States of NOAA

Once (that I know of), a NOAA employee accused me of "ranting" in one of my published works about the administration for which he worked.

According to the *American Heritage Dictionary of the English Language*, the noun "rant" is defined thus: "violent, loud, or extravagant speech." This reference to oral expression hardly fits the written word.

As a transitive verb (one that takes a direct object, for those of you who have forgotten your high school English grammar), the said dictionary defines the verb "to rant" thus: "to exclaim with violence or extravagance." Again, the reference to the written word fails to apply. Besides which, it is difficult if not impossible for an author to assert violence when merely writing.

As an intransitive verb (one without a direct object to receive the action of the verb), the dictionary defines the verb "to rant" thus: "to speak or declaim in a violent, loud, or vehement manner; rave."

But I quibble. The fact that I tell it like it is obviously irks the folks at the National Oceanic and Atmospheric Administration. The fact that they deserve such contempt just as obviously has fallen upon deaf NOAA (r)ears.

Like Hitler invading Poland, NOAA has no intention of stopping its advance of invasive empire building by means of expanding an existing sanctuary or creating new ones. It is bent on world domination, and will not cease its malicious tactics until it possesses complete totalitarian control of the entire underwater realm, in saltwater and fresh. What else can you expect from a government administration that thinks of itself as "planet stewards?"

Groundwater may be next on NOAA's agenda. Then comes rain.

If NOAA perceives my observations as rants, so be it. The difference between rant and elocution is in the ear of the listener. Now, let's get down to facts.

Not So Little Jack Horner

NOAA has fingers in so many pies that it is difficult to know where to start my so-called rant. Or "tirade:" a word that is equally as incorrect grammatically, as it refers to spoken expression.

I prefer the word "diatribe," which is defined as "a bitter and abusive criticism or denunciation; invective." Not only does that word possess a flair of grammatical acumen with regard to my writings about NOAA, but it applies accurately to NOAA's actions with regard to its gross abuse of power, so that the Administration justifiably warrants such sarcasm and vilification. (How's *that* for a rant? Or a diatribe?)

I will start by writing about my specialty: shipwrecks.

The Billy Mitchell Caper

I have written at length about the German warships that were scuttled by means of aerial bombardment or by naval gunfire off the Virginia portion of the Delmarva Peninsula. To recapitulate: Along with Ken Clayton, in 1990 we discovered and dived on the German battleship *Ostfriesland* at a depth of 380 feet. This discovery dive was so momentous that it was reported in newspapers nationwide.

The *Ostfriesland* was one of Germany's most prized warships. She was the flagship of the 1st Squadron before and during World War One. She was celebrated not only on a Christmas card (above), but on a commemorative stamp (left).

Over the next five years we discovered and explored the cruiser *Frankfurt* (at a depth of 420 feet), the destroyer *G-102* (at 350 feet), and three U-boats (285 feet, 275 feet, and 230 feet): six of the nine warships that were taken from the Kaiser's fleet and brought to the United States for study purposes in 1919. Again, these discovery dives were so remarkable that a television crew accompanied us, then broadcast a multi-part news report that was seen across the country.

In addition to magazine articles, I wrote about these discoveries in a number of my books: *Ultimate Wreck Diving Guide* (1992), *Shipwrecks of Virginia* (1992), *Ironclad Legacy* (1993), *The Lusitania Controversies* (1999), *Deep, Dark, and Dangerous* (2005), *Shadow Divers Exposed* (2006), *Shipwreck Sagas* (2008), *The Kaiser's U-boats in American Waters* (2010), *NOAA's Ark: the Rise of the Fourth Reich* (2013), and *The Great Navy Wreck Scam* (2015).

In order to enable technical divers to visit these historic shipwrecks, I provided the precise locations of those warships that we actually explored, and the approximate locations of those that we did not. Some of the succeeding divers also wrote and spoke about their experiences on the scuttled German warships, particularly J. T. Barker, who posted details of his dives on his website, where they are still available for all to read.

Over the years, I also gave lectures and slide presentations about these underwater events in numerous States of the Union.

In September 16, 2012, NOAA issued a press release in which it claimed to have "discovered" the same shipwrecks that Clayton and I had discovered more than two decades earlier. As you can ascertain by my writings, television appearances, and lectures, I did not keep our discoveries secret. By the time of NOAA's fallacious announcement, the German warships that I called "The Billy Mitchell Wrecks" were old hat.

Now NOAA claimed the "discovery" of what it called "The Billy Mitchell Fleet." As you can see from above, by that time I had written about our various shipwreck discoveries in ten books, the focus of one being exclusively about NOAA and its sordid history of lies, deception, and administrative abuse. There is no way that NOAA could feign ignorance of our discoveries of the Billy Mitchell Wrecks, especially as NOAA maintains a library of my nautical history books, and as my dives on the *Ostfriesland* were brought out in court hearings during two of my four *Monitor* lawsuits against NOAA in the 1990's.

This was not the first time that others had taken credit for my accomplishments. Probably it would not be the last. This particular case was simply another in a long list of measures that NOAA has taken to rewrite history: first by neglecting to give credit where it was due, and second by writing me out of NOAA's sordid history of villainy.

As an example, despite the fact that my four federal lawsuits against NOAA forced the hostile government administration to permit access to the Monitor National Marine Sanctuary, neither my name nor these cases are mentioned anywhere on NOAA's website. George Orwell predicted such a government method of changing history in *1984*.

NOAA now claims that it permits recreational diving on the *Monitor*, without not-

The United States of NOAA

ing that it does so only against its wishes, solely because it was forced to do so by legal decree and at the behest of the United States Congress. By cleverly wording its statements, NOAA makes it seem as if they always permitted recreational diving: a deceptive practice that is a common tactic in its administration.

NOAA went so far as to claim that its search for the Billy Mitchell wrecks started years before NOAA's so-called "discovery." It would have taken no more than a few minutes of research to obtain the location of the wrecks from my books. But NOAA's press release was written in a vacuum, as if the locations of the wrecks were not already widely known: standard NOAA newsmanship.

Not content with taking credit that was undeserved, NOAA took a swipe at the recreational diving community by claiming, "we have evidence that divers have damaged some of them."

The question that is begged by this prejudicial statement is: How can divers have damaged a wreck which NOAA claimed to have just discovered? Furthermore, if divers did in fact damage this wreck, then NOAA could not have discovered it. Ipso facto (Latin for "by the fact itself"), recreational divers must have discovered it.

Another question that is begged is: How could a diver possibly damage a wreck that was bombarded to perdition, then crashed to the seabed in more than 300 feet of seawater, has lain in a corrosive environment for ninety-one years, and now lies badly rusted and largely collapsed? Furthermore, under these conditions, how could NOAA *identify* so-called diver damage and distinguish it from natural deterioration.

Again, this is just another case of NOAA fakery: making an unsupported allegation that ridicules the true discoverers who found the wrecks before they did.

J. T. Barker solved one of these conundrums for me. On one of his expeditions to the *Ostfriesland*, his dive buddy (name withheld in order to prevent NOAA from harassing him) found a loose porthole lying on the sand next to the wreck. He recovered the porthole. Afterward, Barker posted on the Internet the story of his dive and the recovery of the porthole. This porthole recovery is what NOAA called "damage," despite the fact that the porthole was not beaten free of wreckage.

Now read the quote carefully: "we have evidence that divers have damaged some of them." The statement is carefully worded: NOAA did not claim to have *seen* any damage, but claimed to have evidence of it. The evidence was Barker's Internet posting. NOAA relied this posting as "evidence." Although it was true that a porthole was recovered, the so-called "evidence" was purely hearsay.

NOAA exaggerated this lone event to pretend that recreational divers had damaged "some of them:" a falsehood which implied that more than one wreck was "damaged."

NOAA has refused to release the locations of the wrecks that they "discovered." Here are the Billy Mitchell wreck locations that are in my possession:

Ostfriesland	37-09.396 / 74-34.562	36825.0 / 41589.0
Frankfurt	37-11.940 / 74.34.475	26827.1 / 41611.7
G-102		26827.3 / 41611.8
V-43	37-16.893 / 74-32.163	
U-117		26877.7 / 41595.3
U-140	37-11.940 / 74-45.410	26874.1 / 41574.5
UB-148	37-09.449 / 74-45.266	26873.6 / 41569.1

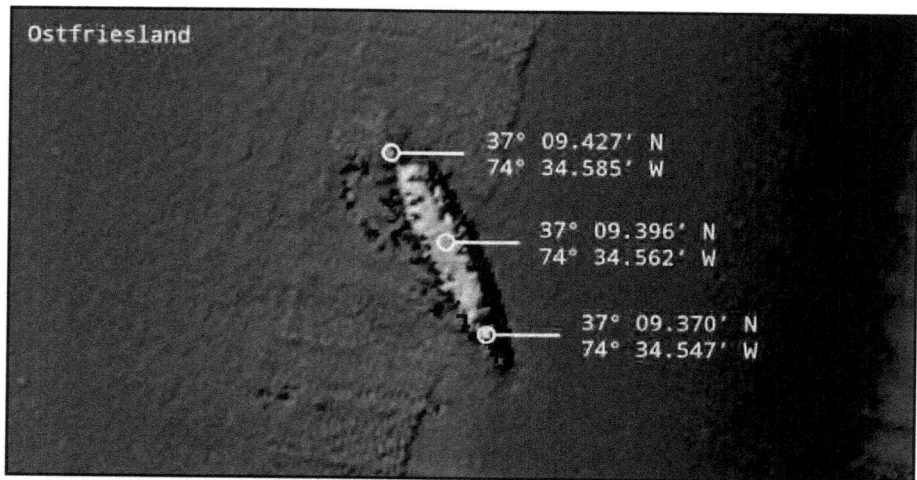

NOAA's multi-beam image of the *Ostfriesland*. This is the only wreck for which NOAA willingly provided the location. That is because I had already made the location public knowledge by publishing the coordinates in my books. By way of example, NOAA has still refused to allow the public to know the location of the *Monitor*, a wreck for which it "permits" recreational diving, and on which it prohibits fishing. One might ask: how can an angler stay away from a location that is unknown to him. By way of another example, NOAA has not provided the public with the location of the *YP-389*, which is discussed below. Don't worry; I have published the location. By these examples my readers can see that NOAA does not truly work *for* the people, but *against* them, by withholding public information from the public that is funding the Administration.

YP-389

I wrote extensively about the *YP-389* in three of my books: *Track of the Gray Wolf* (1989), *Shipwrecks of North Carolina: North* (1993), and *The Fuhrer's U-boats in American Waters* (2006).

In 2009, NOAA issued a press release in which it claimed to have "located and identified the final resting place of the *YP-389*" on August 7 of that year. This statement was written in such a way as to give the impression that NOAA *discovered* the wreck site. In fact, the *YP-389* was discovered in 1973 by a Duke University expedition that was searching for the Civil War ironclad *Monitor*. That expedition resulted in the finding of twenty-one wrecks. NOAA simply obtained the records of that expedition, then went straight to the previously recorded locations, and deployed a remotely operated vehicle (ROV) to photograph the wrecks.

Although NOAA identified the wreck from photographic images, it did not discover the wreck. NOAA specializes in newsmanship: cleverly crafting language in such a way as to lead readers into inferring something that was not specifically stated. Creating deception is all in the way the story is told.

I gave the wreck's historical location as 34° 53' North / 75° 31' west; also as: south of the Diamond Shoals, 5 to 8 miles northeast of buoy No. 4 of the Hatteras mine area. The actual location turned out to be 34-56.445 / 75-23.900.

Although NOAA is a government administration, and all information it gathers belongs to the public, it refused to release the location of the wreck to the taxpayers who funded NOAA's expensive search efforts. Like all journalists, the actual GPS coordinates were provided by a private source whose anonymity I must maintain.

When I first heard about the finding of the *YP-389*, my first thought was: Why was NOAA spending money in search of shipwrecks? Its mandated mission has nothing to do with shipwreck research or private hunting expeditions. So who authorized the expenditures for a project that had nothing to do with NOAA's reason for existing?

NOAA provided the answer. According to a press release, the search for the *YP-389* was the first leg of NOAA's Battle of the Atlantic expedition. I will return to this subject in the following section. But let me state here and now that embedded in the press release was information about a three-week-long expedition that NOAA had conducted the previous year, on the known and oft-visited sites of the British armed trawler *Bedfordshire*, and the German U-boats *U-85*, *U-352*, and *U-701*. Furthermore, NOAA noted that these surveys were only "part of a larger multi-year project to research and document a number of historically significant shipwrecks."

For fun, NOAA personnel also made all-expenses-paid recreational dives on the *Keshena* and *Dixie Arrow*.

I repeat, NOAA did not find the wreck on its own. The wreck was discovered in 1973 by a Duke University ocean survey. The role that NOAA played was in photographing the wreck with "high definition imagery."

In keeping with its attitude toward the public, NOAA refused to release these images to me when I requested them.

Bluefields and U-576

I first wrote about the German U-boat *U-576* sinking the *Bluefields*, and the U-boat's immediate loss with all hands, in *Track of the Gray Wolf* (1989). I wrote about them again in *The Fuhrer's U-boats in American Waters* (2006).

The historical location I gave for the *Bluefields* was 34° 46' north / 75° 22' west; for the *U-576* I gave 34° 51' / 75° 22'.

NOAA found the *Bluefields* at 34-45.695 / 75-30.297; the *U-576* at 34-45.733 / 75-30.449. The two wrecks lay some seven hundred feet apart: slightly more than a city block.

According to one NOAA press release, NOAA spent *seven years* and searched *several hundred square miles* of ocean in its hunt for the long-lost U-boat. How much money was spent on this seemingly pointless and self-indulgent pursuit went unannounced. Even though the American people paid for the expensive quest, as usual NOAA refused to divulge the locations of either wreck. I obtained the GPS numbers from a confidential source.

The date given in the press release for the finding of the U-boat was August 24, 2016. The *Bluefields* was found "in August."

In one of NOAA's press releases – there were many, for NOAA is known for tooting its horn as loud and as often as possible – NOAA admitted that it was the result of a scheme "to survey and document vessels lost during WWII off the North Carolina coast." This scheme – or scam – was "part of the NOAA Battle of the Atlantic Research Project."

In the same press release, NOAA stated with its standard grandiosity, "NOAA's mission is to understand and predict changes in the Earth's environment, from the depths of the ocean to the surface of the sun."

So why the concentration on World War Two losses? There was no correlation between them and the Earth's environment. In reality NOAA was looking for ammunition.

Not the kind of ammunition that is found on World War Two wrecks, but the kind that NOAA can use to expand its authority.

According to another NOAA press release, "Data collected on the *U-576*, *Bluefields*, and *YP-389*, three sites that have never been visited by people since their loss in 1942, will prove invaluable to Monitor National Marine Sanctuary as it continues to develop approaches to better protect these resources and share this history with the broader public."

In other words, all this time and money was spent so that NOAA could justify expanding the boundaries of the Monitor National Marine Sanctuary to encompass all the waters off the coast of North Carolina: the create a huge mega-sanctuary over which NOAA would have complete totalitarian control, and in which fishing and diving would be disallowed. Stated differently, NOAA was hyping the "importance" of inanimate objects on the bottom of the sea in its bid to prevent hardworking commercial anglers and charter boat skippers from earning their living. And this is to say nothing about the economic collapse that would result from the loss of the tourist trade.

NOAA keeps claiming that it wants to "protect" and "preserve" these wrecks. Yet except for the *Monitor*, NOAA has done nothing to protect or preserve the hundreds of wrecks that are already under its aegis. In fact, NOAA has never defined the words "protect" and "preserve," or the *kind* of protection or preservation that it would initiate if it ever did start to "protect" and "preserve" them.

In NOAA's usage, "protect and "preserve" are euphemisms for "control."

NOAA also claims that it needs to expand the sanctuary so it can study the wrecks that were sunk in the Battle of the Atlantic. Yet no one is stopping NOAA from studying the wrecks now. Just like everyone else, NOAA has free reign to study shipwrecks to its heartless content – or, as far as its funding will allow. It does not need to have the wrecks in a sanctuary in order to study them, which it has already proven by its years-long searches.

What NOAA really wants is exclusivity over shipwrecks; that is, full possession with all other contenders excluded.

In NOAA's statement above, it claimed that it wanted "to share this history with the broader public." So far it has neglected to share much information with that public. Not only does it refuse to share locations, so that the "broader public" can study or otherwise have access to and study these wrecks, but, other than a few sample pictures, it has not released the video footage or "high definition imagery" which NOAA is required by law to share with the public. I know this is true because I contacted NOAA and asked for digital copies of footage and photographs, and NOAA refused to allow me to have copies of imagery which, as an American citizen and taxpayer, I own.

The Prevarication Business

Adding insult to injury, NOAA issued a press release in which it claimed, "*U-576* was seen on August 24 for the first time since WW2." This statement contains two blatant lies.

NOAA is so used to lying that in this case it lied about itself. NOAA's press release people must have forgotten that they had already issued a press release about the discovery of the U-boat – *two years earlier*. Apparently, NOAA just makes up stories as it goes along, and issues false statements that draw attention to itself in the present, regardless of what it stated in the past. Perhaps NOAA should keep better records of its falsifying press releases.

In a previous press release, which was "revised" on October 21, 2014, "After poring over historical records and sweeping the seafloor with cutting-edge technology, NOAA researchers have pinpointed the long-buried wrecks of the freighter *Bluefields* and German U-boat *U-576* off the North Carolina coast. The discovery of these two vessels, which met their end in a pivotal naval skirmish in 1942, sheds new light on a bloody yet little-known chapter in American history: the Battle of the Atlantic.

The press release contains a number of misleading or untruthful statements. Let's examine each one in detail.

First, there was no need to "pore" over historical records because those records were well known and had long been published and were in the public eye. As noted in the previous section, I wrote two books about the Battle of the Atlantic, and many other books succeeded mine. By the time NOAA started to "pore" over historical records, hundreds of books and magazine articles had been published about the so-called Battle.

Second, the wrecks were not buried, either long or short. Had they been buried, NOAA would not have been able to located them by using side-scan sonar equipment. Side-scan sonar shows only those objects that protrude above the seabed; it cannot see objects that are not exposed.

Third, the naval skirmish was in no way pivotal. It was just another routine U-boat attack among hundreds. More than a hundred Allied vessels and a dozen U-boats were sunk in the Eastern Sea Frontier alone, and that does not count how many were lost in the other American sea frontiers. If NOAA truly believed that the incident was pivotal, it neglected to mention why. It just made an unsupported allegation, then dropped the subject altogether.

Fourth, the location of the two hulks shed no new light on anything – except, for what it's worth, about how far off was the navigation of Navy and merchant vessel captains, plus aircraft pilots, who plotted the attack position incorrectly. Again, NOAA offered nothing to substantiate any "new light," or attempted to explain what was learned about the Battle of the Atlantic from the location of the wrecks.

Nonetheless, NOAA makes such empty-headed statements all the time. Worse, NOAA gets away with it. The public is led to believe that NOAA spent millions of dollars on accomplishing something great, and doesn't even realize that nothing was accomplished that is going to change history or add new knowledge to the Battle of the Atlantic. Little if any useful information can be revealed by studying collapsing steel hulks on the bottom of the sea.

The Incredible Mr. Limpet

The second blatant lies is that by the time NOAA got around to photographing the U-boat two years later, J. T. Barker had already shot videotape footage of the wreck. He announced his successful photo mission on Facebook and on his website. This is the same website from which NOAA learned that divers had "damaged some of them."

So we already know that NOAA habitually monitored Barkers website. This means that NOAA possessed certain knowledge that he had shot video of the U-boat before NOAA's boat even left the dock.

Barker was the owner and operator of the dive boat *Under Pressure*. He developed an ingenious method of observing and visually exploring ultra-deep shipwrecks in such a way that it obviates the need for decompression. He not only demonstrated the principles behind its efficacy, but he shot foot of the *U-576* in a 2.8-knot current at a depth of 700 feet.

Barker got the idea from a basic rig that his commercial fishing pals used, then modified it to compensate for current and depth.

Drop cameras are not a new invention. They were developed during World War Two as a means to examine tankers and freighters that had been sunk by German U-boats off the American eastern seaboard. How fitting that Barker first employed his rig on a German U-boat off the American eastern seaboard. The basic system has evolved over the years, not only from refinements in configuration but from advances in technology. The still camera has now been replaced by a video camera.

Anyone can lower a video camera over the side of a boat. Obtaining comprehensible footage without losing the rig is another story. The inherent problem is aiming the camera and keeping it aimed in current. Drop lines twist constantly in the water; cameras sail in current. The result is a camera that springs like a top and points mostly in the wrong direction.

Barker's crucial improvement was a stabilizing system. For a mounting bracket he used a homemade contrivance of his own design. On this he mounted a GoPro video camera in a waterproof housing. He positioned two lights so that their beams aligned with the direction in which the lens was pointed. Now came the stabilization add-ons.

First he suspended a 10-pound weight below the rig, on a line whose breaking strength was less than that of the drop line. The length of the weighted line was 10 feet longer than the relief of the wreck. The weight maintained the verticality of the rig. If the weight snagged in wreckage, the weight line would break instead of the drop line.

Then he added large vanes or rudders that kept the lens pointing into the current as the boat drifted over the wreck. The rig was then lowered by means of a commercial bandit fishing rig. The bandit rig (or reel) was extremely useful for retrieving the video platform; reeling it in by hand from 700 feet could prove exhausting.

This rig may sound simple but a great deal of thought went into choosing the parts and assembling the components in order to achieve the desired results.

The camera rig can also be used on shallow wrecks by anchoring the boat and letting out anchor line until the boat is positioned over the wreck.

Barker called his innovative deep-sea camera rig Mr. Limpet, after a character in the movie which is the title of this section. Don Knotts played the eponymous role.

Barker's fellow explorers on this exploratory expedition were Phil Jones and Michele Peabody. The three of them shared the charter fee. Chris Romine cut the wings and Matt Hannum provided the pool after hours and helped in testing the rig.

As Barker so aptly noted, "Getting the gear cost: housing $399, GoPro $299, [raw materials for] Mr. Limpet rig to make $20, cost of the boat around $160 each. Being the first to get video . . . priceless."

NOAA's political pull and power enabled it not only to control the dispensation and distribution of news, but to both rewrite history in the manner of George Orwell's Ministry of Truth, and to ignore facts that contradicted its promotional story line.

It was for reasons like this that I wrote *NOAA's Ark: the Rise of the Fourth Reich*.

The Potsdam Agreement

With regard to the *U-576*, a NOAA press release claimed, "The U.S. recognizes Germany's ownership" of the U-boat's wreckage. This is another blatant lie. The U.S. most certainly does *not* recognize Germany's ownership of the *U-576* – or any other U-boat that Nazi Germany owned or operated during World War Two.

At NOAA's insistence, the Germany Foreign Office claimed, "In legal succession to the former German Reich, the Federal Republic of Germany, as a rule, sees itself as the owner of formerly Reich-owned military assets, such as a ship or aircraft wreckages."

In reality, the so-called "rule" does not apply. Anyone who has studied the history of World War Two U-boats cannot possibly be ignorant of the Potsdam Agreement. After the capitulation of Nazi Germany, the Allies issued the terms of unconditional surrender in a document known as the Potsdam Agreement. The Potsdam Agreement stipulated that Germany was to be stripped of all – and I stress the word "all" – of its military arsenal. This included military arms and ammunition, army vehicles, navy vessels, and in particular –emphasized by name at the insistence of Winston Churchill – *all* U-boats. Furthermore, Germany was never again permitted to build, buy, or own U-boats.

This means that the successor German government does not and never has owned the wreckage of Nazi U-boats.

NOAA's statement in the first sentence of this section is a deliberate falsehood that NOAA has perpetuated in order to ingratiate itself with the current German regime. The current German regime cannot possibly be unaware of the Potsdam Agreement, so it too is perpetuating a lie.

In actual fact, and despite NOAA's contention to the contrary, the U.S. recognizes the Potsdam Agreement to which it was a signatory. The U.S. does not recognize the current German regime as the owner of any part of the Nazi war machine.

The current German regime may be the legal successor to Reich-owned non-military assets, but not to any of the Reich-owned war machines and vessels.

The U.S. Navy has also jumped onto the U-boat propaganda bandwagon because it is fighting with NOAA over ownership of wrecks. The Navy is now involved in a scheme to wrest title of more than 23,000 wrecks worldwide from the public domain to Navy control: a ruse that will include U-boats from both world wars.

NOAA, the Navy, and the current German regime are all engaged in a global conspiracy to disregard the Potsdam Agreement in order to promote their own agendas with regard to warships in general and U-boats in particular: a three-way fight for illegal ownership and authoritarian custody. None of them has expressed any willingness to preserve the wrecks from the forces of nature: by means of cathodic protection on metal-hulled wrecks, by means of coating wooden-hulled wrecks with retardant paint as a way to protect them from wood-boring organisms, by installing supports on collapsing hulls, by building cofferdams around wrecks to protect them from waves and deep ground swells, or by any other means.

I informed NOAA, the Navy, and the public about international law in relation to the Potsdam Agreement in *Shipwrecks of North Carolina: South* (1992), *Shipwrecks of Rhode Island and Connecticut* (2004), *Shadow Divers Exposed* (2006), *NOAA's Ark: the Rise of the Fourth Reich* (2013) and *The Great Navy Wreck Scam* (2015).

NOAA's Persistent Territorial Demands
(Shades of the Shade of Adolf Hitler)

Hitler was known for saying, "This is my last territorial demand." Unfortunately, he reiterated that statement ad nauseam as he continued to gobble neighboring nations, and then not so neighboring nations. His real goal was to take over the world. Now, NOAA is dedicated to taking over the underwater world. And not just the seabed but the water column above it and the surface interface.

NOAA has a number of fingers in underwater pies for both the expansion of existing sanctuaries and the creation of additional ones.

I have already mentioned the proposed expansion of the Monitor National Marine Sanctuary. The enormity of this proposed expansion is, well, enormous. This sternly regulated sanctuary is centered on the Civil War ironclad *Monitor*, and consists of a column of water that is one mile in diameter, with radii extending half a mile from the wreck site.

NOAA wants to expand the boundaries of this sanctuary a million-fold!

NOAA's short-term goal is to create a new sanctuary without seeming to create one, by expanding the boundaries of the existing sanctuary to encompass all the ocean off the State of North Carolina to a hundred miles offshore, and giving it the pretentious name of Battle of the Atlantic National Marine Sanctuary.

But NOAA does not intend to stop there.

Canyons and Seamounts
The Tip of the Iceberg

Already in the works is the proposed expansion of the Stellwagen Bank National Marine Sanctuary, which, in keeping with the proposed expansion of the Monitor NMS, would include all the waters off the State of Massachusetts beyond the three-mile territorial limit.

Regulations for this important long-time commercial fishing area will be "Subject to such terms and conditions as the Secretaries deem appropriate." Letting secretaries control regulations without input from the fishing industry is akin to having game lands in which hunting is not permitted: a contradiction in terms if there ever was one. The word for this kind of control is totalitarianism.

Now watch how the progression works.

In addition to expansion of the Stellwagen Bank NMS, NOAA has already appropriated some 5,000 square miles of seabed that is collectively called the "Northeast Canyons and Seamounts Marine National Monuments," with the same simple but global regulations that I quoted two paragraphs above. To wit: commercial fishing has been banned altogether. Trawling and dragging are outlawed. Anchoring a vessel is prohibited.

This monument is located off the Grand Banks, and includes the Lydonia Canyon, Gilbert Canyon, Oceanographer Canyon, Bear Seamount, Physalia Seamount, Retriever Seamount, and Mytilus Seamount.

At the present time, NOAA is also attempting to take permanent possession of at least four other canyons: the Hudson Canyon (off New York and New Jersey), the Wilmington Canyon (off Delaware), the Baltimore Canyon (off Maryland), and the

Norfolk Canyon (off Virginia.

NOAA collectively calls these canyons the Urban National Marine Sanctuary.

Next to go in NOAA's creeping jurisdiction will be (between the previously listed canyons from north to south): Hendrickson Canyon, Toms Canyon, Carteret Canyon, Lindenkohl Canyon, Spencer Canyon, Poor Mans Canyon, and Washington Canyon.

This agglutination process is yet another foot in the door and up the public's ass. NOAA's ultimate long-term goal is to make the entire Eastern Sea Frontier (from Maine to Florida) one huge mega-sanctuary with highly restrictive regulations. In fact, when NOAA reps speak at public meetings about proposed sanctuaries and expansions, they use a coastal map that shows the boundaries of the wartime frontiers that were formulated by the Navy after the outbreak of World War Two.

Now you can see where NOAA is headed.

The Robbery of the Outer Banks

Like spreading cancer, NOAA's creeping jurisdictional expedient is to create a number of small isolated sanctuaries – with each one proposed to be NOAA's last territorial demand – then gradually expand their boundaries, and finally stitch them together the way NOAA did off the coast of California.

I explained this insinuating process in my book, *NOAA's Ark*, but Californians did not heed my warning. Now all the offshore waters of the country's third largest State suffer from severe restrictions with regard to boating, fishing, and diving. Like Poland was to Hitler, this was not NOAA's last territorial demand.

NOAA is invading the eastern seaboard in a number of places and in several ways. As noted above, for years NOAA has been trying to expand the Monitor National Marine Sanctuary in order to control all the waters off the coast of North Carolina. Strong opposition from individuals, organizations, local communities, and Congressional representatives, has so far blocked this expansion, but NOAA keeps trying to overrun the American version of the Maginot Line.

The region that will be the most adversely affected by NOAA's excessively restrictive regulations is called collectively the Outer Banks. These barrier islands already suffer from obstructive regulations because many of the sandy beaches and inland swamps and forests are national wildlife refuges under the "management" (read "control") of the National Park Service.

Dare County commissioners are well aware that local businesses will be adversely affected by additional intrusion, and noted this in their letter to NOAA. In order to temper Dare County's strong disapproval of expansion, in its records and memoranda to Congress, NOAA used the euphemism "concerns" to supplant the accurate descriptive word "opposition." This makes it seem that "concerns" are of little consequence, thus hiding from Congress the true nature of local input.

Dare County, which hosts the Outer Banks and its seaside resorts, "strongly objects to any expansion of the sanctuary or the creation of additional Marine Sanctuaries." In the county's letter to NOAA, titled "Position of the Dare County Board of Commissioners," the commissioners emphasized their opposition on several grounds. Thus:

"Expansion of the [Monitor] Sanctuary could result in the entire body of ocean waters off the Dare County seashore becoming a gigantic Marine Sanctuary in the future, which would result in highly restricted access that would devastate recreational and commercial fishing and seriously harm the economic stability of Dare County."

And Dare County ain't just whistling Dixie. Dare County's fears have already been executed in the Florida Keys National Marine Sanctuary, where NOAA's restrictive regulations and whimsical attitude has put numerous people out of business and forced others to lose their livelihood. NOAA enforces more stringent regulations whenever it feels like it, with no prior notice and without input from anyone or any other regulatory agency. NOAA does whatever it wants whenever it wants, stakeholders be damned.

Dare County Position Letter: "Dare County has witnessed first-hand, how promises made by other well-intended federal superintendents have later been set aside by those who follow after they have retired or are reassigned." As County Commissioners noted, "Ironclad verbiage is needed to make sure that promises made today guarantee public access tomorrow for responsible SCUBA divers, and for recreational and commercial fishing."

Despite these bona fide objections, NOAA steadfastly refuses to make any such "ironclad verbiage." NOAA wants a blank check so it can do anything it wants any time it feels like doing it.

Let me now demonstrate how NOAA's latest scheme for global domination is working in combination with other proposals (or territorial demands).

NOAA Beery
or, NOAA's Latest Con Game

NOAA is now using shills to promote its nefarious goal to take possession of all the waters off the eastern seaboard, and ultimately beyond.

According to the dictionary, a shill is "one who works as a decoy, as in a confidence game, by posing as a customer or an innocent bystander."

To set the stage, NOAA started advertising for shills in 2012, in its mammoth 212-page "Monitor National Marine Sanctuary Draft Revised Management Plan." Now, when non-NOAA employees submit suggestions for new sanctuaries, NOAA can claim that they were derived in response to NOAA's plea for areas that needed NOAA's "protection." (Read "control" for "protection.") This shell game is an ingenious way for NOAA to swindle the public without seeming to make the proposal, by giving the appearance of distancing itself from the designation process.

As Shakespeare might have written, a fraud by any other name would smell as rank.

NOAA used this kind of deception to propose a sanctuary that would encompass Sandy Hook, the bay, the surrounding waters, the rivers that feed the bay, and the land that borders the waterways.

I remind my readers that the rivers that feed the bay do not constitute a "marine environment." The dictionary definition of "marine" is "of or pertaining to the sea."

NOAA has a history of exceeding its authority and ignoring its Congressional mandate to "protect" the marine environment. NOAA has already moved into the freshwater of Lake Huron by creating the Thunder Bay National Marine Sanctuary – against strong opposition from stakeholders and local residents.

Fierce restrictions abound. For example, whenever inlets to marinas and boat launches became clogged with silt, the State of Michigan routinely dredged the lake bottom in order to facilitate safe passage. But according to sanctuary regulations, dredging constitutes "disturbing" the bottom and the plants and animals that live in the mud. As a result, a number of marinas have gone out of business because, as a result of clogged inlets, they can no longer cater to local and itinerant boaters; they cannot rent slips because they are inaccessible from the lake, so boaters must go elsewhere. The same is true for public launch sites, whose access to the lake has been compromised by depths too shallow to let pleasure boats pass.

The same regulations will apply to the proposed Sandy Hook NMS.

Worse yet, NOAA plans to include adjacent *land* in the sanctuary. I reiterate: NOAA's Congressional mandate pertains to the offshore marine environment in international waters beyond the State and federal three-mile territorial limit. In no way does its mandate permit NOAA to usurp State and personal property.

If this stepping stone is emplaced, the next phase will be to expand the Sandy Hook NMS farther upstream and along the New Jersey coast. It will also spread offshore.

Add expansion of the Hudson Canyon NMS to the mix, as well as the Urban National Marine Sanctuary, and . . . well, you can see where this is heading. NOAA would then control Hudson Bay, the Mud Hole, the Hudson Canyon, and parts of the New Jersey and New York coasts. Do not let this happen to the eastern seaboard, or fishing and diving will become activities of the past.

Another Freshwater But Not So Refreshing Drink

Not content with proposing to expand the Thunder Bay NMS by adding another one hundred square miles to the existing sanctuary, in order to control more shipwrecks, NOAA has also proposed to takeover more than one *thousand* square miles of Wisconsin freshwater. Again, the purpose is to control more than three dozen known wrecks plus other "cultural resources" which NOAA refuses to identify, as well as nearly one hundred additional wrecks that have yet to be discovered.

This sanctuary would include all the waters of western Lake Michigan off the counties of Manitowoc, Sheboygan and Ozaukee, right to the beach. In other words, as soon as a bather stepped off the shore into the cool refreshing lake, he would be stepping into NOAA regulated territory. Perhaps bathers would not even be allowed to step into the lake, for fear of contaminating the water with the microbes on their feet.

Anglers will no longer be permitted to fish from the bank. Judging by past experiences, particularly in the Florida Keys, you can take that to the bank. No matter what NOAA states now, after it gains control of sanctuary waters, it can change the regulations anytime, anyhow, in order to suit its fancy. NOAA's promises guarantee only that the people are bound to get screwed.

In the eighteenth century, statesman Edmund Burke stated, "Those who don't know history are doomed to repeat it." This quote has been restated, rehashed, and paraphrased ever since, yet people still refuse to learn by its portent. Anyone who knows the facts of NOAA's past actions can infer the conduct of NOAA future actions.

To alert Governor Scott Walker of the perils of letting NOAA take control of all of Wisconsin's submerged bottomlands, I sent him a copy of *NOAA's Ark: the Rise of the Fourth Reich*. Undoubtedly, he has heard only NOAA's side of the proposal: a side that is backed by lies and false promises. My book presents the true history of NOAA's past actions, so that he and the people he represents will know what to expect should they cede Wisconsin's portion of Lake Superior to NOAA.

NOAA's Procrustean Bed

Fortunately, I am not the only one who is posting warnings about NOAA's totalitarian attitude. Wisconsin citizen, lawyer, and riparian landowner Judith Perlman published some eye-opening facts about NOAA's sanctuary proposal, and how NOAA's mishandling of other sanctuaries has adversely affected adjacent inhabitants.

As noted above, NOAA claimed that the reason behind the Wisconsin proposal was to protect shipwrecks and other unnamed cultural resources. Before I proceed with Perlman's observations, I need to remind my readers that when Congress passed the Marine, Protection, Research, and Sanctuaries Act in 1972, the purpose of the Act was to create *marine* sanctuaries in order to "preserve, restore, or enhance areas for the conservational, recreational, ecological, research or esthetic values in coastal waters." Coastal meant the seaside: saltwater beyond the three-mile territorial limit. As reiterated previously, "marine" means "of or pertaining to the sea." There is no way in which this congressional mandate can be misunderstood by educated representatives.

Additionally, there was no mention of shipwrecks. The act referred only to the marine ecosystem.

NOAA has taken it upon itself to "protect" (read "control") shipwrecks, but there was never any congressional intention that NOAA should create its authority to do so.

With regard to the Wisconsin sanctuary, Perlman noted that NOAA's proposed regulations empower it to exercise authority over any "sanctuary resource," which includes "any living or nonliving resource of a national marine sanctuary that contributes to the conservation, recreational, ecological, historical, educational, cultural, archaeological, scientific, or aesthetic value of the sanctuary." The only resource that NOAA left out was the kitchen sink. Or did it?

Perlman found that NOAA defined "shipwreck" as any "piece of debris . . . regardless of where taken, removed, moved, caught, collected or harvested." Thus, as Perlman noted, shipwreck "can be a piece of driftwood, beach glass or metal found anywhere." This includes the kitchen sink.

Not only that, but Perlman pointed out that "NOAA never studied whether the shipwrecks need further protection. It proposes to do so only after the sanctuary is designated." In other words, NOAA wants a blank check and offers nothing but empty promises in return. Let me reiterate that in all the years since the first sanctuary was created, NOAA has protected – truly protected, as from natural deterioration – only one shipwreck: the *Monitor*, and it did so by breaking the wreck apart in order to salvage discrete parts. Every other wreck under NOAA's control has been left to rust or rot.

Perlman cited examples of NOAA's excessive authority. A NOAA employee "took photos of and stopped a local organization from using their metal detectors on a public beach." I stress the word "public," because in NOAA's vocabulary, everything that is public belongs to NOAA.

Perlman found that "NOAA ticketed a couple in a California sanctuary who picked up beach rocks for 'unlawful mineral extraction'." The absurdity of this incident speaks for itself.

Perlman learned that once NOAA takes control of Wisconsin's bottomlands, Wisconsin's fine of $5,000 per violation – that is, a real commercial violation, not picking up a stone – would be increased to $130,000 per violation per day." And guess who gets to keep the money. If you guessed NOAA, put a gold star on your forehead. But don't get the gold star from a NOAA-controlled beach.

Perlman ascertained that "the National Marine Sanctuary Act allows NOAA to assess and collect fees for the conduct of any activity under a special-use permit, including 'the fair market value of the use of sanctuary resources.' This gives NOAA the right to charge for activities we presently enjoy along the lake."

Let me stress that those activities to which Perlman alluded we now enjoy *for free*. And guess who establishes the fair market value? NOAA, of course.

Perlman noted, "Our Lake Michigan recreational areas will come under the control of a federal bureaucrat, which could mean permit fees and expensive project requirements."

Perlman observed, "there is no accountability for taxpayer dollars."

Finally, Perlman stated, "Until now, the federal government has bullied its way through our community with a 'sell job' that has deliberately omitted facts necessary to make an informed decision. The whole proposal is a house of cards built on nothing."

Further affiant sayeth naught. In other words, "That's all, folks."

Mellowing out in Mallows Bay

As long as I am on a kick to discuss NOAA's freshwater annexations, I should mention the Potomac River, which divides Maryland from Virginia. Mallows Bay is a small bay on the Maryland side of the river where more than a hundred obsolete wooden-hulled merchant vessels were scuttled in the 1920's. It soon became a junk yard to which other unwanted hulks were towed and disposed.

Mallows Bay is a small indentation in the Potomac River. The wrecks are concentrated in an area of approximately one-quarter square mile.

Using that tiny spot as the kernel for another large acquisition, NOAA wants to create the Mallows Bay–Potomac River National Marine Sanctuary. The proposed sanctuary will encompass forty miles of the Potomac River, and is intended to include all the major tributaries along that length: Belmont Bay, Powell's Creek, Mattawoman Creek, Chicamuxen Creek, Quantico Creek, Chopawamsic Creek, Widewater Creek, Potomac Creek, Nanjamoy Creek, and Port Tobacco River – some *fifty-two square miles* in all.

In other words, the total area that NOAA wants to usurp is *more than two hundred times* the space in which the shipwrecks are located.

All of these tributaries plus the Potomac River itself possess countless docks and piers that protrude into the river, all of which will become beholden to NOAA in order to remain in existence. Permits will be required in order to make repairs. Boat motors might be outlawed because their propellers will churn the mud in shallow water.

Needless to say, this major artery between the national's capital and the Chesapeake Bay will be strangled by sanctuary regulations. Major waterside municipalities rely on tourism and access to the river for their livelihood. When NOAA takes all this away, and refuses to allow dredging so that marina and public boat launch sites can remain open, the area will wither away under the guise of NOAA's definition of "preservation."

All for a bunch of rotting hulks that will undoubtedly be left to rot.

Shipwrecks in Mallows Bay.

The Runaway Sanctuary Invasion

NOAA has not forgotten the other Great Lakes. Also in the works is the Lake Erie Quadrangle National Marine Sanctuary. This sanctuary would encompass all the Pennsylvania waters in the lake: 759 square miles of lake bed.

This sanctuary would join the proposed Erie Niagara National Marine Sanctuary, which would encompass all the New York waters in Lake Erie, as well as the New York waters of eastern Lake Ontario.

The adjoining western portion of Lake Ontario would be annexed as the Great Lake Ontario National Marine Sanctuary.

In short, the entire American side of Lakes Erie and Ontario would be taken in one fell swoop, which would leave no free water in either of those lakes.

Also on the books are three sanctuaries in Lake Superior: the Lake Superior NMS, the Keweenaw NMS, and the Chequamegon Bay NMS. After designation, these three sanctuaries would be expanded until their borders joined, so that the entire American side of Lake Superior would be one huge mega-sanctuary.

Did I miss any? I don't know. Sanctuary proposals are spreading like cancer cells that threaten to kill the host by taking away every waterborne freedom in the country.

If NOAA gets its way, all five of the Great Lakes will eventually be joined to become one gigantic mega-mega-sanctuary. All these sanctuaries are being created not to protect a rare or fragile marine environment, but specifically to take absolute control of shipwrecks.

The American Great Lakes Ports Association was quick to provide "a list of the types of activities restricted at existing marine sanctuaries: over-flights by aircraft, aquaculture, seabed cables, mineral extraction, commercial shipping, commercial fishing, recreational fishing, size and speed restrictions on watercraft[,] and discharges."

Clearly, NOAA has no "last territorial demand." It wants the entire underwater world plus the adjacent lands. And "adjacent lands" can be expanded to include everything in the homeless of the free and landless of the brave.

Soon there won't be any free water left in or off the United States of NOAA.

Shipwrecking the Economy

To introduce this section, let me reiterate that the Marine Protection, Research, and Sanctuaries Act has nothing to do with shipwrecks. Yet NOAA has spent an enormous amount of taxpayers' money to create a list of what it calls "potentially polluting wrecks in U.S. waters." That should read "BS" instead of "U.S." I have dived on a number of wrecks on the list and found them to be completely empty of cargo because their bulkheads collapsed decades ago.

NOAA utilizes scare tactics as a way to convince Congress to give more money to NOAA in order to study a potential problem that has already been studied and resolved. As long ago as 1967, the U.S. Coast Guard studied the problem in its Sunken Tanker Project. The Coast Guard found that every World War Two wreck that divers examined first hand, contained no cargo in its holds because the holds were open to sea, and the cargo had already leaked out a drop at a time, so that no global contamination ever existed.

Yet NOAA is still pushing this outdated agenda.

I have personally dived on more than a dozen of the wrecks that are on NOAA's list of nearly one hundred, and never observed intact cargo holds. Yet NOAA cries that these dozen wrecks may contain more than a million barrels of "potentially polluting" oil. NOAA has to be aware of this information because I wrote about these wrecks in my Popular Dive Guide Series.

NOAA is striving to bring a dead issue back to life as a money making scheme.

NOAA has advanced from marine protection to the shipwreck business. Miners used to shout, "There's gold in them thar hills." NOAA had adapted this clarion call to the underwater realm. Money is to be made not in the wrecks themselves, but in charging people to see them.

Incontinence

NOAA has its controlling and expansive eye on territories that are located elsewhere than the continental United States.

Because it is so remote, you have probably never heard of the Fagatele Bay National Marine Sanctuary. It's located on the island of Pago Pago in the South Pacific. This sanctuary was created to "protect" a "tiny volcanic bay, barely 160 acres in size." It was the smallest sanctuary in the system. At one-quarter square mile in area, it comprised one quarter of the area of the Monitor NMS, which totals one square mile.

In 2012, this miniscule sanctuary was expanded from one-quarter square mile to *13,581 square miles.* That's right, folks. The sanctuary is now 54,324 times larger than its original size. The newly named National Marine Sanctuary of American Samoa is one fifth the size of Texas. Perhaps it doesn't compare with the size of Poland when Hitler invaded that country in 1939, but it's still a respectable annexation: a tactic that NOAA employed after it gets its figurative foot in the door.

Now you can see how dangerous it is for the freedom of the public when NOAA creates a new sanctuary. The amount that a sanctuary can be expanded has no limits other than the total surface area of the planet. Next stop, the Moon!

Taking possession of lunar maria (dead seas) may seem like an exaggeration, but who knows how big NOAA's dreams for conquest go?

With the swipe of a pen, Fagatele went from being the smallest of NOAA's possessions to the largest. Keep in mind that the ocean area that NOAA annexed lies in international waters. This means that NOAA now controls sea lanes that once belonged to the world. Now every nation on the globe must bow to NOAA's wishes or pay exorbitant fines for violating little-known regulations. Thus NOAA can now tax every person on the planet.

Now for the stickler. The people who are affected the most by NOAA's overly restrictive regulations are the local inhabitants who rely – or used to rely – on these waters for their livelihood. As soon as NOAA achieved totalitarian authority over this vast ocean area, it initiated catch limits that have put some commercial fishing operations out of business. Harvest restrictions presently limit the amount of profit that struggling operations can earn.

These bag limits refer not only to crabs, lobsters, and bottom fish that live and reproduce in the sanctuary permanently, but to pelagic fish such as tuna that merely pass through the sanctuary. Closure periods reduced the amount of time which commercial anglers were permitted to remain at sea to 62 days. This means that anglers were forced to remain unemployed for ten months of the year.

All fishing vessels that worked in the sanctuary were required to obtain permits before they could begin fishing. Furthermore, NOAA restricted the length of a fishing vessel's hull, thereby reducing the amount of product that anglers could stow in the hold, which further reduced an angler's ability to sustain profitability.

Local anglers complain constantly and bitterly about these and other overly restrictive regulations, but they can do nothing about the situation because NOAA makes the laws irrespective of stakeholders' needs to eat and stay in business.

NOAA was well aware of "the extent to which American Samoa is engaged in and dependent on fisheries resources economically, socially, and culturally," but imposed restrictive regulations anyway.

Approximately 98 % of American Samoa's exports consisted of canned tuna. Thousands of jobs were lost when the largest cannery on the island was forced to close due to lack of product to can. Other canneries found it impossible to operate at full capacity; the reduced workload led to layoffs and shorter hours.

Both native inhabitants and long-time residents had to leave their homeland in order to find work elsewhere.

In short, NOAA strangled the local workforce and destroyed the territory's economy . . . all because it wanted to exercise its authority to the detriment of the people.

Sorry, Charlie.

Getting into the Act

As you can see, NOAA has no "last" territorial demand. NOAA wants to continue creating and expanding sanctuaries until it controls the entire underwater world. I know I already stated that, but it bears repeating.

NOAA is continuously taking possession of vast ocean areas, lakes, rivers, and both lakeside and riverside dryland property. Look at some of the other sanctuary nominations that NOAA has under review:

        Alaska – Aleutian Islands
        Alaska – St. George Unangan Heritage
        California – Chumash Heritage
        Florida – Eubalaena Oculina
        . . . and more on the way

NOAA aggrandizement is not local. It is global. It must be stopped before it metastasizes and goes totally out of control . . . Actually, it already *is* already out of control, and has been since its designation. There is only one way to deal with the situation before the American people are strangled to death by overly restrictive regulations.

The National Marine Sanctuary Program must be abolished!

NOAA's Plans Are Trumped

As the old saying goes: There's good news and there's . . . great news!

Okay, so the saying doesn't go exactly like that. But in this case the good news is great news.

In April 2017, President Donald Trump issued an executive order which imposed "a halt on designating or expanding any National Marine Sanctuary, unless the action 'includes a timely, full accounting from the Department of the Interior of any energy or mineral resource potential in the designated area.' "

Furthermore, Trump planned to review "all such designations and expansions over the past decade." This means that new sanctuaries which the public has been protesting could be undesignated and returned to the public, and that past sanctuary expansions could be repealed and the sanctuaries reduced to their original size.

This is equivalent to building a wall around Nazi Germany, and freeing occupied territories that the Nazis had invaded and conquered.

'Nuff said.

Trump hopes to undo what ex-President Barak Obama did. Trump issued this executive order not because so many stakeholders, anglers, and divers were protesting NOAA's abuse of authority and abolishment of personal freedom, but because NOAA's unwarranted sanctuary formations and expansions restricted the exploration and production of offshore drilling for oil and gas.

Trump: "Renewed offshore energy production will reduce the cost of energy, create countless new jobs, and make America more secure and far more energy independent."

According to Trump, NOAA's greed has deprived America of "potentially thousands and thousands of jobs and billions of dollars in wealth."

NOAA's power thrusts and global initiative to annex every shipwreck in American waters, thence beyond, is reminiscent of the quote that is attributed to Hitler: "Tomorrow the world."

Americans should rejoice over Trump's new directive. But remember the words of Thomas Jefferson: "The price of freedom is eternal vigilance." No doubt NOAA will fight to keep the submerged property that it has stolen from the American people over the years. So, while Americans are rejoicing, they should not let down their guard against future NOAA treacheries and perfidies.

Some cancers require constant monitoring in order to prevent recurrence. NOAA is one of them.

NOAA issues aside, I am not otherwise particularly enamored by the way the current President has acted, or enacted. Instead of President Trump, I prefer to think of his title as President Trumpery. The definition of trumpery is "showy but worthless finery; bric-a-brac; nonsense; rubbish; deception; trickery; fraud." At least one of those definitions is appropriate. But not in Trump's handling of NOAA.

Above the Law

NOAA's executives and employees are driven by what is known as "libido dominandi," a Latin phrase which translates as "the lust to dominate." Judging by the language in which the phrase was coined, this psychiatric condition has been in existence for a long time.

For NOAA, it started long before Congress passed the Marine, Research, Protection, and Sanctuaries Act. It started as soon as the National Oceanic and Atmospheric Administration was given dictatorial powers to penalize the commercial fishing industry for fishing under overly restrictive rules and regulations that NOAA created as a way to enrich itself by establishing grossly excessive fines for minor mistakes, misunderstandings, and misdemeanors that could have been avoided had NOAA been inclined to warn anglers instead of by feeding off them.

NOAA operates with no oversight or any system of checks and balances. It is a totally self-governed parasite with no accountability to anyone but itself. It is beyond the pale of law, like "a den of vipers and thieves," as President Andrew Jackson once said when he abolished the Second Bank of the United States.

For example, "The Commerce Department's inspector general released a report . . . that found serious flaws in NOAA's fisheries enforcement and law enforcement operations – describing an unbalanced system, too heavy on criminal investigation, that has created a 'dysfunctional relationship' between NOAA and the fishing industry."

What brought this situation to light was the congressional investigation of NOAA's "heavy-handed fisheries enforcement," during which NOAA's Law Enforcement Director Dale Jones was accused of the "unauthorized destruction of more than 100 files at law enforcement headquarters in Silver Spring," Maryland.

The investigation brought to light NOAA's "systemic, nationwide" issues plaguing the fisheries enforcement program, in which NOAA created a "highly charged regulatory climate" with regard to "innocent mistakes or misunderstandings" and minor infractions that were nothing more than misdemeanors.

Representative Madeleine Bordallo, chairperson of the House Oceans and Wildlife Subcommittee, put the situation in a nutshell: "As the top cop at NOAA and a longtime investigator himself, Dale Jones must be acutely aware that shredding documents during a federal investigation raises serious questions about his commitment to a full and fair look at all the facts. At a time when transparency and accountability in the way our government operates is of utmost importance, this type of behavior cannot be condoned, and Mr. Jones should step aside until the IG's [Inspector General] investigation is completed."

Representative John Tierney not only wanted Dale Jones to be "relieved of his duties," but wanted his entire department overhauled. Tierney: "People come in and treat these fishermen like common criminals."

And the NOAA beat goes on . . .

"Save the sharks"

I will start this section with a parable. In the 1800's, American settlers and ranchers were having trouble protecting their farm animals and range herds from natural predators: primarily wolves and mountain lions. The way people dealt with the situation was to shoot the marauding animals on sight. They reasoned that the fewer predators that lived by preying on their stock, the more stock survived to feed them and to export to cities where the meat was needed to stave off starvation of the urban populace.

It made sense then; it still makes sense today. Wild animals are kept at bay by keeping their numbers to a minimum. In addition to protecting farm stock from predation, game animals such as deer abound for recreational hunters.

Occasionally I have scuba dived from a fishing boat on which anglers fished between dives. Often their catch was bitten in two by sharks before the anglers could reel their fish to the surface. This represented a frustrating financial loss because there was no market for fish heads.

Every once in a while they caught a shark on a baited hook. In order to increase the odds in their favor, to make anglers the apex predators instead of sharks, they killed the sharks in order to reduce the number of their competitors. They also sliced open the belly of gravid sharks and killed the unborn progeny as well. It all made sense.

Unborn dogfish shark.

Now NOAA has joined a consortium of shark-huggers who want a worldwide ban on fishing for sharks. None of these sharks are rare or endangered species. They are predators that compete with commercial anglers for fish biomass.

At the same time, NOAA enforces strict regulations regarding limits on the number of fish that anglers are permitted to keep, the reason being that schools of food fish supposedly suffer from achieving sustainable limits (although this so-called logic is debatable).

The irony here - or the stupidity - is that NOAA now supports legislation that would ban fishing for the predators that create the biomass shortage for commercial anglers. This is equivalent to raising wolves and mountain lions, then releasing them in barnyards and ranch land so they can prey on cattle that produce milk or meat for market, thus reducing the amount of harvest available for consumers while increasing the price of the product.

Anyone with an ounce of white matter between his ears can see that saving sharks is nonsense. The fewer sharks that inhabit the ocean, the more fish are available to catch and feed starving consumers. If the Sustainable Shark Fisheries and Trade Act is passed, NOAA will have sole discretion on implementing contradictory regulations.

A Whale of a Tale, or a Tale of a Whale, or a Tale of Woe

A tragedy in the making commenced on November 22, 2016. A juvenile humpback whale was chasing a school of Atlantic menhaden when prey and predator entered Moriches Inlet, on Long Island, New York. The menhaden escaped over the sandy shoals but the 30-foot-long whale stranded in the shallows.

Local residents who heard the whale bellowing rushed to the rescue as crowds gathered to offer whatever help they could provide. Before long, volunteers arrived on the scene fully equipped to handle the situation. Scuba divers boated to the site and poured water on the skin of the 15-ton whale, in order to keep it moist and to prevent it from overheating. In short order a tugboat arrived along with a dredger and a barge with a backhoe on board.

The dredger started to dig a channel from deep water to the stranded whale. The tug was prepared to tow the whale into the channel and let it swim to safety. These workers were nearing completion of their task, but NOAA intervened before the community effort could be effected. NOAA's first act of command was to warn away the lifesavers under threat of arrest. NOAA claimed jurisdiction under the Marine Mammal Act.

I could drag out this sad saga for three more days, the way NOAA did, but it would serve no useful purpose.

Despite the long-time rallying cry of "Save the whales," NOAA refused to accept any and all help that could have saved the whale, including appeals from New York's governor. If NOAA would just have gotten out of the way of the people who were truly interested in the whale's health and safety, that whale might be alive today.

Instead, NOAA stood by idly, watched the marine mammal weaken day by day, and did nothing to ease its suffering or save its life. After watching the animal struggle for three days, NOAA on-site personnel killed it.

The hue and cry among the populace was long and loud. So long and loud that NOAA was forced to respond to what had become a national heartbreak. NOAA had the unmitigated gall to claim that it was "unaware of offers to help until it was too late."

What bullshit!

In response to my Facebook posting of the incident, local diver Paula German replied to NOAA's claim, "This is not true. NOAA was on the boat that kept us from helping the whale! I spoke to him with others on the coast guard boat. We told him what we wanted to do and had a barge 200 feet from his boat."

Were NOAA employees both deaf and blind, or did they ignore offers of help because they were power mongers whose sole purpose in life was to exercise their authority?

That's NOAA for you.

Ask yourself this question: Is this the kind of outfit you want to rule your life?

THE LUSITANIA CONTROVERSIES
THE TWO-VOLUME
HISTORY OF WRECK-DIVING

There is more to a book than its title. There is the subtitle. A subtitle is an explanatory device which describes the topic of a book more fully than its title. A case in point is The Lusitania Controversies. At first glance the title implies the sole subject of the Lusitania. But each of the two volumes possesses a subtitle which explains in greater detail the global premise of which the Lusitania is but a part.

Together, both volumes present the entire history of wreck-diving, from its meager beginnings in the 1950's to the advent of technical diving in the 1990's.

Book One is subtitled Atrocity of War and a Wreck-Diving History. One quarter of the volume is devoted to the construction, career, sinking, and aftermath of the Lusitania. Three quarters are devoted to the history of wreck-diving and to autobiographical experiences of the author, who became an essential element in wreck-diving and a pioneer in technical diving. Coverage extends to 1979, and includes a section on the author's first Doria trip, in 1974.

Book Two is subtitled Dangerous Descents into Shipwrecks and Law. This volume continues the history of wreck-diving from 1980; describes numerous dives on ever-deeper shipwrecks; a number of incredible penetrations into the vast interior of the Andrea Doria, including the recovery of two bodies; and details the beginning of mixed-gas diving to the point at which an expedition to the Lusitania became practical. The volume concludes with a detailed description of the 1994 Lusitania expedition (of which the author was a part) and subsequent legal activities.

The two volumes are larger than the sum of their parts. They comprise biographical content with incredible underwater adventures: some hair-raising, others deadly, all exciting: a fascinating excursion into the real world of wreck-diving and the evolution of the activity.

Navigation equipment in the *Lusitania's* wheelhouse: telemotor, telegraph, and gear head of the manual helm.

Books by the Author

The Popular Dive Guide Series

Shipwrecks of Maine and New Hampshire
Shipwrecks of Massachusetts: North
Shipwrecks of Massachusetts: South
Shipwrecks of Rhode Island and Connecticut
Shipwrecks of New York
Shipwrecks of New Jersey (1988)
Shipwrecks of New Jersey: North
Shipwrecks of New Jersey: Central
Shipwrecks of New Jersey: South
Shipwrecks of Delaware and Maryland (1990 Edition)
Shipwrecks of Delaware and Maryland (2002 Edition)
Shipwrecks of the Chesapeake Bay in Maryland Waters
Shipwrecks of the Chesapeake Bay in Virginia Waters
Shipwrecks of Virginia
Shipwrecks of North Carolina: from the Diamond Shoals North
Shipwrecks of North Carolina: from Hatteras Inlet South
Shipwrecks of South Carolina and Georgia
Shipwreck Potpourri

Shipwreck and Nautical History

Andrea Doria: Dive to an Era
Deep, Dark, and Dangerous: Adventures and Reflections on the Andrea Doria
Great Lakes Shipwrecks: a Photographic Odyssey
The Great Navy Wreck Scam
The Fuhrer's U-boats in American Waters
Ironclad Legacy: Battles of the USS Monitor
The Kaiser's U-boats in American Waters
The Lusitania Controversies: Atrocity of War and a Wreck-Diving History (Book One)
The Lusitania Controversies: Dangerous Descents into Shipwrecks and Law (Book Two)
The Nautical Cyclopedia
NOAA's Ark: the Rise of the Fourth Reich
Shadow Divers Exposed: the Real Saga of the U-869
Shipwreck Heresies
The Shipwreck Research Handbook
Shipwreck Sagas
Stolen Heritage: the Grand Theft of the Hamilton and Scourge
Track of the Gray Wolf
The $25 Dollar Wreck of the Robert J. Walker
Underwater Reflections
USS San Diego: the Last Armored Cruiser
Wreck Diving Adventures

Books by the Author

Dive Training
Primary Wreck Diving Guide
Advanced Wreck Diving Guide
The Advanced Wreck Diving Handbook
Ultimate Wreck Diving Guide
The Technical Diving Handbook

Nonfiction
The Absurdity Principle
Lehigh Gorge Trail Guide
Lehigh River Paddling Guide
Wilderness Canoeing

Science Fiction
A Different Universe
A Different Dimension
A Different Continuum
Entropy (a novel of conceptual breakthrough)
A Journey to the Center of the Earth
The Mold
Return to Mars
Second Coming
Silent Autumn
Subaqueous
Tesla and the Lemurian Gate
The Time Dragons Trilogy
    A Time for Dragons
    Dragons Past
    No Future for Dragons

Sci-Fi Action/Adventure Novels
Memory Lane
Mind Set
The Peking Papers

Supernatural Horror Novel
The Lurking: Curse of the Jersey Devil

Vietnam Novel
Lonely Conflict

Videotape or DVD
The Battle for the USS Monitor

Visit the GGP website for availability of titles:
http://www.ggentile.com/index.html

Enter the wild, exciting, and exotic world of Gary Gentile: author, lecturer, photographer, explorer, and deep-sea wreck-diver. Enter a world of adventure and thrills tempered by poetry and subtle beauty. Gary will take you to shipwrecks, show you marine life, and explore the great outdoors the way no one else can.

Gary has written 67 books, published nearly 4,000 photographs, discovered more than 40 shipwrecks, and led a life of adventure.

Of the thousands of decompression dives that Gary has made, 200 of them were on the Grand Dame of the Sea: the *Andrea Doria*. He was the first scuba diver to enter the First Class Dining Room, from which he recovered many examples of elegant china. He also recovered and restored hundreds of items of jewelry and souvenirs from the Gift Shop, located at a depth of 220 feet. More important, he discovered and recovered a number of ceramic panels that once adorned the walls of the First Class Bar. These colorful panels were the work of famed Italian artist Romano Rui.

In the early 1990's, Gary was instrumental in merging mixed-gas diving technology with wreck-diving. His dive to the German battleship *Ostfriesland*, at a depth of 380 feet, triggered an unprecedented expansion in the exploration of deep-water shipwrecks, and the advent of helium mixes as a breathing medium. He wrote the first book on technical diving: *Ultimate Wreck Diving Guide* (1992), which was later expanded to *The Technical Diving Handbook* (1998).

In 1994, Gary participated in a mixed-gas diving expedition to the *Lusitania*, which lies at a depth of 300 feet.

Gary has specialized in wreck-diving and shipwreck research, concentrating his efforts on wrecks along the eastern seaboard, from Newfoundland to Key West, and in the Great Lakes. He has compiled an extensive library of books, photographs, drawings, plans, and original source materials on ships and shipwrecks. He has conducted surveys on numerous wrecks, some of which have been drawn in the form of large-sized prints that are suitable for framing. He has either discovered or been the first to dive on scores of previously unknown shipwrecks.

Over the years he has rescued from the ravages of the sea many thousands of shipwreck artifacts, making him a leading authority in recovery techniques. He has gone to great lengths to preserve and restore these relics from the deep, and to display them to thousands of interested people, divers and nondivers alike. Throughout the years, these artifacts have been displayed at various museums, symposiums, and club-oriented exhibitions.

Gary has written scores of magazine articles, and has published thousands of photographs in books, periodicals, newspapers, brochures, advertisements, corporate reports, museum displays, postcards, film, and television. He lectures extensively on underwater topics, and conducts seminars on advanced wreck-diving techniques, high-tech diving equipment, and wreck photography.

His books are primarily novels of science fiction and adventure, and nonfiction volumes on wreck-diving and on nautical and shipwreck history. The Popular Dive Guide Series will eventually cover every major shipwreck along the east coast of the United States.

There is also another side of Gary's life: that of an outdoor adventurer. In this guise he has climbed rocks and mountains, backpacked through country high and low, bivouacked in the snow, and paddled his canoe through rapids and down untamed

Author's Bio

Gary steadies Bart Malone's tanks after they returned from a dive. (Courtesy of Bart Malone.)

wilderness rivers - often for weeks at a time. His longest trip lasted a month, when he and five companions paddled 380 miles down the George River in Labrador. For three weeks straight they did not encounter another human being, or see signs of civilization. Gary embraces total self-sufficiency in the wilderness.

He has captured on film all of these wonderful outdoor adventures, as well as the splendor of nature's colorful scenery. He has given slide presentations to dive clubs, hiking clubs, canoe clubs, elder hostels, church groups, cub scouts, boy scouts, power squadrons, Naval associations, Civil War societies, Masonic lodges, Mensa, corporate functions, scientific organizations, and many, many other groups too numerous to mention.

He gave most of these presentations and workshops not only in dozens of State and Provinces in the U.S. and Canada, but also in Australia and Scotland.

In other work-related ventures, Gary owns and operates a publishing business, does shipwreck artifact appraisals, handles research and consulting jobs, and is sometimes employed as an expert witness in legal matters and court cases.

In 1989, after a five-year battle with the National Oceanic and Atmospheric Administration, Gary won a suit which forced the hostile government agency to issue him a permit to dive the USS *Monitor*, a protected National Marine Sanctuary. Media attention that was focused on Gary's triumphant victory resulted in nationwide coverage of his 1990 photographic expedition to the Civil War ironclad. He then had to fight NOAA for three more years to keep the wreck open for the public in perpetuity. Gary continues to fight for the right of access to all shipwreck sites.

Join now in this photographic extravaganza. See the beauty of nature under the waves; explore the interior of an armored cruiser; stand in awe of a warship's turrets; dive wrecks from Nova Scotia to Florida and in the Great Lakes; learn how to save and show those precious, sea tainted relics; sit in on workshops on advanced wreck-diving techniques and high-tech diving equipment; take a tour of that renowned Italian passenger line that divers long to touch: the *Andrea Doria*. Through slides and video, experience the Civil War ironclad *Monitor* as it used to lay on the sandy bottom before the engine and turret were salvaged, and learn about Gary's eight year battle with NOAA, and the precedent-setting court decision which forced NOAA to make the wreck accessible to the public. See the remains of the *Lusitania* in 300 feet of water, and learn how a complex mixed-gas wreck-dive is conducted. Sit in awe at nature's rugged charm. All this and more awaits your pleasure.

Let Gary bring it all to you.

www.ingramcontent.com/pod-product-compliance
Lightning Source LLC
Chambersburg PA
CBHW051046160426
43193CB00010B/1086